Housing Possession Duty Desk

a practical guide

Simon Mullings is a housing law specialist caseworker at Edwards Duthie Shamash Solicitors. He has more than 20 years' experience in legally aided social welfare law and most of those years have been spent delivering duty advice and representation in six county courts (three now sadly defunct) throughout East London. He is a contributing author of LAG's *Legal Aid Handbook* and co-editor of *Justice Matters*. He is co-chair of the Housing Law Practitioners Association and was named Social Welfare Legal Aid Lawyer of the year in 2020.

Sue James is director and solicitor at Hammersmith and Fulham Law Centre and a specialist in housing law. She is a founding trustee of Ealing Law Centre and has worked in law centres for most of her career. She is an experienced court duty advocate having spent the last 15 years delivering and running two duty schemes in West London. In 2017 she won the Legal Aid Lawyer of the Year Outstanding Achievement Award. She is co-editor of the *Legal Aid Handbook* and *Justice Matters* and writes a regular column for *Legal Action* on access to justice, housing and legal aid.

The Legal Action Group is a national, independent charity which campaigns for equal access to justice for all members of society. Legal Action Group:

- provides support to the practice of lawyers and advisers
- inspires developments in that practice
- campaigns for improvements in the law and the administration of justice
- stimulates debate on how services should be delivered.

Housing Possession Duty Desk

a practical guide

Simon Mullings and Sue James

Supported by

THERIUM ACCESS

SUPPORTING ACCESS TO JUSTICE

LAG the access to justice charity

Legal Action Group
2021

This edition published in Great Britain 2021
by LAG Education and Service Trust Limited
c/o Oliver Fisher Solicitors, Royalty Studios,
105-109 Lancaster Road,
London W11 1QF
www.lag.org.uk

British Library Cataloguing in Publication Data. A CIP catalogue record for this book is available from the British Library.

FSC
www.fsc.org
MIX
Paper from responsible sources
FSC® C020438

This book has been produced using Forest Stewardship Council (FSC) certified paper. The wood used to produce FSC certified products with a 'Mixed Sources' label comes from FSC certified well-managed forests, controlled sources and/or recycled material.

print ISBN: 978 1 913648 16 9
eBook ISBN: 978 1 913648 17 6
bundle (print and eBook) ISBN: 978 1 913648 18 3

Typeset by Refinecatch Ltd, Bungay, Suffolk
Printed in Great Britain by Hobbs the Printer, Totton, Hampshire

This book is dedicated to all duty advisers – past, present and future.

Foreword

by The Hon Mr Justice Knowles CBE

It is easy to view legal proceedings for the possession of residential property too narrowly. They do concern the enforcement of contracts, and legislation of some complexity. But they are about savings and homes and business. They involve government, corporations, charities and individuals. They have an impact on markets. They can concern allegations about payment, but they can also be about issues from unlawful behaviour to protection from violence.

It is no surprise to find claimants and defendants who are vulnerable. It is no overstatement that the practice and procedure of housing possession law can alter lives (of claimants and defendants alike), and families and communities.

The COVID-19 pandemic has altered and deepened all of these dimensions. Its impact on health, employment, and the economy, has brought more and new claimants and defendants into range. The implications of the grant or refusal of an order for possession have become more serious than ever. The heightened consequences of homelessness for the individuals involved, the communities in which they live, and for stretched local authorities, are obvious.

There are many, many thousands of possession cases. As sometimes happens with scale, a concerted effort is needed to avoid focus slipping away from the individual features of the case and the circumstances of its parties. It is too easy to create a conveyor belt, to base assumptions upon experience that is no longer applicable, to leave underlying issues unaddressed, to assume that possession proceedings are just about orders for possession.

In all this the duty adviser plays the pivotal role. A source of legal advice to the tenant or borrower. Bringing a renewed opportunity for negotiation with the landlord or lender. Ready in appropriate cases to provide a gateway to more detailed assistance, and to alternative dispute resolution. With the professional experience and independence to speak to any authorities involved and to represent in court.

Wise claimants appreciate them just as much as do the defendants they serve.

As the preface puts it, the duty adviser is the legal equivalent of the A&E doctor. And that accurate parallel says so much for the importance of the role and the respect it deserves. Imagine facing proceedings for possession of your home without advice. Then imagine that in the pandemic.

The Master of the Rolls Working Group on Possession Proceedings has striven to work across, and with contributions from, the entire sector. As its chair, I have learned many things. I mention four. First, the readiness of claimants and defendants to recognise they share a common interest in the system working. Second, that the system had weaknesses that were revealed rather than caused by the pandemic. Third, that a better system is within reach.

A fourth thing I learned was about the quiet, informed, leadership that the authors of this book provide in this field. This book is just one example of a contribution they make with enormous knowledge and deep professional and personal integrity.

This book makes a typically modest claim to serve as a practical guide. It is that, but it is so much more. It serves those who make the system work. To all of them, and to the remarkable authors, I pay respectful tribute.

Sir Robin Knowles CBE
February 2021

Preface

As legal aid shrinks and housing lawyers become scarce, it is at the door of the court where most people now receive advice and assistance on their housing case. Duty advisers are the legal equivalent of A&E doctors – and as such, we need to be prepared. We hope that this book will be the essential guide in your toolkit on the frontline of defending possession proceedings.

A day as a duty adviser is a challenging experience – but one that is undoubtedly rewarding. It is where we can make greatest change, in a relatively short amount of time, by keeping a roof over someone's head. Clients are often distressed. It is necessary to build trust, marshal the facts, apply the law, negotiate, and then, if no agreement is reached, be prepared to fight the case before a judge. All in 20 minutes.

For experienced duty advisers, we hope that this will be a guide through the change in possession proceedings – now known as the 'Overall Arrangements' – following the lifting of the stay on proceedings as well as being a useful reference book and aide memoir. For those embarking on duty representation for the first time, or almost, we hope that this handbook gives you the tools needed to be a fearless advocate for those who face losing their home.

As a duty adviser, you get to see almost every type of case, but arrears of rent and mortgage are prevalent. The withdrawal of legal aid for welfare benefit cases in 2013 was a short-sighted decision by the government, as it is those cases that now end up in court – where the costs are higher both financially and emotionally. A very high proportion of rent arrears cases have a benefit issue at their heart, and benefit cases are increasingly complex with the welfare reform programme.

A lot of time on the duty scheme can be spent looking at the universal credit journal of a client (often on their phone) and trying to fathom what exactly has happened. Adjournments are necessary to investigate the benefit issue further – but where do we send these clients? And what happens if they can't get access to an adviser before they are next in court?

There are structural problems in the housing and the welfare systems that we see daily on the duty scheme. To make real change to protect tenants (and landlords, for that matter), we need to amend the benefit rules around the benefit cap, the bedroom tax, backdated benefit, direct payments, sanctions, the two-child rule and more. These problems existed before COVID-19. It is a shame that the government did not take the opportunity during the 2020 stay in possession proceedings to address them alongside the Overall Arrangements for re-commencing possession proceedings.

Most egregious is the failure to do away with no-fault evictions and most mandatory grounds for possession. If you have a system that forces landlords to go to court to obtain a possession order, why take away the judge's discretion in making that order? Taking someone's home away because they have a benefit problem makes no sense – but is happening across England and Wales daily.

Doing duty advice is already an act of resistance to the idea that a person's home is simply a transactional arrangement, a matter of terms in a contract. Duty advisers insist on the statutory and other protections that exist. However, if we can, we must call for those protections to be extended, for the solutions to possession proceedings to be put in place before possession proceedings are even contemplated, to get upstream of rent and benefits and financial and social problems, and ultimately to make last-minute assistance at the door of court genuinely a last resort, rather than the inevitable consequence of cuts to welfare and access to justice.

In our practice and in writing this book, we have relied heavily on LAG's *Legal Action* magazine. *Legal Action*'s monthly 'Housing: Recent Developments' column is essential reading. Alongside the big UK Supreme Court and Court of Appeal cases of the day, you will find useful gems of unreported county court possession cases which, while not binding judgments, can be very persuasive and can be used extensively on duty. However, don't just *read* your copy of *Legal Action*. When you have your notable victories in court or successfully argue an unusual point, send a summary of them to LAG for inclusion in 'Housing: Recent Developments'. In the current context, whereby most housing cases are dealt with by duty solicitors, it is vitally important that we share our knowledge and experiences, and the great satisfaction that you got from saving someone's home can be multiplied many times by telling us how you did it so that many more homes can be saved.

In a fairer system, this book might not need to exist – but while it does, we hope it assists duty advisers to help tenants and borrowers to remain in a decent, stable, secure home.

We continue to learn through the doing of and writing about housing law and practice. We hope you do too through the reading of it.

Our thanks to the brilliant and wise Esther Pilger, who ran with our idea of a book for duty advisers and supported us throughout, as well as Carol Storer OBE and the LAG team. We would also like to thank Angus King, Jeinsen Lam, Mike Norman, Marina Sergides and Zia Nabi who read all or part of the first draft, which helped to shape the guide and make it a better book. Any errors are ours.

The authors pay tribute to HHJ Jan Luba QC, Nic Madge and Derek McConnell in particular, alongside those others who have written *Defending Possession Proceedings* (DPP) since 1987, those who write it now and those who will come to write and develop it in the future.

Sue James would like to thank Simon Mullings for putting in the heavy lifting (to use his own words) in this book and for his friendship and generosity, as well as always being ready with a song. And, of course, to Ben and Harry – always.

Simon Mullings would like to thank co-author Sue James and David Emmerson OBE. Lastly, always, and most of all, Melanie Jean Warner – previously unimaginable things can be achieved if only someone believes in you.

Sue James
Simon Mullings
February 2021

Contents

Abbreviations

AA	attendance allowance
AJA 1970	Administration of Justice Act 1970
AJA 1973	Administration of Justice Act 1973
ASB	anti-social behaviour
ASBI	anti-social behaviour injunction
CB	child benefit
CCA 1974	Consumer Credit Act 1974
CMI	current monthly instalment
CPR	Civil Procedure Rules 1998
CPRC	Civil Procedure Rule Committee
CTC	child tax credit
DCJ	Designated Civil Judge
DLA	disability living allowance
DPP	*Defending Possession Proceedings*, Legal Action Group
DWP	Department for Work and Pensions
EA 2010	Equality Act 2010
ECHR	European Convention on Human Rights
ECtHR	European Court of Human Rights
EESA	enhanced employment support allowance
ESA	employment and support allowance
FCA	Financial Conduct Authority
FOS	Financial Ombudsman Service
FSMA 2000	Financial Services and Markets Act 2000
FSMA(RA)O 2001	Financial Services and Markets Act 2000 (Regulated Activities) Order 2001 SI No 544
HA 1980	Housing Act 1980
HA 1985	Housing Act 1985
HA 1988	Housing Act 1988
HA 1996	Housing Act 1996
HAT	Housing Action Trust

HCEO	High Court Enforcement Officer
HLPA	Housing Law Practitioners Association
HMO	house in multiple occupation
HPCDS	Housing Possession Court Duty Scheme
HRA 1998	Human Rights Act 1998
IPO	interim possession order
IS	income support
JSA	jobseeker's allowance
LAA	Legal Aid Agency
LASPO	Legal Aid, Sentencing and Punishment of Offenders Act 2012
MCA 2005	Mental Capacity Act 2005
MCOB	Mortgage Conduct of Business Rules
MHCLG	Ministry of Housing, Communities and Local Government
MPTL-RA	Managed Payment to Landlords – Rent Arrears
MR	Master of the Rolls
NINO	national insurance number
NRLA	National Residential Landlords Association
PCG	Pension Credit Guarantee
PCOL	Possession Claim Online
PEA 1977	Protection from Eviction Act 1977
PIP	personal independence payment
PRPSH	Private Registered Provider of Social Housing
PSED	public sector equality duty
R date	review date
RA 1977	Rent Act 1977
RMC	Regulated Mortgage Contract
RSL	Registered Social Landlord (see para 1.17 for use in this book)
S hearing	substantive hearing
SMI	Support for Mortgage Interest
TPD	third party deduction
UC	universal credit
UCHE	universal credit housing element
WTC	working tax credit

CHAPTER 1

How to use this book and terms used

How to use this book

1.1 This book is not *Defending Possession Proceedings* (DPP). That leviathan text has been the definitive guide to possession proceedings since 1987, and its authors are amongst the foremost of housing lawyers. Two or three of them practically invented the idea of housing law.

1.2 DPP runs to some 1,224 pages in its current edition. Housing law is not standing still, and successive governments and the courts appear to have as a prime objective an increase in page count of housing law texts. DPP has comprehensively covered each and every development, and will doubtless continue to do so. In some cases it has predicted and analysed problems in housing law where practitioners, law-makers and judges had not even noticed them. In short, it has been and remains the essential text for anyone involved in possession proceedings, from advisers to solicitors to barristers to judges.

1.3 And then there is the fact that DPP is 7cm thick and weighs 1¼ kilograms.

1.4 However, since the advent of the Legal Aid, Sentencing and Punishment of Offenders Act 2012 (LASPO) and the legal aid reforms in its wake, most housing possession law has been conducted by duty advisers working in the county court under the Housing Possession Court Duty Scheme (HPCDS), emergency on-the-day assistance and advocacy, funded by legal aid and available to anyone who is at risk of losing their home. The skills and knowledge required to represent a tenant or borrower with only five minutes to take instructions, perhaps even less to talk to the opponent, and only a half share of five to 10 minutes to convince a judge, are somewhat different to those employed when carefully drafting a pleading or preparing for a day-long trial.

1.5 That said, and for all the high-tempo, knockabout atmosphere of housing possession duty day, there is skill and knowledge and resilience and confidence required to do the job. It is just that those skills and that knowledge have to be deployed in double time. Duty advisers need quick access to information sufficient to sketch an outline of a case or legal principle to persuade a judge that a person should not lose their home. This book seeks to provide that quick access, while also elucidating some of the legal and practical issues that are all part of housing possession duty day.

Tables

1.6 There are no tables of statutes, regulations or case-law in this book. While statute, regulation and case-law is important to duty work, and we have referred to that which we think the duty adviser needs, this is a practical guide to duty advice and (a point we will return to often) the much larger DPP is the right place for a more finely detailed and conventional account of the law which requires tables.

Sticky notes

1.7 To make the best use of this handbook, we suggest that you read it before you get to court, although we recognise that it probably won't be all in one go. We suggest that you familiarise yourself with the chapter headings so that you know where to look for something as and when the need arises at court. We envisage the handbook being a personal copy (rather than shared in the office) – one that is splattered with sticky notes, biro markings and ends up being sufficiently dog-eared to signify regular use.

Summaries

1.8 We have tried to provide summaries and to draw out key concepts in grey break-out boxes. We hope that is useful while recognising that readers have different practices and experiences, and therefore naturally have different ideas as to what is 'key'. We hope we have pleased some of the people some of the time.

Wales

1.9 Readers will be aware that housing is a devolved matter in Wales, and in this book we have tried to acknowledge where the law or practice is different in Wales. We would be happy to be informed of anything we have missed for future editions.

Appendices

1.10 We have provided checklists for tenant possession, tenant warrant, mortgage possession and mortgage warrant cases (appendix 1). These have been developed over many years of duty work. They are one sheet only for convenience. We hope they are helpful for you, but add to or take away and change them to suit the way you work.

1.11 We have also provided wording which may help with precedent letters (appendix 4). Again, these are short. That is deliberate. We have included what we think is standard, but not included elements which of necessity require tailoring to the client's needs. We hope that they are some help, but you will have to add your own material, skill and knowledge to make sure your letters to your clients are as effective as possible.

1.12 We have included text for the outcomes of 'substantive (S) hearings'. Because 'review (R) dates' are new to us, we have not attempted to predict how those letters should work. We may look to include R date outcomes text in a future edition if R dates remains relevant, and it may be possible to put more material up online if it seems helpful.

1.13 What we have provided is draft consent orders to use at the R date (appendix 3). We have included what we have predicted at the time of writing the court will want to see. Again, if it seems appropriate to add to these, we will.

1.14 Relevant rules and practice directions are included (appendix 6). You also have the 'Overall Arrangements for Possession Proceedings in England and Wales' of the Master of the Rolls Working Group on Possession Proceedings, which currently govern the way possession claims are listed and dealt with (appendix 9).

1.15 At the time of writing, there are three different time periods of differing notice period requirements, which are also different between the two different jurisdictions of England and Wales. Notice periods have never before been such a complex subject. We have provided the details in schedules taken from the GOV.UK website, and hope it helps to have those to hand in this book (appendix 7).

Terms used

Claimant and defendant

1.16 We have tried to keep to using the terms 'claimant' and 'defendant' when appropriate and only used 'tenant', 'landlord', 'lender' and 'borrower' when we want to be specific.

RSL

1.17 We have used the acronym RSL (for Registered Social Landlords) to refer to housing associations and other providers of social housing who are not local authorities or Housing Action Trusts (HATs). We appreciate that PRPSH (Private Registered Providers of Social Housing) is the formal title for such organisations in England, but RSL (i) is in much more common usage and will not cause any confusion by its use in this book and (ii) is still the formal title in Wales.

Conditional possession orders

1.18 We are using the term 'postponed possession order' mostly in the sense of where a possession order is made but the date for giving up possession is postponed on terms to be complied with by the tenant. If the tenant breaches the terms, there is a mechanism in the order for the landlord to ask the court, to apply on written notice to the tenant, to fix the date for possession which would then make the order into an 'outright possession order'.

1.19 We distinguish an outright possession order where the date for giving up possession is extended for up to a maximum 42 days by calling that kind of order a 'postponed outright possession order'.

1.20 We use the term 'suspended possession order' knowing that it is imprecise but is well-known and understood.

Counterclaims, set off, additional claims, Part 20 claims

1.21 We refer to 'counterclaims' and to 'set off' in this book because we are in the business of defending possession proceedings. We are looking at claims that defendants may assert in order to set off arrears and prevent possession orders. These claims may be counterclaims or they may more simply be 'set off', but the main thing is that they are asserted in order to prevent a possession order being made. We don't bother much with the distinction between a 'counterclaim' and just 'set off' because it does not arise in practice on duty. Other types of claims under Civil Procedure Rules 1998 (CPR) Part 20 may do other things which are outside of the scope of this book.

Master of the Rolls Working Group's Overall Arrangements

1.22 We refer throughout to the 'Overall Arrangements' – these are the Master of the Rolls (as Head of Civil Justice) Working Group on Possession Proceedings, 'Overall Arrangements for Possession Proceedings, in England and Wales: "The Overall Arrangements"'

(17 September 2020: Version 1.0). These are reproduced in appendix 9 below. The Overall Arrangements explain how possession proceedings should be conducted following the lifting of the stay on proceedings (implemented on 26 March 2020 in response to the COVID-19 pandemic) from 20 September 2020.

Defending Possession Proceedings

1.23 We refer to the *guvnor* of housing textbooks, *Defending Possession Proceedings* (Jan Luba QC, Nic Madge, Derek McConnell, John Gallagher and Sam Madge-Wyld, 8th edn, Legal Action Group, 2016) as 'DPP' throughout, and the debt owed to it by our practical guide to housing possession court duty work is self-evident.

What is a duty adviser? What is duty advice?

- These may seem to be strange questions to be asking at this point in the book, but they are important ones that define the limits of what a duty adviser can achieve at a possession hearing.
- A duty adviser is not the same as a legal representative in the traditional sense, and duty advice is not the same as representation by an advocate briefed in advance about the claim and the defendant's response to the claim. A legal representative generally has much more opportunity to consider the case, to seek evidence and test the evidence, and to formulate the arguments in advance of a hearing.
- Most experienced (deputy) district judges are keenly aware of the limits of the instructions that can be taken on the duty day, including time constraints and also the less than ideal working environment of the court building setting. The paperwork that the duty adviser may have to work with may be incomplete. The defendant may have caring obligations or other circumstances whereby their focus is by necessity not fully on providing a clear account of their circumstances.
- If a judge does not deal with the hearing with an appreciation of those limitations, then it is worth politely reminding them, not least for the benefit of the transcription should that be needed at later date.

- This is particularly important in the current situation where R date advice is available and might have been given to a defendant and first possession hearing are now listed for 15 minutes and it may be felt by judges that they can get into the detail more than when hearings were listed for five minutes.
- For example, lengthy discussion about the nature of a defence that is proposed and the evidence that might be marshalled to support that defence is a possible indication that the judge is not taking into account the short amount of time and the circumstances in which the duty adviser must work.
- It is legitimate to remind the judge of those circumstances in which the duty adviser obtains instructions and the limits of R date advice, if indeed it was provided, and refer to the test that the judge should apply when deciding how to deal with the case. See chapter 5 on defences. It may be remarked that the rules giving rise to the test have not changed.

Conclusion

1.24 We hope that we have given you enough form and substance to fight off every landlords' and mortgagors' application for possession. We are open to any suggestions where we can improve on practice, and welcome suggestions from practitioners. We are working in an area of law and practice that is in flux and constantly growing. We have made the text as comprehensive and as up-to-date as possible to November 2020.

CHAPTER 2

The court and the duty day

Key points

- Housing Possession Court Duty Scheme (HPCDS) sessions are conducted in the county court before district judges or deputy district judges.
- In this chapter we try to give a sense of the setting, the roles of each of the participants and the texture of a court duty possession day from the perspective of the duty adviser.
- Prior to the COVID-19 public health crisis, most possession claims were issued by a landlord or lender and then listed for a hearing. The duty adviser would see any tenant/borrower defendant who wanted advice and representation on the day.
- COVID-19 has caused the government and the judiciary to radically alter the procedure, and we set out how 'review (R) dates' and 'substantive (S) hearings' will work at the time of writing under the Master of the Rolls Working Group on Possession Proceedings' 'Overall Arrangements'. See 1.22 above and appendix 9 below for details.
- Some of those arrangements are specific to local courts and so a duty adviser will need to make themselves familiar with those arrangements, such as how defendants get in touch for R advice and how agreements at the R advice date stage are communicated to the court.
- The importance of R date advice may be in settling the claim – but much more often it will be in giving advice as to how a defendant can put themselves in the best position for the S hearing.
- At the S hearing, the court usher co-ordinates everything leading up to going into the court room itself. The authors cannot stress enough how important it is to have a good relationship with the usher.
- Duty advisers need the soft skills of empathy, calm professionalism and the ability to listen. That goes as much for negotiating with an opponent as it does for taking instructions from the defendant.

Listing pre COVID-19

2.1 Prior to the COVID-19 pandemic crisis, possession claims were mostly block listed. In some busy courts, a block list might consist of 60 cases each listed for five minutes and proceeding at a rapid pace. Of those, the duty adviser could expect to be instructed in anything between five and 25 of those cases.

2.2 While a very busy day might seem daunting, an experienced duty adviser will use the fact of the shortness of time for the court to consider each case to their clients' advantage. Where there is any dispute as to fact or law, the court has little option but to adjourn cases where it has only five minutes to consider the case. In these circumstances, it is not hard to persuade the judge that the threshold for a defence is met or there is a need of more information giving rise to an adjournment.

2.3 In less busy courts there will be a much lower number of cases. There might be more time to consider the facts, and the arguments to be deployed to achieve the desired outcome must be more carefully constructed.

2.4 The listings can include social landlord cases, private landlord cases, accelerated possession listed hearings and mortgage cases. The courts tend to try to list similar cases together, and in busy courts it is not unusual to have a whole day of local authority possession cases.

2.5 Additional warrant suspension application cases tend to be listed in the morning before the main list and just after the lunch adjournment in the afternoon or at the end of the court day.

2.6 On 27 March 2020 a general stay was announced by the Master of Rolls on possession proceedings in response to the COVID-19 public health crisis. That stay was in place until 20 September 2020. It was clear that different arrangements would be needed when the stay was lifted in order to meet the following strategy outlined in the document 'Overall Arrangements for Possession Proceedings in England and Wales: "The Overall Arrangements"' produced by the Master of the Rolls Working Group on Possession Proceedings:

> 4. The strategy reflected in the Overall Arrangements is directed to (a) reducing volume in the system by enabling earlier advice and increasing settlement, (b) taking account, within limits that the law has imposed, of the effect of the pandemic on all parties, and (c) maintaining confidence in the fairness of outcomes. These objectives are also relevant beyond the legal system, including to the economy and to homelessness.

Listing after 20 September 2020 – the lifting of the stay

2.7 The listing of the cases following the lifting of the stay is dealt with in the Overall Arrangements document developed by the Master of the Rolls Working Group.

2.8 This includes the innovation of the 'review (R) date', which is a review conducted by the judge of the papers filed by the claimant, as well as an opportunity for the defendant to get free, non-means-tested advice from a duty adviser prior to any hearing. In general, 10 R dates are listed for each duty day.

2.9 The first substantive hearing is now called an 'S hearing' and these will be listed at least 28 days after the R date.

2.10 S hearings are also listed 10 per day, but because they are traditional type hearings with the parties being at court, they are listed at 20-minute intervals to ensure social distancing in the court building, including in the waiting areas. All are face-to-face, unless the parties agree otherwise or some other contingency arises preventing a face-to-face hearing.

2.11 The hearings are listed for 15 minutes, with the remaining five minutes allocated to social distancing and safety arrangements such as court cleansing. Possession hearings have always been flexible as to exactly how much time they are in court regardless of the time estimate, and so it will probably vary from case to case as to exactly how much time each case will be before the judge.

2.12 With 15 minutes to hear each case it is expected there will be more scrutiny by the judge as to the factual background of the case than in the previous block listed five-minute hearings. In addition, the judge and parties should have the benefit of the R bundle of documents (see below) which should be more fulsome and helpful than the Possession Claim Online (PCOL) claim form and particulars of pre COVID-19 hearings.

2.13 The duty adviser may have to fit R advice in around whatever of the 10 substantive hearings they are instructed on, but at the time of writing most organisations have told us that they will deal deploy two advisers on any given duty day – one to conduct R date advice and one to do the S hearing at court.

2.14 The time for the judge to consider the review date claims is at the end of the court day – and so if orders settling cases at the R date are to be put before the judge then R advice must be completed by the end of the S hearings if possible. Arrangements to get orders to the court will be specific to each court and will involve a dedicated email address.

2.15 As previously, warrant applications and other miscellaneous applications and hearings, including accelerated possession claims listed for hearing, will be fit in around the listed S hearings.

2.16 The Overall Arrangements document sets out a suggested schedule for hearings on S dates, but is keen to reiterate that listing is a judicial function.

Enhanced information, COVID-19 Case Marking and R date bundle

2.17 The Overall Arrangements, alongside Civil Procedure Rules 1998 (CPR) Practice Direction (PD) 55C 6.1 and 6.2, require claimants to set out in one form or another what knowledge the claimant has as to the effect of the COVID-19 pandemic crisis on the defendant and/or their dependants. This may be done by way of the activation notice in cases which require that (see chapter 3 on CPR PD 55C) or in new cases, at the S hearing.

2.18 The effects that are to be reported are not just medical, but may be financial due to loss of employment or other reason. The claimant is only required to consider making enquiries about the effects of the pandemic crisis. Nevertheless, a failure to do so might be argued by a duty adviser on the issue of reasonableness to make a possession order in relevant cases and may be considered to be, for example, an unlawful fetter on discretion in public law defence cases.

2.19 COVID-19 information provided by the claimant may lead to court mark the case with 'COVID-19 Case Marking' or the case may be marked on request by the claimant or defendant and is not limited to COVID-19 effects on the defendant. The claimant may wish to inform the court that they have been affected by the pandemic and that should figure in the court's consideration of what order to make.

2.20 The Overall Arrangements state that the information required is as follows (footnotes to para 30):

> Covid-19 Case Marking by a Defendant will require the following information from the Defendant:
>
> - brief details of the particular hardship faced by the Defendant;
> - whether there were material arrears outstanding before March 2020;
> - whether the Defendant has been placed on furlough, and whether the Defendant offered or paid a related proportion of rent or borrowing arrears;
> - whether the Defendant has obtained universal credit since March 2020, and whether the Defendant offered or paid a related proportion of rent or borrowing arrears;
> - whether the Defendant has been unable to earn by reason of Covid-19;
> - whether the Defendant has been shielding;
> - what proposals the Defendant has to pay the rent or borrowing arrears.

Covid-19 Case Marking by a Claimant will require the following information from the Claimant:

- brief details of the particular hardship faced by the Claimant;
- whether the Claimant has received assistance under a Covid-19 scheme, including (where a Landlord) with any borrowing by the Landlord in respect of the property.

2.21 The purpose of COVID-19 marking is to indicate that the case may be suitable for settlement (see appendix 8 for what we know about the mediation pilot), draw the court's attention to the pandemic-related medical or financial issues in the case, to assist with listing priorities and decision and to help with monitoring. Judges have told the authors that their courts will literally mark the files with a large letter 'C' in marker pen.

2.22 Claimants will also need to provide to the court at least 14 days before the R date (see below) an electronic bundle, with a paper bundle allowed as an alternative. It is implied in the Overall Arrangements that the clamant should try to provide the defendant with an electronic bundle as well. As will be seen in relation to R advice below, if the claimant does not produce an electronic bundle to the court and/or the defendant, then that will cause difficulties with R advice, which is very likely to be conducted remotely.

2.23 The contents of the bundle are not specified. Duty advisers would want to see notices and tenancy agreements, protocol checklists and other helpful documentation – but these are not prescribed.

2.24 The Overall Arrangements state that there are new rules in respect of rent arrears cases requiring the claimant to provide an up to date rent statement for the last two years or, it may be assumed from when the tenancy started if more recent than two years.

2.25 CPR PD 55A 2.3(2) requires the particulars of claim to include:

> ... in schedule form, the dates and amounts of all payments due and payments made under the tenancy agreement for a period of two years immediately preceding the date of issue, or if the first date of default occurred less than two years before the date of issue from the first date of default and a running total of the arrears;

2.26 But CPR PD 55B allows for a summary only of the arrears to be provided if the claim is issued by PCOL and if a rent or mortgage statement covering the full term or a minimum period of two years has already been sent to the defendant prior to commencing proceedings. The claimant is then required to serve an updated schedule not more than seven days after issue of the proceedings and must give evidence of having done so (CPR 55 PD 55B 6.2 and 6.3; and see chapter 3 below).

2.27 What duty advisers need to see is the updated schedule; the tenancy agreement; the notice relied on; and any pre-action protocol checklist, and if they are giving R advice remotely, they will need that in electronic form. However, the documents are not prescribed for the R date bundle and so it is to be seen whether they are regularly included and whether judges are alert to the directions at PD 55B 6.2 and 6.3. Certainly duty advisers will need to note for themselves and advise the defendant what information they had while giving R advice as that may need to be communicated to the judge at the S hearing on the issue of what if any progress was made following a R advice, and also to monitor whether the appropriate rent or mortgage schedule information has been provided by the time of the S hearing.

What do you need at court?

- This book!
- Calculator
- Phone and charger (advise not to rely on calculator on phone)
- Laptop/tablet – This will be necessary to obtain the R date bundle if the duty adviser is giving R date advice from court.
- Checklist forms to record client instructions (see appendix 1):
    - tenant possession;
    - tenant warrant;
    - mortgage possession;
    - mortgage warrant.
- A means that suits you of keeping documents together and separate from other documents – this can be as simple as a folded piece of scrap paper as a makeshift 'wallet'.
- Something that you can write a quick note on for the defendant to take away if needed.
- Details of local advice agencies and other signposting details, such as foodbanks etc.
- Pens (more than one)
- Sticky notes
- Water
- Food
- Your or your organisation's business cards
- Print-out of main benefits rates – see: www.rightsnet.org.uk/resources/benefit-tax-credit-rates

- Number(s) of local authority homelessness offices – if an application to suspend a warrant does not succeed, your client may need to contact the council in a hurry.
- If there is case-law you find you use often, keep a print-out with you.

What do you need generally? (non-exhaustive list)

- *Defending Possession Proceedings* book
- *Legal Action* magazine
- Updates – Nearly Legal, Arden Housing View, Lime Legal, various barristers' chambers' updates
- Housing Law Practitioners Association (HLPA) membership and bi-monthly training
- An up-to-date notion of your organisation's capacity to take on new cases under legal aid or otherwise and of the advice sector locally
- Colleagues to talk to inside and/or outside of your organisation

The R date

Overview

2.28 The purpose of the R date is twofold. First and foremost, it allows an opportunity for the tenant to get free, non-means-tested legal advice and assistance in advance of the hearing of the claim for possession. Secondly, the judge will consider the claim papers to make sure that they comply with the rules, protocols and Overall Arrangements, and may make directions or even strike a case out (unlikely in the vast majority of cases) if they do not.

2.29 When the claim form is served on the tenant, only the R date will be listed and there is prominent information urging the tenant to obtain advice from the duty advice service in advance or under the Housing Possession Court Duty Scheme (HPCDS). The arrangements for obtaining this advice is provided on the documentation.

2.30 In some courts it appears that the S hearing will be automatically listed for 28 days after the R date. In others, the S hearing will only be listed at the R date. In either case the intention of the Overall Arrangements (not always followed by all courts, it has to be said) is that the S hearing date will not be communicated to the tenant initially. This is to provide more incentive for the tenant to obtain advice at the R date.

How it works

2.31 R date advice may be delivered remotely by telephone or video, or may be face-to-face.

Face-to-face R advice

2.32 At the time of writing, in the light of the COVID-19 crisis it is inconceivable to us that the county courts will be able to host face-to-face R date advice in most if not all court buildings because of the need for social distancing. That may of course change, but at this time, it seems likely that if face-to-face R advice is to be delivered it will be because the provider is able to accommodate this at their own offices. We do not think that will be a widespread practice, at least at first.

2.33 The R date is part of the duty day at court and so face-to-face R advice would mean having one duty adviser at court conducting S hearings and one adviser elsewhere conducting face-to-face R advice. That may prove uneconomical for some organisations to sustain, but other organisations may in any event be conducting their duty days in that way.

Remote R advice

2.34 It is anticipated that most R advice will be conducted remotely, and mostly by telephone. While it is true that the remote nature of this advice may limit how effective it can be, it must be recalled that this is an entirely new piece of advice that did not exist before and so for tenants it is well worth engaging with.

2.35 The duty adviser conducting remote R advice should have access to the electronic claim bundle that the claimant is required by the Overall Arrangements to provide 14 days before the R date. If a paper bundle only has been provided, then that will not be available to a remote duty adviser and so that fact should be noted that the judge at the any later S hearing can be informed.

2.36 If the duty adviser does get access to the bundle, either from the court or the defendant, they will wish to go through that with the tenant and obtain instructions as to how the current situation came about. Checklists to assist with taking instructions appear at appendix 1 below.

2.37 The claimant or their representative must be available to speak to, and the duty adviser's primary purpose is to negotiate a settlement of the claim in the usual way. It is hoped that this R advice and negotiations can lead to a significant number of S hearings not needing to go ahead. Such an outcome is good for both landlord and tenant, but also helps with relieving pressure on the court system of the large backlog and ongoing demand for court resolution of possession claims.

2.38 An outcome from the R date which will obviate the need for an S hearing will of course include adjournments or conditional possession orders if that cannot be avoided. If such an outcome can be agreed, then an order recording the agreement can be put to the judge for approval the same day. Precedent draft orders are annexed at appendix 3 below.

2.39 It may also include the adviser identifying a defence to proceedings of sufficient merit to attract legal aid. If the landlord is not persuaded to withdraw or adjourn proceedings, and if the tenant is eligible for legal aid, then there is an opportunity for the adviser's organisation to grant legal aid under delegated functions in order to prepare a formal defence. In those circumstances an order containing directions for the same can again be put to the judge for approval the same day and that will include provision for the S hearing to be vacated.

2.40 There is a dedicated email address for each court for the purpose of co-ordination between the parties, the court the duty adviser(s) and the claimant's representatives, and this is how an agreed order will be communicated to the judge.

2.41 The duty adviser may propose mediation in cases that they consider are appropriate for referral (see appendix 8). A referral will only place if both parties agree.

The Overall Arrangements and the CPR

The Overall Arrangements are guidance issued by the Master of the Rolls' office to help the court and the judiciary manage the opening up of proceedings. They are not rules or directions. It is unclear to the authors as to the consequences of a court not following these arrangements either in spirit or letter.

What is clear is that in relation to post stay claims, the court's general case management powers at CPR Part 3 are doing a lot of the work in making the Overall Arrangements effective. CPR 3.1, 3.2, 3.3 and 3.4 are the mechanics by which R dates and S hearings occur, along with everything in between.

It may well be that we will need to see the Overall Arrangements in action (and possibly in the breach) to understand how the courts of first instance and any appeal courts would deal with deviation from the arrangements.

For example, those leading the Master of the Rolls' Working Group were at pains to confirm that that there is no intention in the Overall Arrangements that any form of possession order, conditional or otherwise, would be made on the R date. Any such order would give a defendant an absolute right to set it aside but we would hope that no (deputy) district judge would think of making such an order in the absence of the parties.

It will be important to obtain instructions from your client at the earliest opportunity about any effects of the COVID-19 public health crisis on their and their household's health and/or finances including any loss of employment and furlough issues. This is important for the court to know generally, and may justify asking for the file to COVID-19 marked – see 2.17 et seq above.

2.42 If an outcome cannot be reached involving long-term resolution of the claim or the filing of a formal defence (and counterclaim), then the duty adviser will need to provide advice to the tenant as to how they can put themselves in the best possible position by the time of the S hearing. This will of course involve making whatever affordable payments be made to the rent account; dealing with benefits matters; seeking money advice in cases where the tenant has other debt problems; and/or any of the usual advice housing lawyers are familiar with in advising tenants.

2.43 The duty adviser has an obligation under the HPCDS contract to write to the defendant after the R date to record their instructions and to advise them of the issues in the case and the outcome of the R advice. Client care information must also be provided. It is helpful to have a standard letter to record the advice given and the outcome of the R date. It is important that the letter is fully and accurately tailored to the defendant's situation. This letter is likely to determine how the tenant approaches the next stage in the case, whatever the outcome, and so it is very important that the advice is accurate, particularly as regards any action that it is advised that the tenant should take to prepare for any subsequent S hearing. It will be important to advise the defendant to take a copy of the R date advice letter to court, as it could be a different adviser at the S hearing.

2.44 For what it is worth, text for advice letters which may be adopted is at appendix 4 below, but as always the most important part of any precedent letter is what is added to reflect the defendant's situation. We have had some limited experience of conducting R advice at the time of writing, and have had the benefit of anecdotal reports from other duty advisers of their experiences. It appears that the advice to the defendant about how they might prepare for the S hearing is likely to be the most important aspect of R advice, especially in private landlord cases where there is little prospect of settling the case before a hearing.

2.45 R advice is reported to the Legal Aid Agency (LAA) by the client monitoring form issued by the LAA and the fee is the same as for an S hearing – that is the same as under the previous contract: see chapter 16. The only difficulty is that the duty adviser may not get confirmation from the court that a proposed consent order has been approved. In those circumstances, the duty adviser will have to record the outcome that they assume the court has adopted.

2.46 It was important to many members of the Working Group that the R advice should not place unrealistic, or indeed any, expectations on tenants whose cases subsequently came before the judge at an S hearing. Judges at S hearings should not be looking at whether R advice was received and making assumptions about what a tenant ought to have done having had that advice. The reason for that is that the R advice is an entirely new piece of advice and assistance, and its effectiveness is entirely untested and unclear. See below as to how this issue might be dealt with at S hearings.

The S hearing

Overview

2.47 At the start of the stay, among the London courts, there were draft proposals put forward at court user-group meetings that possession claims would have to be done remotely and without duty advice. Happily, those proposals did not survive the Working Group's deliberations. From the beginning there was an assumption in the discussions that the first potential judicial decision-making hearing in any possession claim would be a face-to-face hearing in a court room rather than by any remote means, and that duty advice would be available.

2.48 It is possible for a tenant to request a remote hearing if it suited them, but by default the hearings are in person, at court and with a duty adviser present.

2.49 In order to facilitate that safely, the number of S hearings in a day is limited to 10 in contrast to up to 60 or more in the block possession lists prior to March 2020. Claims are listed every 20 minutes to keep the waiting rooms at court buildings as sparely used as possible. Risk assessments have been carried out at each court to check the arrangements are possible.

2.50 The S hearings will take place in the usual county courts but there is speculation that 'Nightingale courts' may be used in the future for possession actions if it will help to clear the backlog of cases.

2.51 If the matter is not struck out by the judge at the R date for defective paperwork or a settlement is not reached at the R date between the tenant and the landlord, then the matter will proceed to an 'S hearing' 28 days from the R date. Usually the tenant will be informed of the S hearing by an order being sent out following the R date although we have seen cases where the court has sent notice of the R date and S hearing at the same time, which is not what the Overall Arrangements envisaged.

How S hearings work

2.52 The S hearing is very much more like the traditional 'first hearing' in possession proceedings that duty advisers were used to before March 2020. The hearings are longer – 15 minutes for the hearing plus five minutes to allow for social distancing matters – and the tenant may have had R date advice, and in a few cases may have been referred for mediation. The R date advice should not create further expectations in the judge's mind than would have been the case prior to the advent of the R date, and any mediation will not be made known to the judge.

2.53 In other cases, the S hearing may be the first time the tenant has sought any advice and the hearing may be very much like a pre-March 2020 possession hearing.

2.54 A tenant facing an S hearing is entitled to duty advice regardless of whether they have had R advice before. The duty adviser on an S hearing may have been the duty adviser advising at the R date, or might not, depending how their organisation runs their duty days. In any event, the duty adviser will have the claim papers and the hearing bundle from the landlord. They will take instructions from the tenant, perusing and considering any documents the tenant may bring to the hearing. They will then speak to the landlord's representative to get any further information needed and to try to negotiate a settlement.

2.55 If agreement can be reached, then that can be put before the judge in court for approval. If agreement cannot be reached, then the tenant's case must be argued in the court in the usual way.

2.56 Clearly a judge has more time in an S hearing then the notional five minutes in pre-March 2020 block lists. Duty advisers will need to be prepared for a more interrogative hearing than previously. However, it is important to stress once again that there is no intention in the arrangements introduced by the Working Group to create a greater expectation that tenants will have resolved their difficulties in paying rent or other issues by the time of the S hearing, than in any pre-March 2020 case. Judges should be made aware of the deep limitations of R date advice if it appears they are expecting more progress by the time of the S hearing than is reasonable and would have been expected prior to March 2020.

2.57 A range of outcomes are possible at the S hearings, and those have been outlined at chapter 12.

Instructions, negotiations and advice at the S hearing

2.58 For the new S hearings, the duty adviser will obtain instructions face-to-face in the normal way that pertained before the COVID-19 crisis. The courts should have carried out a public health assessment as to the facilities for the duty adviser to see clients face-to-face. It should go without saying that the adviser should be careful about handling documents.

2.59 What will be different about the new S hearings is that there may have been R advice given 28 days or more prior to the S hearing (and in a few cases there may have been mediation activity as well if that pilot scheme is taken up). The duty adviser may have been the adviser to give the previous advice. In those circumstances, the adviser will have a reasonable idea of the issues in the case.

2.60 If the advice and/or negotiation was not conducted by the duty adviser who is at the S hearing, then the nature of the advice and/or negotiation with the landlord is information the adviser will have to ascertain quickly. Asking the defendant for a copy of the advice letter they have received from the adviser on the R date will both assist and speed up any negotiations.

2.61 In all cases whether advice was given or not, it is to be hoped that the R bundle with the full range of documents required will be available to the duty adviser in the format they require and that will be of much more assistance in apprehending the issues in the case than the claim form and particulars of claim alone.

Obtaining instructions and managing hearings

It is obvious but worth reiterating that defendants who have come to court at risk of losing their home can be feeling and can display a range of emotions and behaviours that are not always conducive to taking clear instructions.

Obtaining instructions – client contact

It is not possible to teach all of the soft skills needed to work with anxious and sometimes angry clients, but we can emphasise the need for empathy, calm professionalism and the ability to listen. It is not unusual for duty clients to say that obtaining duty advice was the first time they felt listened to in the whole process, and just the process of listening can sometimes break down understandable defensive attitudes – that goes for claimant opponents as much as it does for defendant clients.

Take opportunities to reassure defendants if possible. It is not unknown for defendants to come to court wondering if they might go to jail and of course they can be reassured about that. An adviser might be able to say that a defendant is unlikely to lose their home. But of course always be realistic and don't promise that things will be fine if that might not be the case. You must not shy away from giving bad news if, for example, a defendant is facing a mandatory order for possession where there is no prospect of a defence. That defendant needs to know their situation and then needs advice as to what to do next.

As with advocacy skills, client contact skills must be developed with experience and by observing more experienced advisers at work.

Obtaining information – your opponent

Anxiety and emotions are not the only barrier to obtaining instructions – some housing possession cases can be complicated for lawyers to understand never mind lay people, and it is not easy for defendants to get across the details that a duty adviser needs.

Use your opponent. Defendants often attend court without any papers or with a great many. You may not know what the case is by just speaking with the defendant.

Once you have met with the defendant go to see your opponent at an early stage. It is essential to ascertain what the claimant wants (e.g. an outright order or an adjournment) and they will usually provide you with a concise statement of the issues in the case.

Ask your opponent for an up-to-date rent account and any witness statements they have prepared since the proceedings commenced. If you are missing any other papers then ask if you can see their file.

Time management

Use your time at court appropriately. If the claimant tells you they are looking for an adjournment then you will not need to spend much more time with the defendant and can move on to the next case. If the claimant wants an outright or suspended order then it will be essential to spend a longer period of time establishing the facts and considering the documents.

It is not unusual to go speak with the claimant a number of times as you go back and forth between defendant and claimant to try to reach a settlement.

The court usher

Pre COVID-19 you may have had a long line of defendants waiting for advice. It is important that you work with the usher and communicate on which cases are ready to go before the judge. You may also have seen a number of defendants but not gone into court. On those cases, inform the defendants to stay close and listen out for their case to be called and you will be called by the usher to represent them. At the time of writing this may not be as relevant as before, but it will still be important to communicate with the usher.

Summary of information to gather

When interviewing clients on the R date or the S hearing the objective is to:

- Identify the relevant legal framework.
- Identify the relevant facts.
- Obtain the facts in the most efficient way – sometimes that will be from papers and interview, sometimes from the other side, sometimes a mix of all of them.
- Identify if the case is discretionary or mandatory grounds for possession.
- Ascertain if there is there a defence.
- Check if the defendant wants to defend.
- Is there a technical argument to delay where the defendant is facing mandatory grounds?
- Decide if this is this a case more suited to negotiation, for example where legal aid will not be available to take the case further.

2.62 Once the claimant's claim is understood, it will be necessary to understand the defendant's case. A checklist of instructions is very helpful on duty because an adviser has very limited time to obtain a lot of information. Specimen checklists are provided in this book (appendix 1). Duty advisers will definitely want to adapt our versions to suit their own way of working.

2.63 The aim of the checklist is to record for the adviser the main facts of the case from which an argument for the desired outcome can be prepared. This includes the main details of the claimant's case, as well as the instructions of the defendant as to their position and that of their household.

2.64 Some elements of the case may be more narrative than a checklist allows. These may include details about health including COVID-19 related issues; about the conditions in the premises;, about work, benefits, debts and other financial issues; and about the history of contact between the defendant and the claimant.

2.65 It is essential for the duty adviser to be realistic about the time spent obtaining instructions from a defendant. One of the skills developed through experience is to be able to manage an interview such that the best use of limited time is made. The duty adviser needs to leave time to be able to negotiate with the claimant's representative, and so it is essential to get the relevant issues in just enough detail to be able to advance the argument for the desired outcome.

2.66 It may be necessary to obtain much of the information from the claimant's representative. That is perfectly normal and should not be seen as any weakness in your client's position. Some defendants, for all sorts of reasons, are simply not adept at managing the information required to successfully manage a tenancy and money. They still enjoy the full protection of the law as any other tenant, and the claimant should assist with providing information about the case.

2.67 This also assists with time management. If the claimant indicates to you that they are prepared to adjourn the proceedings because they are aware of issues in the background that need resolving, then the duty adviser knows that they will not have to spend as much time on that case. If the claimant is seeking a suspended, postponed or outright possession order, then time will need to be spent formulating reasons why that should not happen.

2.68 If a claimant or their representative does not assist with information they clearly have to hand, then that issue may be referred to the judge on the question of conduct of the claimant.

Weekly/monthly payments

How to calculate monthly from weekly

A surprising number of people will calculate a monthly amount by multiplying the weekly amount by four. That is of course wrong.

Usually the best way will be to multiply the weekly amount by 52 weeks, and then divide by 12 months. While not 100% numerically accurate, it is the method understood by most landlords.

How to calculate weekly from monthly

It follows, then, that you can multiply a monthly amount by 12 months and divide by 52 weeks.

Some landlords operate 50 or 51 week rent payments years where there are rent-free weeks. In these cases, it is important when agreeing payments terms to agree that the extra amount against the arrears does or does not need to be paid during any rent-free weeks. It is also necessary to adjust the multiples for the number of weeks the year where rent is payable.

2.69 Negotiations with the claimant or their representatives should be conducted politely and with a view to reaching settlement where possible. The defendant's case should be put at its highest point, and the desired outcome firmly argued for. If negotiations cannot lead to a settlement, then that should be accepted and the matter will have to go before the judge as a contested hearing. It is useful to always remember that even if the adviser believes the claimant or their representative is being unreasonable or even hostile, nothing will be achieved by anything other than courtesy, and the client will still have to have some sort of relationship with the person after the hearing.

2.70 The duty adviser can and should use any advantage of skill or knowledge to advance the defendant's case and undermine the opponent's case, and that includes politely pointing out any difficulties that the opponent may have in making out their case in court. That is a very different matter to getting involved in discourteous exchanges.

2.71 It may be necessary to show to the claimant documents of the defendant, but the adviser must remember to take them back. Likewise, it may be necessary to ask the claimant or their representative if it is possible to show the defendant documents in their possession. That being said, the claimant should have served any documents that they wish to rely on and if they have not, then that might be cause for an adjournment.

2.72 If an agreement as to a desired outcome *can* be reached, then it is important to tie up all of the details of the agreement. If conditions are placed on an adjournment or other order, then the exact conditions must be agreed in full between the parties including amounts; the date for things to be done; the duration of any agreement; and any other details that mean there can be no room for doubt as to compliance. The position as to costs must be also agreed.

2.73 Ultimately if a desired outcome cannot be agreed, then the parties will need to go before the judge and argue the case. The parties have a duty to tell each other what their cases will be in court, and so the adviser must explain what they will be asking for and broadly what their argument will be. It is bad form to raise issues in court which were not discussed outside court.

2.74 The timescales on duty days sometimes mean that discussions are conducted at such speed that things can be missed. Generally judges and experienced representatives are fully aware of this and are robust about the way in which such things are dealt with. It is still worth trying to agree any facts that can be agreed outside of court so as to assist with keeping to the time estimate of the hearing.

Universal credit and complexity

Universal credit (UC) pays monthly and can make it very complicated for tenants to work out what they have to pay and when. It is important when making an agreement with the landlord or pursuing particular terms of an order in the court that the date of the first payment is stipulated to be when the defendant is actually able to make that payment.

Example: You see a defendant on 2 July at court. The defendant has just paid rent from monthly wages or UC housing element (UCHE) which is paid monthly, and will not get another payment until the end of the month. Rent is payable weekly on Monday. The order sought should be '*terms of current rent plus payment of £3.75 per week against the arrears of rent of £xx.xx with the first payment being made on Monday 1st August*'.

The tenant will either have to pay a month's worth of rent and a month's worth of £3.75 (£16.25) so that they are always on or ahead of the payment schedule; OR they must pay their rent on 1 August and then pay the £3.65 every Monday from 1 August.

This is just one example, but it should give you an idea of how you must approach these issues carefully to make sure the defendant can comply with the order they have agreed or which the court orders. It can get very complicated when, as is often the case, the amount of UCHE does not meet the full rent and the amount paid to the rent account varies with the defendant's varying income. The duty adviser will need to work out and advise the tenant how to calculate what to pay to cover everything that needs to be paid, but must also advise the tenant to keep in close contact with the landlord to check that the right amount is reaching the rent account at the right time.

In fact, it is always important to advise the defendant to stay in touch with their landlord to make sure the payments they are making are reaching the landlord and accord with the order that has been made and which the landlord is expecting.

Many tenants will be stretched making even small payments against the arrears. However, if you think it is appropriate, you may advise the defendant to try if they can to pay a little over what had been ordered so that they can get ahead of the order and build goodwill with the landlord. Such goodwill may be invaluable if the defendant has unforeseen problems making payments in the future.

The UCHA and Managed Payment to Landlord – Alternative Payment together might not even meet the rent. Arrangements, direct to the landlord.

Possible UCHE scenarios:

- UCHE pays rent in full and for the same period as the rent is due, eg monthly;
- UCHE pays rent in full but for a different period than the rent is due, eg monthly when rent is due weekly;
- UCHE pays only part rent for the same period as the rent is due, eg monthly and is short by the same amount each month;
- UCHE pays only part rent for a different period than the rent is due, eg monthly when rent is due weekly and is short by the same amount each month;
- UCHE pays only part rent for the same period as the rent is due, eg monthly and the amount varies each month;
- UCHE pays only part rent for a different period than the rent is due, eg monthly when rent is due weekly and the amount varies each month.

You can double these scenarios by adding that for each the UCHE might be being paid to the defendant or might be being paid directly to the landlord.

Lastly, in cases where UC is being paid to the landlord there might or might not be extra payments being made to the landlord (Managed Payment to Landlords – Rent Arrears or MPTL-RA) nominally in respect of arrears. We say nominally because if the UCHE does not meet the rent due, then these payments will not be going to the arrears at all and will simply be topping up the UCHE. The UCHE and MPTL-RA might not even together meet the rent.

You may well come across situations with UC where through payments being made from their entitlement and/or sanctions, people have little or no money to live on. These are distressing cases and a duty adviser needs to be ready to make referrals and/or signpost to various services to try to get benefits problems resolved, and to foodbanks so people can get food. A duty adviser needs to learn what forms of support are available locally because they will need to make referrals in some very hard cases.

Roles and representatives

2.75 The issue of who is representing the claimant and who is fulfilling other roles prior to the litigation and within the litigation is important and should be part of the consideration of the duty adviser and the court. In the case of private landlords where there is no legal representation, it is important to ascertain whether the person at court is the landlord or not.

2.76 In the case of landlords who are individuals, then barring any ill-advised impersonation it should be straightforward to check that the person at court is the landlord. The tenant should be able to identify them. In the case of landlord companies or organisations, then only senior people in the organisation can represent those organisations. If the person at court is not one of those people, then the claim will have to be adjourned as the judge will not be able to hear that representative. The court may need to be reminded of the rules.

2.77 Legal representation where the claimant does not represent themselves is governed by the Legal Services Act 2007. By section 14 it is an offence to carry on a 'reserved legal activity' if not entitled to do so, and reserved legal activity includes the conduct of litigation including representation. Essentially, a person entitled to conduct litigation is a barrister instructed by a solicitor or legal department; a solicitor or a legal executive or a caseworker from a firm of solicitors or from a legal department of the council or a Private Registered Provider of Social Housing (PRPSH) and instructing. Solicitor firms or in-house solicitors will be regulated by the Registered Social Landlord (RSL). Claimants can also be assisted by a barrister through direct access.

2.78 In practice, in local authority, RSL and mortgage cases there is rarely any issue with the identity of the representative at court, be they a legal or other kind of representative, such as a housing officer or rent officer. However, in private possession work there are unregulated organisations such as the one in *Gill & Gill v Kassam* (HHJ Worster, Birmingham County Court, 13 August 2018) – see Nearly Legal, 'Eviction companies, conducting litigation, and defective notices' (https://nearlylegal.co.uk/2018/08/eviction-companies-conducting-litigation-and-defective-notices/) – and duty advisers need to keep the rules in mind.

Landlords, agents and representatives

Role	Identity
Claimant in the proceedings	Landlord(s) If landlord is a company, then the company is the claimant If joint landlords, then both/all must be claimants (CPR 19.3(1))
Serve a notice	Landlord (HA 1988 ss8, 21; PEA 1977 s5; HA 1985 s83(1))

Sign a notice	Landlord or agent
Sign statement of truth in particulars of claim	Landlord or legal representative If Landlord is a company, then 'a person holding a senior position in the company or organisation' (CPR PD 22)
Represent at hearing	Landlord in person or legal representative Legal representative is defined in CPR 2.3(1) (see below). In relation to solicitors' agents see guidance from the Bar Council at www.barcouncilethics.co.uk/documents/393/ If landlord is a company and does not have a legal representative, then arguably the person representing at the hearing should be a person who could sign a statement of truth.

CPR 2.3(1):
[. . .]
'legal representative' means a–
(a) barrister;
(b) solicitor;
(c) solicitor's employee;
(d) manager of a body recognised under section 9 of the Administration of Justice Act 1985; or
(e) person who, for the purposes of the Legal Services Act 2007, is an authorised person in relation to an activity which constitutes the conduct of litigation (within the meaning of that Act),
who has been instructed to act for a party in relation to proceedings;'

In social landlord cases, it is very common for a housing officer to be the person who has signed the statement of truth in the particulars of claim and who is representing the social landlord at court. There is a question in theory as to whether a housing officer fulfils the CPR PD 22 definition, but in practice courts do not take any point on it.

Capacity

2.79 It does sometimes occur on court duty days that a duty adviser will be consulted by a person who may lack capacity to conduct litigation. Experienced lawyers will know that it is not for a lawyer or adviser to adjudicate as to whether a person lacks capacity. In these circumstances, the duty adviser should remind themselves of the definition of capacity in sections 2 and 3 of the Mental Capacity Act (MCA) 2005:

2 People who lack capacity
(1) For the purposes of this Act, a person lacks capacity in relation to a matter if at the material time he is unable to make a decision

for himself in relation to the matter because of an impairment of, or a disturbance in the functioning of, the mind or brain.

(2) It does not matter whether the impairment or disturbance is permanent or temporary.

(3) lack of capacity cannot be established merely by reference to–
  (a) a person's age or appearance, or
  (b) a condition of his, or an aspect of his behaviour, whichmight lead others to make unjustified assumptions about his capacity.

(4) In proceedings under this Act or any other enactment, any question whether a person lacks capacity within the meaning of this Act must be decided on the balance of probabilities.

3 Inability to make decisions

(1) For the purposes of section 2, a person is unable to make a decision for himself if he is unable–
  (a) to understand the information relevant to the decision,
  (b) to retain that information,
  (c) to use or weigh that information as part of the process of making the decision, or
  (d) to communicate his decision (whether by talking, using sign language or any other means).

(2) A person is not to be regarded as unable to understand the information relevant to a decision if he is able to understand an explanation of it given to him in a way that is appropriate to his circumstances (using simple language, visual aids or any other means).

(3) The fact that a person is able to retain the information relevant to a decision for a short period only does not prevent him from being regarded as able to make the decision.

(4) The information relevant to a decision includes information about the reasonably foreseeable consequences of–
  (a) deciding one way or another, or
  (b) failing to make the decision.

And also CPR 21.3(2):

(2) A person may not, without the permission of the court–
  (a) make an application against a child or protected party before proceedings have started; or
  (b) take any step in proceedings except–
    (i) issuing and serving a claim form; or
    (ii) applying for the appointment of a litigation friend under rule 21.6,

until the child or protected party has a litigation friend.

2.80 A duty adviser who suspects a client may lack capacity should make an immediate application for an adjournment of proceedings on the basis of CPR 21.3 before any further step in the proceedings is taken.

It is not a question of proving that the defendant lacks capacity – that is not the role of the duty adviser, but of communicating to the judge that in the duty adviser's view they may lack capacity and that issue needs to be resolved before any further step in the litigation is taken. The duty adviser should indicate that in their view, the fact that the defendant has the assistance of the duty adviser is not enough to confer capacity pursuant to MCA 2005 s3(2).

Evidence

2.81 While there is traditionally not time for the court to consider much in the way of written evidence beyond the claim form and particulars, or oral evidence in a busy housing possession list, the new Overall Arrangements and less busy court lists may allow for evidence to become an issue for the duty adviser. It is beyond the scope of this book to go into all the rules of evidence, but it is worth setting out a checklist of issues for the duty adviser to be aware of the following points:

2.82 An advocate cannot give evidence on behalf of their client. Where the representative is the housing officer, this is sometimes given a rather broad interpretation by the court given that much of the evidence required is already in the particulars of claim and/or any statements that have been filed.

2.83 The claimant can be asked to verify any evidence they rely upon by giving oral evidence including examination of the maker of any witness statement if they can. If they can't, they may be in difficulty relying on it.

2.84 Although examination of a witness is rare in duty hearings, it should always be borne in mind as a tactic if evidence put forward by the claimant is denied by the defendant, particularly in relation to service of the notice.

2.85 Likewise, it can be useful to ask the defendant to give evidence if there is a factual dispute that the adviser thinks could resolve matters, although that must be considered very carefully as the defendant can also be cross-examined and so the adviser would need to be confident that the defendant can verify the facts. Defendants often do not have the paperwork at court to verify their case, and so asking them to give oral evidence can be an effective way of making good the absence of documentary proof.

2.86 The judge can ask questions of either party, either directly or through representatives. A duty adviser learns whether or not to encourage individual defendants to speak directly to the judge, and in the right circumstances that can be a useful tactic. Defendants under pressure in a court setting can be emotional. There is no reason for defendants to have to hide appropriate emotional responses to the prospect of losing their home, and it can be useful to remind the court of the high stakes involved in possession hearings.

2.87 Occasionally a defendant may have sent a statement to the court and may or may not have a copy and/or have sent it to the claimant. The adviser will have to manage that as best as they can – and it is absolutely permissible to ask the judge to be able to see the statement from the court file. It will then have to be shown to the claimant or their representative whether it is helpful or not.

2.88 If the defendant arrives at court with a statement which has not been filed or served, it is one of the jobs of the duty adviser to decide whether it should be relied upon or not. If it is to be relied upon, it will have to be shown to the claimant and handed up to the judge.

Judges and hearings

2.89 Possession proceedings are conducted in the county court and are presided over by a district judge or a deputy district judge. A deputy district judge can be a part-time judge appointed as deputy district judge and can also be a retired judge who is appointed as a deputy district judge.

2.90 Some deputy district judges can therefore have a huge experience of hearing possession claims and others may be relatively new to it. Regardless of the level of experience of the judge, it is both wise and courteous for the duty adviser to set out the law and practice in full for any arguments they are making, while at the same time indicating that the judge may well be fully aware of the law and practice. Judges can be highly knowledgeable and experienced – they may still need reminding of the details of the law. Most judges are grateful for the involvement for the duty adviser because of the duty adviser's ability and skill to get across the factual nub of the case, the relevant law, the discretion which judges must exercise in relevant cases as well as any rules and practice directions which are relevant. In that respect the duty adviser has the normal dual role of the advocate, which is to put their client's case at its highest point; while also serving the court by accurately assisting with explaining the law and practice relevant to the case.

2.91 Female judges are addressed as 'Madam' or 'Ma'am' and male judges as 'Sir'. If the opponent is a barrister, then they are by convention referred to as 'my learned friend' and, while a less established convention, the authors like to call non barrister representatives (solicitors or legal executives) 'my friend'. The claimant may be referred to as 'the claimant' or by their name, eg 'Ms James' or 'Mr Mullings'.

2.92 Possession hearings may be conducted in chambers (a relatively informal room where each party sits at opposite sides of a desk adjacent to the judge's desk) or in a more formal courtroom. The rules and practice are not different in either setting. Advocates (and the duty adviser is an advocate) are usually not required to stand when speaking, and their clients may sit next to them. Usually, as long as it does not disturb proceedings, advocates may take whispered instructions from their clients in hearings, although that will not be possible during the COVID-19 crisis.

2.93 All proceedings are now conducted in open court unless the judge orders otherwise (CPR 39.2). This can be difficult for some tenants and borrowers. The hearing can involve personal details about finances or family circumstances and health which the defendant may not wish to share widely. In mortgage proceedings, there is a danger of unregulated lenders and mortgage rescue operators seeking to gain details of cases where they may seek to profit from those facing mortgage difficulties and needing to sell their home. In appropriate cases the duty adviser may apply to the judge for a hearing to be held in private under CPR 39.2(3). Ultimately it will be for the judge to decide, but many judges are aware that the default position is to have hearings be open and transparent and so the duty adviser will need to make good arguments why that usual position should not be followed.

2.94 In possession claims, the claimant's advocate or the claimant in person usually speaks first and the duty adviser responds. It may be that an agreement has been reached and the adviser is simply there to indicate agreement. In other agreed cases, it may be incumbent on the duty adviser to set out the agreement for the court if they can do so more concisely than the claimant could.

2.95 In other cases, the claim may be contested and the adviser may be making an application for certain things to happen, such as time for an external factor to be resolved and then the matter come back to court, or time for a defence to be filed. In those cases, the adviser waits their turn and then makes their application, setting out the reasons for the order they seek.

2.96 There are important exceptions to waiting one's turn. Where the claim is for a mandatory order for possession and the tenant wishes to bring a counterclaim or dispute the claim on public law grounds, then it may be necessary to ensure that the court does not make any findings of fact on the level of arrears or service of the notice, and in those circumstances it may be necessary to politely ask to make the application before evidence is taken as to those matters.

2.97 The texture and form of hearings is something that duty advisers have to get to grips with by experience, and people new to duty advice would do well to shadow a colleague for some time to observe how the hearings tend to proceed. Different people have different styles of advocacy, but in the experience of the authors, courtesy to the judge and the opponent never goes down badly and often goes down well.

2.98 Court hearings are recorded and if there is an appeal then the transcript of the recording will be obtained for that purpose. Therefore it is important for the duty adviser to make sure that everything that needs to be said to establish the defendant's case, is said. That way it will be on the transcript if the issue of the arguments put to the judge are in issue in an appeal. It is also worth recalling and reminding the judge if necessary that the judge must give reasons for their decision.

2.99 When the hearing is concluded, it is important to make sure that the exact details of the outcome are recorded in writing. These may include obligations on the defendant which are the conditions on which they keep their home. If there is anything that was not quite understood or heard, it is perfectly proper to ask the judge to repeat them in order to ensure that the outcome is recorded.

2.100 That includes any preamble to the order. If that matter has to come back to court, the next judge will read the preamble so it forms an important part of the outcome of the hearing even if it is not part of the order itself.

After the S hearing

2.101 After the hearing and outside of the courtroom, the duty adviser will need to explain the outcome to the defendant and make sure they understand. Where conditions and/or obligations have been placed on the defendant those need to be explained accurately and in detail. It will often help to have the defendant take a note or to make a note for them. They may have obligations to fulfil very quickly so they need to leave the court building understanding what they have to do. The defendant may have been waiting some considerable time for their hearing and may be under a lot of stress. They may be anxious to get out of the court building for all sorts of reasons. They are of course at liberty to do so, but the adviser's job is to do everything reasonably possible to get them the advice they need before they leave the building.

2.102 An adviser may be able to help by signposting to other forms of advice such as law centres, citizens' advice or other generalist agencies. It is good practice to have the details of local forms of advice for the courts where advisers are working so they can pass these on. It is even more helpful for the duty adviser to build relationships where possible with local advice centres so that such signposting can be more effective.

2.103 In cases where the hearing has not gone well, it can of course be very difficult to advise the defendant as to what has happened and what their options are next. It is important to provide that advice, though, because that may steer them to making the right choices in very difficult circumstances.

2.104 In cases where the defendant is going to keep their home, whatever the kind of order it can be helpful to encourage a short post-hearing discussion between them and their landlord or lender. Traditionally cases that end up in court often have a background of poor communication between landlord and tenant or borrower and lender, and so anything that can be done to encourage future communication about difficulties will be helpful.

2.105 If it is intended for the duty adviser or their organisation to see if they can assist the defendant further, perhaps with a defence or other matters, then while it is not required to take the defendant's telephone number for any other purpose, it is a good idea to get it for that purpose.

2.106 Under the HPCDS contract, the adviser is obliged to write to the defendant recording their instructions, the negotiations undertaken and the outcome of the hearing. It may be helpful to have a precedent letter for each of the different types of cases advisers come across on duty to assist to communicate the advice the defendant needs. We have included some precedent letters which can be adapted to suit individual advisers' or organisations' practices (see appendix 4).

2.107 However, it is important that the letter is fully and accurately tailored to the defendant's situation. This letter is likely to determine how the defendant approaches the next stages in the case, or their conduct in relation to the tenancy, whatever the outcome – and so it is very important that the advice is accurate, particularly as regards any conditions set for an adjournment, postponed order or suspended order. As always with precedent letters, the most important part of the letter is the information that is added to the precedent to tailor the letter to the recipient's need for advice. The letter of advice to a duty client is often the last piece of expert legal advice they will have for some time, or even ever. It is important to make that advice count to help the client retain their home in the future.

CHAPTER 3

Pre-action protocols, CPR Part 55 and practice directions

Key points

- In this chapter we get to grips with the protocols, rules and practice directions which govern the way in which possession proceedings work.
- At the time of the writing, the 'Overall Arrangements' issued by the Master of the Rolls Working Group on Possession Proceeding are in force, and while they are designed to work with the existing framework, they do extensively change the mechanics of possession claims leading up to issue and up to and including the first hearing ('S hearing').
- The importance of the protocols, rules and practice directions cannot be overstated, and they are reproduced in full in the appendices to this book. In mandatory grounds for possession cases they are sometimes the last line of defence, literally as well as metaphorically.
- While it is neither possible nor necessary to know all of the protocols, rules and practice directions by heart, duty advisers do need a good working knowledge of the principles in order to know when the arguments arising from them can be deployed.
- There is no applicable pre-action protocol in private possession cases, but compliance with Civil Procedure Rules 1998 (CPR) requirements can be key to trying to defend proceedings or buy time for a defendant.

Introduction

3.1 Possession proceedings are governed by Civil Procedure Rules 1998 (CPR) Part 55 and the three associated practice directions (PDs). These outline the procedure to be followed by claimants and defendants when bringing and defending a claim for possession. These rules and directions supplement the general rules and directions for litigation in the county court and they represent a very distinct and evolved code for possession claims.

3.2 A good working knowledge of the relevant protocols, rules and practice directions, and the 'Overall Arrangements for Possession Proceedings in England and Wales: "The Overall Arrangements"' issued by the Master of the Rolls Working Group on Possession Proceeding, is needed by duty advisers as these often form the basis of negotiations in the first instance and representations in the court if required. Few advisers will be able to learn all of that by heart, and so we have annexed them in the appendices to this publication for easy reference (appendix 9).

3.3 Duty advisers should bear in mind that for nearly all judges the importance of the protocol is a matter of context and whether a breach is material to the issues at hand. Duty advisers should raise all breaches of the protocol, but should be looking to demonstrate how fairness and justice between the parties is affected by the breach wherever possible.

Pre-Action Protocol for Possession Claims by Social Landlords

Overview

3.4 The Pre-Action Protocol for Possession Claims by Social Landlords applies to all social landlords – essentially local authorities and RSLs. It does not apply to private landlords. The protocol expressly refers to 'social landlords' which suggests that it does not apply to private landlords who are letting accommodation in any way pursuant to the local authority's duties to homeless people under Housing Act (HA) 1996 Part 7, but that may be arguable.

3.5 The aims are set out in the protocol itself at 1.4:

- to encourage more contact between parties prior to the issue of proceedings;
- to enable resolution without the need for proceedings; and
- to focus the issues if the claim must go to a court hearing.

3.6 The extent to which the protocol can be relied upon in proceedings is set out firstly at 1.5:

- the court should take into account whether the protocol has been followed when considering what orders to make;
- the tenant's vulnerability should be considered at an early stage (if known to the landlord):
  - whether the tenant lacks capacity to defend the proceedings;
  - whether any issues arise under the Equality Act (EA) 2010.

3.7 The effect of the protocol is further outlined at 2.14 where the court is directed it may make orders in respect of costs, orders for adjournments and even strike out or dismiss all of a claim if the landlord does not comply.

Rent arrears

3.8 Part 2 of the protocol is specifically about possession claims based on rent arrears, and sets out a number of obligations on the landlord, which can be summarised as follows:

- Contact the tenant as soon as possible when arrears accrue.
- Discuss cause of arrears, tenant's finances, entitlement to benefits where applicable and repayments.
- Use that information to try to agree repayment arrangements.
- Provide quarterly rent statements showing rent due and sums received for the past 13 weeks. Emphasis is placed on them being 'in a comprehensible format' which is sometimes a live issue at hearings.
- In applicable cases, apply for payments from the Department for Work and Pensions (DWP) from benefits. This is an important provision.
- Offer assistance with housing-related benefits – another important provision.
- Advise the tenant to seek financial advice from eg Citizens Advice, a Law Centre, a debt advice or other appropriate agency.

3.9 Paragraph 2.6 is a very important provision to bring to the court's attention where there is an outstanding housing benefit or universal credit housing element (UCHE) claim where the tenant can show they have provided the information requested for the claim and payments to cover any liability not being met by housing-related benefits have been made by the tenant. In those circumstances, the protocol says that proceedings should not be started. If these are the circumstances in which proceedings have been started, the adviser should ask for the claim to be struck out.

3.10 Likewise, 2.9 strongly suggests that proceedings should not be commenced if the tenant is keeping to a payment arrangement. If the tenant ceases to comply then warning of proceedings should be given.

3.11 The protocol continues to impose obligations on the landlord right up to and even beyond the first hearing (S hearing). Not less than 10 days before the hearing, the landlord should provide a rent statement (a provision which is beefed up by both practice directions and the Overall Arrangements) and details of what it knows about any housing benefit or UCHE claim. This last point needs to be considered alongside the earlier protocol requirements to seek to discuss and offer help with benefit issues, and so it is not sufficient for a landlord to say they don't know anything if they have not made efforts to find out.

3.12 The landlord should inform the tenant of the hearing and advise them to attend. The landlord should also still be looking to see if any repayment arrangements can be agreed, and if in place, should agree to the case being adjourned. If there is any cessation of an arrangement, the tenant is entitled to a warning before the landlord restores proceedings – 2.13(c) of the protocol thereby extends the effect of the protocol even beyond the first substantive hearing.

3.13 Paragraph 2.15 informs the court that its consideration as to whether it is reasonable for a possession order to be made can be influenced by the tenant's conduct under the protocol. The obligations of the tenant under the protocol are less defined, but landlords will point to a lack of co-operation when trying to persuade the judge to make orders, and those submissions might broadly map on to this provision.

Mandatory grounds

3.14 Part 3 of the protocol deals with cases where the landlord contemplates and brings claims for possession based on mandatory grounds. The purpose of Part 3 is set out in 1.3, and this is helpful for the adviser to have in mind. Paragraph 1.3 recognises that even in mandatory cases, human rights, public law and/or Equality Act defences may be available to a tenant and therefore Part 3 seeks to ensure that the information required by the court to consider if there any such defences available is before the court at the hearing. See chapter 10 below for discussion of these cases.

3.15 In the context of social landlord claims seen on duty lists, this will be cases brought pursuant to:

- HA 1988 Sch 2 ground 8;
- HA 1988 Sch 2 ground 7A;
- HA 1988 s21;
- HA 1985 s84A;
- HA 1996 ss127–128 (introductory tenancies);
- non-secure tenancies and licences;
- housing co-op tenancies.

3.16 The requirements in these cases are that prior to proceedings being issued the landlord must write to the tenant with the underlying reasons as to why it seeks possession and asking for details of their personal circumstances or other matters they may wish to have taken into account, and must take those into account. It is made clear this should be a separate document from the notice of proceedings but could be served alongside such a notice.

3.17 When issuing such a claim, a schedule should be included, setting out compliance with the request to the tenant to provide details of any matter to be taken into account, and what consideration was given to any response, along with details of the underlying reasons for the claim. The schedule should also include any information the landlord wants the court to consider in respect of proportionality.

3.18 Part 3 is good example of how the whole protocol works in practice and in context. A failure to ask the tenant to provide information as to personal circumstances will not itself mean that a judge should not make an order if there is no argument that can be made that any such information that would give rise to a defence exists. However, if there is such information that the social landlord had not taken into account because they did not ask for it (but at the hearing it is as yet unclear that that information would give rise to a defence which meets the relevant criteria for public law, human rights or EA 2010 defences), then it can be argued that the proceedings should at least be adjourned for that information to be provided and for the landlord to consider whether to proceed with the claim or not.

3.19 Part 3 is therefore very important because it is often all that is available to try to prevent an outright possession order being made. The weight to be given to compliance with Part 3 can be argued before a judge to be particularly high as a matter of fairness and justice between the parties (and indeed Article 6 (right to a fair trial) of the European Convention on Human Rights (ECHR)) given that it applies to mandatory orders for possession.

3.20 While there is not the same obligation written into this protocol to set out compliance with the protocol on a practice form to be brought to the hearing (as in the mortgage protocol, below), the Overall Arrangements provide that the claimant should bring an account of compliance to the hearing.

Pre-Action Protocol for Possession Claims based on Mortgage or Home Purchase Plan Arrears in Respect of Residential Property

3.21 The mortgage and home purchase plan protocol has very similar aims as to Parts 1 and 2 of the rented property protocol. The obligations on the lender are:

- when arrears accrue, provide information to the borrower required under regulatory provisions, as to the amount for arrears, the outstanding balance as well as interest and charges;
- to seek information about whether there is a tenant;
- advise the borrower to contact the local authority and to get independent debt advice;
- discuss as to the reasons for arrears, whether temporary or long-term and whether a payment plan is possible;
- consider a request to change the date of the month for payments, and give reasons if a request is refused;
- respond promptly to any proposals from the borrower (in writing if declined);
- if the lender suggests a payment plan it must set out the proposals clearly, and the implications, and give the borrower time to consider;
- the lender must pre-warn the borrower of action to bring a claim if an arrangement is breached.

3.22 Similar to the rented property protocol, there is an important provision at 6.1 to bring to the court's attention where there is an outstanding mortgage interest payment or UC claim, or other source of assistance with paying the mortgage or purchase plan. Where the borrower can show that they have provided the information requested for the claim, in those circumstances the protocol says that proceeding *must* not be started and we emphasise this so that readers will note the stronger language in this protocol. In addition, a claim must not be started if there are financial difficulties and time is needed to seek or fulfil an appointment for debt advice, or there is a reasonable expectation of better financial circumstances arising from employment or a lodger. If these are the circumstances in which for example proceedings have been started, the adviser should ask for the claim to be struck out.

3.23 A lender must consider postponing proceedings if a borrower can show evidence of marketing the property to be sold. Reasonable time must be allowed for a sale where the borrower is actively marketing the property. In order to take advantage of this, the borrower should have provided full details of the marketing of the property to the lender. A borrower should be warned if the lender intends to start proceedings because the property has not been sold.

3.24 Paragraph 7.1 makes clear that proceedings should be a last resort and requires the lender to consider measures to sustain the mortgage or agreement such as:

(a) extend the term of the mortgage;
(b) change the type of mortgage;
(c) defer payment of interest due under the mortgage;
(d) capitalise the arrears; or
(e) make use of any Government forbearance initiatives in which the lender chooses to participate.

3.25 Paragraph 7.2 makes clear what the court should take into consideration if there is a tenant in the property. These provisions need to be considered alongside the Mortgage Repossessions (Protection of Tenants etc) Act 2010 by which the tenant of a borrower may apply to the court in mortgage possession proceedings to delay the date for possession to be given up by up to two months (see chapter 11 below).

3.26 Lastly, the protocol provides that in circumstances where a borrower has made a complaint to the Financial Services Ombudsman about the lender's intention to bring possession proceedings then the lender must consider postponing proceedings to await the investigation by the Financial Ombudsman Service (FOS). Where they do not intend to wait, then they must give notice to the borrower of the reason for not waiting and their intention to proceed.

3.27 Helpfully in mortgage cases, CPR PD 55A (section 55.8, para 5.5) provides that the claimant must bring two copies of form N123 (the protocol checklist) to the hearing so duty advisers can have the requirements and their compliance to hand and if not there should be grounds to ask for an adjournment.

The overriding objective – CPR Part 1

When making any decision in a case, including on any application to adjourn, the judge has to have in mind the principles laid out in the 'overriding objective' to deal with the case justly and proportionately. They will weigh up, for example, the amount of money involved, the importance of the case and complexity of the issue and balance that with the need to deal with the case expeditiously and with minimum cost. It will be important that the duty adviser has this in mind, and in some cases addresses this directly.

If the case is of low value or has already had adjournments, the judge may be more reluctant to adjourn the case again or delay a decision further. We anticipate that this may be a live issue as the new listing of cases means there will be more time to deal with the case and pressure on the courts to get through as many possession hearings as possible.

It will be important for the duty adviser to address the court on this and to stress the importance of the case to the defendant – the loss of the home and the impact of an order being made on the family.

CPR Part 1 – Overriding Objective

1.1 The overriding objective

(1) These Rules are a new procedural code with the overriding objective of enabling the court to deal with cases justly and at proportionate cost.
(2) Dealing with a case justly and at proportionate cost includes, so far as is practicable–
(a) ensuring that the parties are on an equal footing;
(b) saving expense;
(c) dealing with the case in ways which are proportionate–
  (i) to the amount of money involved;
  (ii) to the importance of the case;
  (iii) to the complexity of the issues; and
  (iv) to the financial position of each party;
(d) ensuring that it is dealt with expeditiously and fairly;
(e) allotting to it an appropriate share of the court's resources, while taking into account the need to allot resources to other cases; and
(f) enforcing compliance with rules, practice directions and orders.

1.2 Application by the court of the overriding objective

The court must seek to give effect to the overriding objective when it–
(a) exercises any power given to it by the Rules; or
(b) interprets any rule subject to rules 76.2, 79.2 and 80.2, 82.2 and 88.2.

1.3 Duty of the parties

The parties are required to help the court to further the overriding objective.

1.4 Court's duty to manage cases

(1) The court must further the overriding objective by actively managing cases.
(2) Active case management includes –
  (a) encouraging the parties to co-operate with each other in the conduct of the proceedings;

(b) identifying the issues at an early stage;
(c) deciding promptly which issues need full investigation and trial and accordingly disposing summarily of the others;
(d) deciding the order in which issues are to be resolved;
(e) encouraging the parties to use an alternative dispute resolution procedure if the court considers that appropriate and facilitating the use of such procedure;
(f) helping the parties to settle the whole or part of the case;
(g) fixing timetables or otherwise controlling the progress of the case;
(h) considering whether the likely benefits of taking a particular step justify the cost of taking it;
(i) dealing with as many aspects of the case as it can on the same occasion;
(j) dealing with the case without the parties needing to attend at court;
(k) making use of technology; and
(l) giving directions to ensure that the trial of a case proceeds quickly and efficiently.

CPR Part 55 – claim form and other requirements

3.28 This section will not be a long and detailed exploration of the rules and practice directions, but instead will pull out the issues relevant to a duty adviser advising on the 'review (R) date', and advising and representing at the 'substantive (S) hearing'.

3.29 The starting point is that county courts each have their own geographical jurisdiction for possession claims, and if the claim form is lodged at a court which does not serve the subject address then the claim will be sent to the correct county court.[1]

3.30 The claim is started by a claim form N5 (unless it is an accelerated possession claim – for which see 3.49 below). The claim form must be accompanied by the particulars of claim and the content of the particulars is dealt with in Part 16 and PD 55A – see 3.44 below.

3.31 The pre-pandemic position was that the tenant would be served with the claim form not less than 21 days before the hearing, which

1 It is understood that there is in fact one 'county court' and many court buildings but for ease of explanation we are referring to each county court building as a different county court.

would have been listed not more than eight weeks after issue of the claim, unless the court extended or shortened the time under CPR 3.1(2)(a) or the claim was against trespassers in which case the defendant would be served not less than five days before the hearing.

3.32 However, the Working Group on Possession Proceedings' Overall Arrangements – including R dates and S hearings – have led to those dates being extended by new PD 55C para 4, which provides for an extended interim period currently expiring on 28 March 2021 and that the first substantive hearing may be listed 'when or after' the claim form is issued – see 3.62 et seq below.

3.33 It is commonly known that a tenant does not need to file a defence before a first hearing (S hearing) in possession proceedings. They may bring a defence to the hearing but in many cases they will not. Where the tenant has a potential defence, the tenant or duty adviser will be asking the court to adjourn proceedings to allow time for a defence to be prepared filed and served in advance of a further hearing. However, it is important to recall that CPR 55.7(3), while permitting a tenant to take part in the hearing, does make clear that they are at risk on costs by a failure to do so. However, this is rarely invoked.

3.34 CPR 55.8 ('The hearing') is the key provision for duty advisers. First, it makes clear that the tenant is at risk of a possession order being made at the first substantive hearing (not the R date) and or any adjournment. This reminds us that, if the landlord's papers are broadly in order and they can prove their case, then it is incumbent upon the tenant to provide a reason why possession should not be granted to the landlord.

3.35 This is CPR 55.8:

> (1) At the hearing fixed in accordance with rule 55.5(1) or at any adjournment of that hearing, the court may–
> (a) decide the claim; or
> (b) give case management directions.

3.36 We should pause here and note that CPR 24.3 provides that summary judgment under that rule may *not* be made in residential possession proceedings against a defendant if they are a mortgagor or a tenant, or a person holding over in a Rent Act (RA) 1977 or HA 1988 protected tenancy. Therefore, the power to make a possession order at the first substantive hearing arises from CPR 55.8(1)(a).

3.37 We discuss defences and counterclaims, including the test that the court should apply when deciding whether to adjourn proceedings and give case management directions in more detail at chapter 5 below.

3.38 CPR 55.10 applies to mortgage proceedings, and places requirements on lenders to write with details of the hearing to 'the tenant or the occupier', 'the housing department of the local authority within which the property is located' and 'any registered proprietor (other than the claimant) of a registered charge over the property'. Evidence must be provided to the court of having done so. A failure of this obligation will lead to an adjournment of the claim or even the claim being struck out in some cases.

3.39 A provision is also made for unauthorised tenants of borrowers to apply to the court if a suspended possession order is made against their landlord/the borrower.

3.40 Section II of CPR Part 55 concerns accelerated possession proceedings. A duty adviser will encounter accelerated proceedings only if the matter has been listed for a hearing and so in this book we will simply deal with the elements of accelerated proceedings that are relevant to that. This is dealt with primarily in the commentary to PD 55A below, but it is worth noting that it is in CPR 55.14(1) that the requirement for a defence within 14 days of service of the N5b claim form is set out and that it should be on form N11B. The filing of a defence is what may trigger the court to list a hearing pursuant to CPR 5.16. However, that rule makes clear that a late defence may also trigger the listing of a hearing and even if there is no defence, the judge must list a hearing if they are not satisfied that the landlord's claim is made out.

3.41 CPR Part 55 does not require reasons to be given on the order listing accelerated possession claims for a hearing, but often judges will give their reason for not being satisfied that the claim is made out. While that is a useful starting point for a duty adviser advising on such a claim, advisers also need to be alert to any other possible points the judge may have missed on the papers.

3.42 Section III of Part 55 concerns interim possession orders which in the authors' experience do not occur on Housing Possession Court Duty Scheme (HPCDS) lists.

3.43 CPR 55.29 is a provision brought in on 25 June 2020 to replace and extend the stay which had previously been imposed by PD 51Z. The stay lasted until 20 September 2020 and is now lifted. The procedure for cases which were affected by the general stay under PD 51Z and CPR 55.29 is dealt with by CPR PD 55C and set out at 3.62 et seq below.

CPR PD 55A

3.44 This practice direction supplements the general provisions of CPR Part 55, while PD 55B and PD 55C concern specific points. Again, as with the commentary to CPR Part 55 above, we will concern ourselves with the issues relevant to a duty adviser advising on the R hearing or the S hearing.

Particulars of claim

3.45 Highly relevant is the requirements for contents of the particulars of claim starting at PD 55A 55.4. It is essential for a duty adviser to scan claim documents for the required information, much of which is obvious, but some provisions are worth particular attention. The failure of a particulars of claim to include this information should allow an argument for at least an adjournment and directions for the claimant to amend their claim. Judges should be asked not to overlook such breaches of the practice directions or to allow immediate amendment without re-service. It should be argued that the tenant or borrower is entitled to notice of the claimant's case to allow them to consider and seek legal advice.

3.46 The following provisions of PD 55A 55.4 are particularly useful:

- 2.1(3) – The claim must 'state the ground on which possession is claimed'; this should be read in conjunction with 2.4B below.
- 2.3–2.3A – These set out the requirements for rent and arrears information in rent cases. It is legitimate to argue that strict compliance with these provisions is necessary. This needs to be read in conjunction with 3.84 et seq below.
- 2.4B – 'If the possession claim relies on a statutory ground or grounds for possession, the particulars of claim must specify the ground or grounds relied on.' Because it is the particulars of claim that must specify the statutory ground relied upon, the claimant cannot rely on the notice setting out the grounds. This, along with 2.1(3) above is often used by duty advisers to defeat or delay claims for possession, even if a mandatory ground is relied upon. See also PD 55B 6.2A below in relation to Possession Claim Online (PCOL) claims.
- 2.5–2.5A – A long list of requirements for mortgage possession particulars of claim. Advisers will generally want to use a checklist (see appendix 1 below) to ensure compliance in these cases.
- 2.6 – This is relevant to trespass claims and requires information as to interest in the land or the basis of the right to possession and

the circumstances in which it is said that the land is occupied without licence or consent.

- 2.7 – A landlord claiming possession in relation to a demoted tenancy must include a copy of the statutory notice of proceedings for possession (HA 1996 s143E).

The hearing

3.47 PD 55A 55.8 deals with evidence at the hearing, and can be useful to a duty adviser. The claimant may bring details of rent or mortgage arrears up to date by way of written evidence verified by a statement of truth or orally on the date of the hearing. However, if there is a dispute as to evidence and the maker of the statement is not present, then the court should be asked to adjourn the proceedings pursuant to PD 55A 55.8 para 5.4.

3.48 PD 55A 55.8 para 5.5 only applies to mortgage cases but does not say so. It is useful in that it requires the claimant to bring two copies of form N123 to a hearing, which is the protocol pre-action checklist. The language is that the claimant *must* bring the form, and so it follows that there must be an adjournment if the claimant fails to do so. While not in the practice direction, the Overall Arrangements now include a similar provision (but without a prescribed form) in rented accommodation proceedings.

Accelerated possession claims

3.49 Section II of PD 55A is relevant to accelerated possession proceedings. The parts relevant to this book are 55.18 paras 8.3 and 8.4, which deal with the court's consideration at a hearing of a tenant's application for a possession order to be postponed for up to 42 days pursuant to HA 1980 s89. The test for postponing the order is confirmed as being that the court must be 'satisfied that exceptional hardship would be caused by requiring possession to be given up by the date in the order of possession'.

Orders fixing a date for possession

3.50 Section IV of PD 55A deals with the procedure when a postponed possession order has been made under HA 1985 s85(2)(b) in respect of secure tenancies or under HA 1988 s9(2)(b) in respect of assured tenancies. See also chapter 12 below. It provides that where the terms of a postponed order have been breached then an application for a date for possession to be fixed may be made. That must be on written notice to the tenant of not less than 14 days and not more than three months. That notice must contain information set out in PD 55A 10.4, and must include a request for the tenant to reply. It must also inform the tenant of their right to apply to the court to try to prevent a date for possession being fixed.

3.51 If the landlord proceeds with an application, then the notice and any reply must be attached along with details of the up-to-date position. PD 55A 10.9 provides that while the date for possession may be fixed by the judge considering the papers without a hearing, a judge may also list a hearing of their own accord.

3.52 The hearing concerning the fixing of a date for possession may therefore arise either from the tenant making an application to prevent a date for possession being fixed or because the court has listed the hearing of its own volition having considered the landlord's application. Either way the papers for the application to fix the date should be perused to check compliance with section IV of PD 55A.

3.53 PD 55A 10.10 makes clear that the hearing cannot be used by the tenant to revisit the decision that it was reasonable to make a possession order.

CPR PD 55B

3.54 This practice direction concerns Possession Claims Online, known as PCOL, which are allowed by CPR 55.10A. PCOL claims may be started online by claimants if they meet the criteria in PD 55B 5.1.

3.55 PD 55B 6.2A is confirmation that the requirement for statutory grounds to be stated in the particulars of claim applies equally to PCOL claims (see 3.46 above).

3.56 PD 55B 6.3A through to 6.4 contain important provisions regarding the information provided to the tenant and the court in respect of rent arrears claims:

> 6.3A Paragraph 6.3B applies where the claimant has, before commencing proceedings, provided the defendant in schedule form with–
> (1) details of the dates and amounts of all payments due and payments made under the tenancy agreement, mortgage deed or mortgage account–
>   (a) for a period of two years immediately preceding the date of commencing proceedings; or
>   (b) if the first date of default occurred less than two years before that date, from the first date of default; and
> (2) a running total of the arrears.

> 6.3B Where this paragraph applies the claimant may, in place of the information required by paragraph 6.3, include in his particulars of claim a summary only of the arrears containing at least the following information–
> (1) The amount of arrears as stated in the notice of seeking possession served under either section 83 of the Housing Act 1985 or section 8 of the Housing Act 1988, or at the date of the claimant's letter before action, as appropriate;
> (2) the dates and amounts of the last three payments in cleared funds made by the defendant or, if less than three payments have been made, the dates and amounts of all payments made;
> (3) the arrears at the date of issue, assuming that no further payments are made by the defendant.
>
> 6.3C Where the particulars of claim include a summary only of the arrears the claimant must–
> (1) serve on the defendant not more than 7 days after the date of issue, a full, up-to-date arrears history containing at least the information required by paragraph 6.3; and
> (2) either–
> (a) make a witness statement confirming that he has complied with sub-paragraph (1) or (2) of paragraph 6.3A as appropriate, and including or exhibiting the full arrears history; or
> (b) verify by way of oral evidence at the hearing that he has complied with sub-paragraph (1) or (2) of paragraph 6.3A as appropriate and also produce and verify the full arrears history.
>
> (Rule 55.8(4) requires all witness statements to be filed and served at least 2 days before the hearing.)
>
> 6.4 If the claimant wishes to rely on a history of arrears which is longer than two years, he should state this in his particulars and exhibit a full (or longer) schedule to a witness statement.

3.57 What this means for duty advisers is as follows.

- PCOL particulars almost always only have a summary of the rent arrears.
- PD 55B 6.3A provides that this summary is allowable but only when the landlord has already served a schedule of arrears before proceedings that goes back two years or the last zero balance, is in schedule form with dates of rent due and receipts and has a running total of arrears. The duty adviser needs to check that this has been done and if it has not then that should be notified to the judge and the claim should be adjourned.
- Even where a summary rent schedule is allowable, PD 55B 6.3B provides that the summary must still show the arrears at the date of the notice, the last three rent payments and the arrears at the

date of issue. Absent any of that information and the judge may be informed and an adjournment to correct the defect sought.

- PD 55B 6.3C then stipulates what must happen is that no more than seven days after issues of proceedings, a full up-to-date rent schedule must be served on the defendants. That must comply with 6.3 and so must include:
  1) the dates and amounts of all payments due and payments made under the tenancy agreement, mortgage deed or mortgage agreement either from the first date of default if that date occurred less than two years before the date of issue or for a period of two years immediately preceding the date of issue; and
  2) a running total of the arrears.
- The landlord must ether make a statement that they served the full schedule described in 6.3A prior to proceedings and exhibit the full up-to-date rent schedule required by PD 55B 6.3C or give oral evidence at the hearing as to the pre-issue 6.3A schedule being served and also produce the 6.3C schedule.

3.58 These are quite onerous requirements and duty advisers are often able to get claims adjourned for failure to comply with these provisions. They need careful explanation to judges who are not familiar with the provisions. The best way is to go through each requirement in turn, explaining whether the landlord has complied or not or whether the claimant can provide evidence of having complied or not.

3.59 These provisions are capable of being used in mandatory HA 1988 Sch 2 ground 8 proceedings and can be the last hope for a tenant facing a mandatory ground 8 possession order.

3.60 It is unclear how these provisions affect what is required in the bundle of documents which the claimant must lodge before the R date and which should be made available to the duty adviser on the R date. It is to be hoped that it becomes practice for the full schedule of arrears to have to be made available to the R date duty adviser electronically to assist with R advice in default of which the claim should not proceed. However, that is not clear from the rules, practice directions and Overall Arrangements.

3.61 PCOL is also available for tenants to use to file a defence. This can mean that a tenant seeking help on duty may have filed a defence through PCOL of which they do not have a hard copy to show to the duty adviser. It is often the case that where a tenant has filed a paper defence form, then they still don't have a copy to show to the duty adviser and the landlord's representatives must be asked if they have a copy or failing that the court should be asked.

CPR PD 55C

3.62 CPR PD 55C 'Coronavirus: temporary provision in relation to possession proceedings' is part of the mechanism to bring into effect some elements of the Overall Arrangements. It came into force on 23 August 2020 and, at the time of writing, is due to end on 30 July 2021. This is because they are designed as temporary arrangements due to the coronavirus public health crisis. Therefore, as things stand, the requirements of the parties set out in the practice directions and the temporary amendment of CPR 55.5 will cease to apply after 30 July 2021.

3.63 The first substantive clauses are in section two and relate to the way in which stayed claims are to come back to the court's attention. Paragraph 2.1 provides that in most of those stayed cases a reactivation notice must be filed and served. If in those cases no such notice is filed and served by 30 April 2021 then the claim will be stayed generally. If a party then wants the claim to be considered by the court they will have to make an application to lift that stay.

3.64 All stayed claims brought before 3 August 2020, where a final order for possession has been made, will require a reactivation notice – it is unclear what precisely is meant by 'final order'.

3.65 If a claim was brought on or after 3 August 2020 or if a final possession order has been made, then a reactivation notice is not required.

3.66 By para 2.3, a reactivation notice must:

(a) confirm that the party filing and serving it wishes the case to be listed, relisted, heard or referred; and
(b) except in proceedings relating to an appeal, set out what knowledge that party has as to the effect of the Coronavirus pandemic on the Defendant and their dependants.

3.67 In rent arrears cases (other than those relating to an appeal) an up-to-date rent account for the last two years must also be filed and served with a reactivation notice.

3.68 It is unclear what happens if the notice is filed and served without those other documents, or if the tenant wants to dispute a notice that says the claimant has no knowledge of any effect of the coronavirus pandemic on the defendant and their dependants. Certainly a duty adviser coming across this should argue that the court should at least adjourn any hearing where that has occurred and give directions for the practice direction to be complied with.

3.69 Paragraph 2.5 provides that any trial date set prior to 27 March 2020 will be vacated unless the reactivation notice and other documents including in some cases fresh dates to comply with existing directions is filed and served 42 days before the listed trial.

3.70 Having received a reactivation notice, the court must give at least 21 days' notice to the parties of any new or relisted hearing.

3.71 What sort of hearing is listed if (i) a reactivation notice is required, (ii) directions had already been set but (iii) the parties do not propose fresh directions? Currently this is unclear, but the best guess is that an R date is listed.

3.72 Paragraph 4.1 deals with any claim where a first hearing has not yet been listed. Paragraph 4.1 modifies CPR 55.5 such that the court does not have to list a hearing at the same time it issues a claim form and the first substantive hearing that is listed can be more than eight weeks. This provision allows for the R date to be listed and conducted and for there to be no substantive first hearing if the matter can be resolved by way of the R date duty advice. However, at the time of writing, some courts are simply listing an R date and also listing an S hearing on a date 28 days later. That does not seem to be the intention of the Overall Arrangements at para 32 which reads: 'Generally speaking, the Court will not fix a date when it issues the claim form' – but as listing is a judicial matter, it is up to the court.

3.73 Paragraphs 5.1–5.4 deal with cases where case management directions were in place before 20 September 2020 and provides that a party filing and serving a reactivation notice must also file and serve proposed fresh dates to comply with those existing directions or state that no new direction are needed. They must also give a statement as to whether the case can be heard by video or audio link.

3.74 Unless there is a specific reason why a defendant wants a remote hearing by video or telephone, for example for reasons of accessibility, they would be best advised to indicate they want a face-to-face hearing at court where they can also obtain face-to-face duty advice. A party receiving such a notice and directions must file and serve a response within 14 days if they do not agree with the proposals.

3.75 The authors have a concern (which admittedly may well be academic) which is that it may be open to a party to say that a direction set prior to 20 September 2020 must, unless the court orders otherwise, be complied with within the number of days that were outstanding for compliance at the time any relevant stay was applied. This argument follows the ratio of *Grant v Dawn Meats (UK)* [2018] EWCA Civ 2212 to the effect that when the stay is imposed, time stands still and begins to run again when the stay is lifted.

Example: Let us say there was a direction made on 20 March 2020 for a defence to be filed within 21 days, that is by 10 April 2020. When the general stay was in place on 27 March 2020, the defendant had 14 more days to file and serve a defence but the stay meant that time then stood still. When the stay was lifted on 20 September 2020, then, the defendant still had 14 days to comply, ie by 5 October 2020. The authors think that the *Dawn Meats* case means that a failure to file and serve a defence by 5 October 2020 would be a breach of the order of 20 March 2020 and the claimant may be able to argue that the defendant would need to apply for relief from sanctions under CPR 3.9.

3.76 The argument may be academic, but we mention it here in case it arises in a hearing where a duty adviser is involved. We think the correct argument to be made on behalf of the tenant (in order to sidestep any dispute) would be that *Arkin v Marshall and another* [2020] EWCA Civ 620 and the other appeals against the 2020 general stay made abundantly clear that parties were to be protected from having to take steps in cases and that is also the clear purpose of CPR PD 55C. Therefore, the court should simply direct the defendant to file and serve a defence in a reasonable time and grant relief from sanctions if it deems it necessary to do so.

3.77 For any new claims brought by social landlords on or after 3 August 2020, there is now a requirement for the claimant to bring an account in writing in duplicate of compliance with the applicable protocol – this brings claims by social landlords in line with mortgage claims to an extent. In a mortgage case form N123 is prescribed for this purpose, but no such form is provided for in social landlord cases.

3.78 In all claims after 3 August 2020, a notice must be filed and served setting out what knowledge the claimant has of any effect of the coronavirus pandemic on the defendant and their dependants.

CHAPTER 4

Notices

Key points

- Written notice is required in nearly all cases.
- In some discretionary ground cases the requirement for notice can be waived.
- Checking the service and validity of the notice is one of the most important tasks that fall to the duty adviser.
- If the claimant cannot produce a copy of the notice, and/or cannot prove service of the notice and the requirement cannot be waived, then the judge cannot make a possession order.
- The issues relevant to the validity are:
  - correct notice for the correct tenure;
  - prescribed information;
  - prescribed form;
  - date of service;
  - date by or after which possession proceedings can be commenced;
  - date of expiry by which proceeding must have been commenced;
  - statutory pre-existing conditions for a valid notice to be served;
  - can notice be dispensed with?
- A duty adviser should be prepared to require the claimant to prove service of a valid notice and to cross-examine the claimant's witness on that issue if necessary.
- The issue of the required period of notice has been vastly complicated by amendments to legislation brought about by the Coronavirus Act 2020 and we reproduce comprehensive schedules at appendix 7 below.

Introduction

4.1 The vast majority of cases that come before the duty adviser will involve the need for a written notice to the tenant or occupier prior to the proceedings being issued. Where the occupier does not enjoy the protection of Protection from Eviction Act (PEA) 1977, written notice is not required, but in all other cases there will need to be a written notice. In some cases the court can waive the requirement for a notice.

4.2 We deal with six types of notices in this chapter, and we look to provide assistance to determine the validity of the notice. Issues that arise in the determining the validity of a notice are:

a) correct notice for the correct tenure;
b) prescribed information;
c) prescribed form;
d) date of service;
e) date by or after which possession proceedings can be commenced;
f) date of expiry by which proceeding must have been commenced;
g) statutory pre-existing conditions for a valid notice to be served;
h) can notice be dispensed with?

4.3 Where a notice sets out a ground or reason for possession, it must have the correct facts on it, ie correct level of rent arrears.

4.4 The issue of the period of the notice given – that is the period between (d) and (e) or (f) has been vastly complicated by amendments to legislation brought about by the Coronavirus Act 2020. There are, at the time of writing, three, or in some cases four, distinct periods which determine how much notice must be given to a proposed defendant before possession proceedings can be commenced:

England (all social and private landlords)

- pre-Coronavirus Act 2020 notice period: until 26 March 2020;
- modified notice period: 26 March 2020 to 28 August 2020;
- modified notice period: 29 August 2020 to 31 March 2021;

Wales

Some social landlords

- pre-Coronavirus Act 2020 notice period: until 26 March 2020;
- modified notice period: 26 March 2020 – 28 September 2020
- modified notice period: 29 September 2020 to 31 March 2021.

Some social and all private landlords

- pre-Coronavirus Act 2020 notice period: until 26 March 2020;
- modified notice period: 26 March 2020 to 23 July 2020;
- modified notice period: 24 July to 28 September 2020;
- modified notice period: 29 September 2020 to 31 March 2021.

However, notices to quit for contractual tenancies and licences are *not changed.*

4.5 It is perfectly possible that other changes may come over time. It will be important to stay up-to-date with these changes.

4.6 The authors have thought about how to present this information in a useful and manageable way for advisers. The most comprehensive guide to notice periods is contained in the four documents comprising the guidance from the Ministry of Housing, Communities and Local Government issued for the re-opening of the possession proceedings from 21 September 2020, which can be found here: www.gov.uk/government/publications/understanding-the-possession-action-process-guidance-for-landlords-and-tenants. We have reproduced the relevant notice details at appendix 7 to this book.

4.7 We have not dealt with demotion notices under Housing Act (HA) 1985 s83(4A) and HA 1988 s6A because these do not concern proceedings leading to a loss of home and so are not covered by the Housing Possession Court Duty Scheme (HPCDS) contract.

4.8 Otherwise we attempt below to provide a matrix of requirements (a)–(h) against each type of notice.

Service

4.9 The starting points for understanding the requirements for service of notices are as follows:

4.10 If the landlord wishes to rely on Law of Property Act 1925 s196 for method of service then the agreement must state that s196 is applicable:

> **196 Regulations respecting notices.**
>
> [. . .]
>
> (3) Any notice required or authorised by this Act to be served shall be sufficiently served if it is left at the last-known place of abode or business in the United Kingdom of the lessee, lessor, mortgagee, mortgagor, or other person to be served, or, in case of a notice required or authorised to be served on a lessee or mortgagor, is affixed or left for him on the land or any house or building comprised in the lease or mortgage, or, in case of a mining lease, is left for the lessee at the office or counting-house of the mine.
>
> (4) Any notice required or authorised by this Act to be served shall also be sufficiently served, if it is sent by post in a registered letter addressed to the lessee, lessor, mortgagee, mortgagor, or other person to be served, by name, at the aforesaid place of abode or business, office, or counting-house, and if that letter is not returned by the postal operator (within the meaning of Part 3 of the Postal Services Act 2011) concerned undelivered; and that service shall be deemed to be made at the time at which the registered letter would in the ordinary course be delivered.

4.11 The tenancy agreement may set out methods of deemed service of the notice such as first-class post.

4.12 Otherwise, the landlord must prove that the notice came to the attention of the tenant. In practice, if the judge is satisfied that the method of service was executed by the landlord, ie the notice was put in the post or left at the premises etc then it will be for the tenant to establish why it did not come to their attention.

4.13 The N215 statement of service form is useful to landlords as a way to provide evidence of their having served a notice but also has a useful summary of the deemed service provisions which the court will adopt when deciding whether a notice was properly served on a tenant. For example, service by first-class post is deemed to be the second day after it was posted, provided that is a business day. So, a notice served first-class on a Friday will be deemed served the following Tuesday. This can be worth checking to make sure that landlords have complied with notice periods.

4.14 The landlord, or in the case of joint landlords, one of them, must serve the notice which is apparent from the wording of PEA 1977 s5, HA 1985 s83(1) and HA 1988 ss8 and 21. In the case of a joint tenancy, a notice must be served on all tenants.

4.15 The people who may sign a notice are the landlord or their agent. It is permitted to sign a notice electronically and signatures on accompanying documents have been held to make good a missing signature on the form itself. However, if the signature is absent entirely, the notice will be invalid.

4.16 Where the landlord is a company, the signature must comply with Companies Act 2006 s44(2).

Notices

Notice periods and Coronavirus Act 2020 Sch 29
Important: In the section that follows we have provided the usual notice periods which applied before the Coronavirus pandemic led to legislation to extend notice periods in England and Wales from 26 March 2020.

They might well not be the notice period that is relevant to a notice served on or after 26 March 2020. See 4.4–4.6 above.

We have done this in the expectation that notice periods will at some time revert to these default notice periods. At the time of writing the requirement for the extended notice periods end on 31 March 2021 in England and Wales. That date has been put to a later date by regulations once and may be put back again. The position with notices may be volatile for some time and so the authors considered that we should provide the default pre-pandemic position notice periods here but refer readers to appendix 7 below

> to check the extended notice periods which may apply to any particular notice they are looking at, depending on when it is said to have been served. Duty advisers will also have to have recourse to the usual housing law blogs and updates in order to keep abreast of any further changes to notice periods if they occur.

Notice to quit

4.17 *a) Correct notice for the correct tenure*
Non-secure tenancies, contractual tenancies, including where a tenant has lost statutory tenure, without statutory protection, licences, people left in occupation without rights in the absence of the licences.

b) Prescribed information
Yes – the Notices to Quit etc (Prescribed Information) Regulations 1988 SI No 2201.

c) Prescribed form
None.

d) Date of service
At any time.

e) Date by or after which possession proceedings can be commenced
Default position to 26 March 2020: four weeks (or if it is longer, the period of the tenancy or licence – except for yearly periodic tenancies where the notice period is six months).
Notice to quit for contractual tenancies and licences are not changed.

f) Date of expiry by which proceeding must have been commenced
At any time.

g) Statutory pre-existing conditions for a valid notice to be served
None.

h) Can notice be dispensed with?
No.

Notice of seeking possession (Housing Act 1985 s83)

4.18 *a) Correct notice for the correct tenure*
Secure tenancies with local authority landlord (or rarely RSLs).
Flexible tenancies within the fixed-term.

b) Prescribed information
Must specify the grounds for possession relied upon and the particulars of the ground.

c) Prescribed form
Yes or substantially to the same effect – Secure Tenancies (Notices) Regulations 1987 SI 1987 No 755.

d) Date of service
At any time.

e) Date by or after which possession proceedings can be commenced
Default position to 26 March 2020:

- four weeks and end on the last or first day of a period of the tenancy, except:
- ground 2 – immediately.

For amended notice periods, see appendix 7 below.

f) Date of expiry by which proceeding must have been commenced
12 months after the date in (e).

g) Statutory pre-existing conditions for a valid notice to be served
Grounds for possession HA 1985 Sch 2.

h) Can notice be dispensed with?
Discretionary grounds: Yes if just and equitable to do so.
Mandatory ground: No.

Notice of possession proceedings (Housing Act 1985 s107D)

4.19 *a) Correct notice for the correct tenure*
Flexible tenancies with local authority landlord.

b) Prescribed information
None.

c) Prescribed form
No but must be in writing.

d) Date of service
On or before expiry of the fixed-term.

e) Date by or after which possession proceedings can be commenced
Default position to 26 March 2020: two months.
For amended notice periods, see appendix 7 below.

f) Date of expiry by which proceeding must have been commenced
N/A

g) Statutory pre-existing conditions for a valid notice to be served
See chapter 6 below for the procedure to be followed in relation to flexible tenancies – essentially six months' notice that does not intend to grant another tenancy on expiry, reasons for the same, information as to right to request a review of that decision.

h) Can notice be dispensed with?
No.

Notice of seeking possession (Housing Act 1988 s8)

4.20 *a) Correct notice for the correct tenure*
Assured tenancies (including assured shorthold tenancies) with RSL or private landlords.

b) Prescribed information
Must specify the grounds for possession relied upon and the particulars of the ground.

c) Prescribed form
Yes or substantially to the same effect – Form No 3 Assured Tenancies and Agricultural Occupancies (Forms) (England) Regulations 2015 SI No 620, as amended by Assured Tenancies and Agricultural Occupancies (Forms) (England) (Amendment) Regulations 2016 SI No 443, and from 1 December 2016 by Assured Tenancies and Agricultural Occupancies (Forms) (England) (Amendment No 2) Regulations 2016 SI No 1118.

d) Date of service
At any time apart from ground 7A which then depends on the condition relied on – 12 months from conviction or court finding breach of injunction and three months from a closure order.

e) Date by or after which possession proceedings can be commenced
Default position to 26 March 2020:

- Differs with grounds – of those cases commonly found on duty:
  - 8, 10 and 11 – two weeks;
  - 8A – four weeks;
  - 14 – immediately.

For amended notice periods, see appendix 7 below.

f) Date of expiry by which proceedings must have been commenced
12 months after the date in (e).

g) Statutory pre-existing conditions for a valid notice to be served
Grounds for possession HA 1988 Sch 2.

h) Can notice be dispensed with?
Discretionary grounds: Yes if just and equitable to do so.
Mandatory grounds 7A, 7B and 6: No.

Notice of seeking possession/notice requiring possession (Housing Act 1988 s21)

4.21 *a) Correct notice for the correct tenure*
Assured shorthold tenancies with RSL or private landlords.

b) Prescribed information
N/A

c) Prescribed form
Tenancy commenced *before* 1 October 2015 – No.
Tenancy commenced *on or after* 1 October 2015 – Yes or substantially to the same effect – Form No 6A, Assured Tenancies and Agricultural Occupancies (Forms) (England) Regulations 2015 SI No 620.

d) Date of service
After four months of the original tenancy (whether fixed-term of statutory periodic) or any fresh fixed-term tenancy (not statutory periodic coming into being after a fixed-term tenancy).

e) Date by or after which possession proceedings can be commenced
Default position to 26 March 2020: Two months.
For amended notice periods, see appendix 7 below.

f) Date of expiry by which proceedings must have been commenced
Default: Six months after service of the notice.

g) Statutory pre-existing conditions for a valid notice to be served
A range of issues including matters concerning tenancy deposits protection and information, licensing requirements, retaliatory eviction concerning complaints of housing conditions, energy performance certificates, gas safe certificates, government's 'How To Rent' leaflet, Tenants Fees Act 2019.

h) Can notice be dispensed with?
No.

Notice of possession proceedings (Housing Act 1996 s128)

4.22 *a) Correct notice for the correct tenure*
Introductory tenancies.

b) Prescribed information

- The notice shall state that the court will be asked to make an order for the possession of the dwelling-house.
- It must set out the reasons for the landlord's decision to apply for such an order.
- It must specify a date after which proceedings for the possession of the dwelling-house may be begun.
- It must inform the tenant of their right to request a review of the landlord's decision to seek an order for possession and of the time within which such a request must be made.
- It must inform the tenant that if they need help or advice about the notice, and what to do about it, they should take it immediately to a citizens' advice bureau, a housing aid centre, a law centre or a solicitor.

c) Prescribed form
No.

d) Date of service
During the introductory tenancy including extended trial period.

e) Date by or after which possession proceedings can be commenced
Default position to 26 March 2020:

- not specified but instead driven by the review process;
- tenant has 14 days from notice to request a review. Landlord must then complete the review before the time specified in the notice that proceedings may be begun.

For amended notice periods, see appendix 7 below.

f) Date of expiry by which proceedings must have been commenced
12 months after the start of the tenancy or 18 months is the trial period is extended (otherwise the tenancy becomes secure).

g) Statutory pre-existing conditions for a valid notice to be served
See chapter 6 below for the review procedure.

h) Can notice be dispensed with?
No.

CHAPTER 5

Defences and counterclaims

Key points

- While very often the duty adviser is looking to gain time for the defendant for almost any reason, what the court will want to know is whether there is a defence to the proceedings or not.
- The duty adviser needs to have in mind what the defence (and counterclaim) is or might be even if they are seeking an adjournment for some intervening event, such as a benefit issue, to be sorted out. In that example, the defence would be that it is not reasonable for a possession order to be made while the benefit issue is outstanding.
- A duty adviser may need to give advice to a defendant about how to file and serve a defence if that is directed by the court but the defendant cannot get legal representation.
- Duty advisers need to be familiar with the variety of tests that are required for different defences. For ease they are outlined below from 5.8, but can also be found at chapter 10. Mark those pages with sticky labels.
- In general, and put at its most concise, the position is:
  - in discretionary and Equality Act 2010 defence cases, the defence must be arguable to any degree and not fanciful;
  - in all other cases, it must be seriously arguable.
- The case of *Birmingham City Council v Stephenson* [2016] EWCA Civ 1029 contains important guidance as to the situation when the defendant seeks an adjournment to file a defence.
- Counterclaims can be in respect of disrepair; housing conditions; harassment; breach of covenant for quiet enjoyment; tenancy deposit breaches; and more. In cases where a rent repayment order may be relevant, it should be possible to apply to stay the possession proceedings pending the relevant application in the tribunal.

Introduction

5.1 In almost all cases, the duty adviser is looking for ways to gain time for the defendant – and that may be so that their position can be improved before the case is considered in any detail, or because a defence is possible but just needs time and or advice so it can be prepared. It is important for the duty adviser not to lose sight of the fact that at the first hearing (S hearing) the primary aim for the court is to understand whether the claim is defended or not. The court wants to know (i) if there is a defence (and counterclaim) or not, and (ii) strictly speaking,if there is not then whether a possession order should be made.

5.2 While it might in most cases be fine to explain to a judge an outstanding issue – such as a benefit claim or job prospect – that needs to be resolved before the court can properly consider the case, the duty adviser may at times need to be able to outline what the defence (and counterclaim) is or might be. For example, it would be an outline of a defence to say that it is not reasonable for a possession order to be made while the benefit issue is outstanding.

Defences

5.3 The aim of the duty adviser is to prevent any kind of possession order being made, including conditional orders. The way to do that is to argue that the defendant has a defence or that there are events that need time to transpire that will give rise to a defence. In either of these cases, it will be necessary to show that such a defence has some prospect of success.

5.4 There are practice forms which can be used to set out a defence and which the court sends with the claim form:

- N11R – rented residential premises;
- N11M – mortgaged residential premises;
- N11B – accelerated possession proceeding.

5.5 The form may have been filed or served, or just completed by the defendant, prior to the duty adviser being involved and may be useful in obtaining information about the defendant's circumstances. However, except in the case of accelerated possession claims, the forms are not very good at disclosing a defence. A defendant who is formally represented in possession proceedings will have their defence (and counterclaim) set out in a traditionally pleaded document.

5.6 The duty adviser may wish to let defendants know that they can use the defence forms if the court directs them to file a defence but they cannot get legal representation. In addition, defendants in that position should be advised that the Master of the Rolls Working Group on Possession Proceedings' 'Overall Arrangements for Possession Proceedings in England and Wales: "The Overall

Arrangements"' make clear at para 28 that a simple written account can be considered as a defence and if a defendant uses one of the forms they can also add written statement on a separate page if they wish setting out why a possession order should not be made:

> 28. Court communications will emphasise to a defendant that if he/she has difficulty in completing the forms for a defence, a short statement explaining his/her circumstances and why an order should not be made will suffice.

While it is to be hoped that where a defence (and counterclaim) is to be filed the defendant will get legal advice, there are many cases where the defendant cannot or will not. The Overall Arrangements are helpful in emphasising that the defendant should nevertheless make out their case in writing as best as they can and the court will take it into account.

5.7 At the hearing the adviser needs to ascertain what defence (and counterclaim) might be available and then persuade either the claimant, and if not, then the judge that the defendant should be allowed time to prepare and pursue that case.

5.8 In relation to the test to be met for defences in most duty cases, Civil Procedure Rules 1998 (CPR) 55.8 ('The hearing') is the key provision (although public law and Human Rights Act (HRA) 1998 defences under Article 8 of the European Convention on Human Rights (ECHR) (right to respect for one's private and family life, home and correspondence) have an overlaid test of being 'seriously arguable' – see chapter 10). CPR 55.8(2) needs to be available for instant recall by all duty advisers:

> (2) Where the claim is genuinely disputed on grounds which appear to be substantial, case management directions given under paragraph (1)(b) will include the allocation of the claim to a track or directions to enable it to be allocated.

5.9 This sets the conditions for a possession claim to be allocated to track with directions and sets a working threshold by which it is beyond dispute that the court must allow a claim to proceed as a defended claim. However, it does not in the authors' view set *the* test for the court to allow time and direct that a defence be filed. The language of these provisions is that genuine disputes on substantial grounds give rise to directions including allocation to track or the issuing of allocation questionnaires or an allocation hearing.

5.10 That still allows for directions for a defence to be filed and served where the genuineness of the dispute and/or the substantiveness of the grounds for the dispute are not clear.

5.11 In practice, we come back to the first conclusion to be drawn by CPR 55.8 which is that the judge may decide the claim at a first hearing (S hearing) and so the tenant must demonstrate a reason why the court should not decide the claim by way of a possession order. Any adjournment then allows the tenant to file and serve a defence whether directed to pursuant to CPR 55.8(1)(b) or not.

5.12 A useful summary is set out at paras 13 and 24 of Lewison LJ's judgment in *Birmingham City Council v Stephenson* [2016] EWCA Civ 1029, which we reproduce here because the judgment is not on Bailli or otherwise easily accessible except by the website of Community Law Partnership who brought the case (www.communitylawpartnership.co.uk/wp-content/uploads/2017/03/BCC-v-Stephenson.pdf). At para 13:

> The rules thus envisage that at the time of the first hearing, or indeed at a subsequent hearing, the tenant may well not have served the defence and that judgment should not be entered in default of a defence. Rule 55.8 also envisages that the court may decide the claim without a full trial but it is also right to say that the existence of what appears to be a genuine dispute on substantial grounds is not a precondition to the giving of case management directions under rule 55.8(1)(b).

And at para 24:

> As I have said, I do not consider that the existence of a dispute on substantial grounds is a precondition on the making of case management directions.

5.13 Other guidance in that case is more specific to Equality Act (EA) 2010 defences but it is clear that paras 13 and 24 above are of *general applicability*. So what test should a judge apply to a defendant's assertion that they have or may have a defence to proceedings?

5.14 If the defence meets the CPR 55.8(2) threshold, then it is straightforward to say that case management directions should be made which include allocation to track and the matter proceeds as a defended claim.

5.15 CPR 3.4 deals with statements of case which have been filed and served and which are therefore capable of being considered as to their merits, whereas on duty we are often dealing with cases where a defence is not yet filed and served. Even if the defendant has filed a defence form the duty adviser may argue that that documents should not be considered as constituting the defendant's defence in full if other arguments that did not occur to the defendant can be raised, especially if this is the first time they have had legal advice.

5.16 Case-law (see *Swain v Hillman* [2001] 1 All ER 91) has given guidance as to what the test would be for summary judgment under CPR 24.2 – 'a "realistic" as opposed to a "fanciful" prospect of success' (para 7). CPR 24.2 is expressly not applicable in residential possession cases. However, in *Forcelux Ltd v Binnie* [2009] EWCA Civ 854, [2010] HLR 20, CA parallels were drawn between CPR 55.8(2) and CPR 24 and some argue the 'realistic not fanciful' prospect of success test may be applied by analogy.

5.17 Others point to the express non-applicability of CPR Part 24 to possession claims and argue that in the absence of any other guidance it must be right that the only criteria to be applied to a potential defence is that it is simply 'arguable' to any degree.

5.18 It may be that this point is tested in the Court of Appeal before too long, but the principles that the duty adviser needs to be aware of arising from this discussion are:

- The test for adjourning the proceedings must logically be lower than the 'genuine and substantial' test in CPR 55.8 – relying on *Stephenson*.
- If the duty adviser is able to elucidate what the defence might be, then the duty adviser may say that unless the judge can satisfy themselves that the defence is or would be entirely fanciful or not at all arguable, they must adjourn to allow that defence to be filed and served.
- If there is any more than a cursory discussion of whether the defence passes any sort of threshold then it may be respectfully argued that the judge must adjourn as otherwise the judge will be deciding the case when there is doubt as to whether there is a defence or not.

5.19 There follows a non-exhaustive list of issues that may be raised in defences:

- *Notice* – The relevant notice served in advance of the possession proceedings is invalid, or service of the notice said to be relied upon is disputed.
- *Court papers* – The claim may be defective if the paperwork does not follow the rules or if the landlord has not properly followed the rent arrears protocol – this is unlikely to completely defeat the landlord's claim, but may cause the claim to be delayed while the landlord sorts out its case.
- *Disputed grounds/reasons for possession* – The factual basis of the alleged grounds of possession is disputed. Most commonly this might include the level of alleged rent arrears, or other alleged

breaches of tenancy or of a mortgage agreement or purchase plan. A counterclaim and set off may be involved in this kind of defence – see below.

- *Reasonableness* – In cases where the court has the relevant discretion it may be argued by way of a defence that notwithstanding the claimant making out their ground for possession it is nevertheless not reasonable in all the circumstances for a possession order to be made.
- *Set off* – See 5.20 et seq below.
- *Public law, HRA 1998 (proportionality) or EA 2010 defences* – See chapter 10.

5.20 We should say just for clarity that while CPR Part 15 deals with defences and replies, the rules and practice direction at CPR Part 15 has little applicability to duty advice work within the scope of this book.

Counterclaims and set off

5.21 In rent arrears cases it is reasonably common for a tenant to be able to realistically argue that they have a claim that they can bring against the landlord for damages (compensation) and that any arrears that do exist may be set off by this 'counterclaim', usually for disrepair and in England housing conditions issues, but also for harassment or other reasons. Wales does not yet have a Homes (Fitness for Human Habitation) Act 2018 equivalent.

> ***Example***
>
> A tenant who can show that the landlord has not carried out repairs or has let premises in a condition such that it is not fit for human habitation in England can bring a counterclaim for damages against the landlord. Any damages which are found due to the tenant can then be set off against any arrears found due. The existence of the counterclaim works in possession proceedings to give rise to a defence to proceedings and a counterclaim at the same time.

5.22 It follows that the duty adviser will in these circumstances be asking the court to adjourn proceedings with directions for the defendant to file and serve their defence and counterclaim. Counterclaims can be in respect of disrepair; housing conditions (England only); harassment; breach of covenant for quiet enjoyment;

tenancy deposit breaches; and more. In cases where a rent repayment order may be relevant, it should be possible to apply to stay the possession proceedings pending the relevant application in the tribunal.

5.23 In a rent arrears claim, the defendant's claim against the landlord may merely set off part of or all of the arrears and no more. It would appear that strictly speaking such a case is just an aspect of the defence rather than a counterclaim per se. However, in the context of duty advice and representation the distinction is not relevant as duty advisers will be looking to secure time for an appropriate pleading to be prepared be that a defence, a defence with set off, or a defence and counterclaim. In many cases there is unlikely to be time to work out whether a claim against the claimant will be less than, equal to or more than the claimed rent arrears.

5.24 Bearing in mind the discussion around the test for a defence under CPR 55.8 above, an interesting question arises as to what the correct threshold test would be for a judge to adjourn for a counterclaim to be filed and served. In the context of duty advice, through the test for the counterclaim is less relevant than the test for a defence which would include set off by way of the counterclaim. Therefore, the test that is relevant to the duty adviser is the same as for the defence – arguable and not fanciful.

5.25 While legal aid is not available to bring a standalone claim for damages for disrepair (and/or housing conditions in England), legal aid is available to bring a counterclaim for damages in possession proceedings, as long as the counterclaim acts at least in part as a defence to the proceedings, ie by way of set off. Therefore, the court can be reassured that the tenant will be able to get legal assistance to file and serve a defence and counterclaim.

5.26 A defence and counterclaim is available in mandatory ground 8 cases as in cases where the court has discretion, providing the court can be convinced there is a realistic prospect of the counterclaim bringing the arrears to below the ground 8 threshold. This is important. If the counterclaim would not realistically dispose of ground 8 (eight weeks or two months of rent arrears) then the court may still go on to make a mandatory possession order and adjourn the money claim. The court should be dissuaded from doing so if there is any doubt as to whether the counterclaim is sufficient to dispose of ground 8, and the court should not be trying to decide the merits or quantum (value) of a counterclaim beyond the threshold we outlined above at a first substantive possession hearing.

5.27 We are sure it will be apparent to readers that duty advisers may be arguing both that there is a defence to proceedings such as the level of arrears or service of notice being disputed, and, further there is a counterclaim available to the defendant which may set off any arrears found due.

5.28 CPR Part 20 deals with counterclaims and other additional claims, but is mainly concerned with matters beyond the scope of this book.

Defences in forfeiture cases

5.29 An application for forfeiture is rarely seen on the duty scheme, but for completeness, and just in case, we provide a very brief outline here. It is a means by which the landlord can bring to an end a contractual fixed-term tenancy or lease before the end of the fixed-term. There will need to be a provision in the contract for this, but most do. Forfeiture of a fixed-term tenancy has the same effect as a notice to quit on a periodic tenancy.

5.30 If the tenancy is a Rent Act (RA) protected tenancy forfeiture converts the contractual protected tenancy into a statutory tenancy.

5.31 It cannot be used to terminate Housing Act (HA) 1988 assured and assured shorthold tenancies as HA 1988 s5(1) is the only way to bring an assured tenancy to an end:

> (1) An assured tenancy cannot be brought to an end by the landlord except by–
> (a) obtaining–
> (i) an order of the court for possession of the dwelling-house under section 7 or 21, and
> (ii) the execution of the order,
> (b) obtaining an order of the court under section 6A (demotion order), ...
> (c) in the case of a fixed term tenancy which contains power for the landlord to determine the tenancy in certain circumstances, by the exercise of that power, or
> (d) in the case of an assured tenancy–
> (i) which is a residential tenancy agreement within the meaning of Chapter 1 of Part 3 of the Immigration Act 2014, and
> (ii) in relation to which the condition in section 33D(2) of that Act is met,
> giving a notice in accordance with that section,
>
> and, accordingly, the service by the landlord of a notice to quit is of no effect in relation to a periodic assured tenancy.

5.32 If the tenancy is a fixed-term secure or a flexible tenancy, then any application for forfeiture to the court which results in an order will be made under HA 1985 s82(3) instead. The contractual tenancy will end, and the tenancy will become a period tenancy:

> (3) Where a secure tenancy is a tenancy for a term certain but with a provision for re-entry or forfeiture, the court shall not order possession of the dwelling-house in pursuance of that provision, but in a case where the court would have made such an order it shall instead make an order terminating the tenancy on a date specified in the order and section 86 (periodic tenancy arising on termination of fixed term) shall apply.

5.33 HAs 1985 and 1988 provide a statutory means for terminating either a secure or an assured tenancy, which means the tenant cannot, but also does not have to apply for relief from forfeiture.

CHAPTER 6

Secure, introductory and flexible tenancies (local authority tenancies and licences)

Key points

- Local authority possession claims form the majority of cases in most duty lists and most of those will consist of secure tenancy cases.
- It is an important first step to ascertain the tenancy type and read the particulars of claim.
- Most secure tenancy cases will be rent arrears cases and will therefore be discretionary ground cases.
- These cases involve considerations of whether it is reasonable to make a possession order or not. Benefits to help with rent payments are often an important consideration as are other financial issues, health issues and whether there may be a counterclaim and/or set off.
- There can also be anti-social behaviour cases on both discretionary and mandatory grounds and also other claims with may involve a mandatory order for possession, and so it is important to scour the particulars of claim carefully to understand the case against the defendant.
- There must be compliance with pre-action protocols and Civil Procedure Rules 1998 (CPR) requirements.
- Mandatory grounds cases may be met with public law defences where appropriate.
- Local authority landlords will generally be represented by a local authority officer for rent arrears cases but may have legal representatives for mandatory ground cases.
- It is a good idea to meet and speak with them as soon as possible to help understand the case and what the council is asking for.
- A quick settlement or agreement for directions is possible if the council recognise that there are issues in the background that need resolving.
- If there are disputed facts, see whether or not the officer is in a position to prove their case evidentially, ie as to service of notices etc.

Secure tenancies

6.1 Secure tenancies are tenancies granted by local authorities and are governed by the Housing Act (HA) 1985. They are what most people mean when they talk about council housing.

6.2 They are characterised by the following features:

- *Security of tenure.* A secure tenant may generally remain in their home for as long as they like provided they keep to the terms of the tenancy agreement; for example, they pay their rent, do not use the property for certain illegal purposes and are not a nuisance to neighbours or others.
- *Periodic from the start.* This means that there is not a fixed-term, but instead the tenancy just runs from rental period to rental period. Some secure tenancies start as introductory tenancies for a fixed, but extendable period (see introductory tenancies below), however once they become secure tenancies they are periodic tenancies.
- *Subsidised rent.* Rents under secure tenancies are among the lowest.
- *Local authority landlord.* Although there was a time when some secure tenancies had housing association landlords, those are now rare.

6.3 In order to obtain a possession order, the local authority landlord of a secure tenant must first serve a notice of seeking possession pursuant to HA 1985 s83. That notice must give a certain period of notice which will depend on the grounds relied upon and also when it is served (see chapter 4 above) and must rely on one of the grounds for possession set out in HA 1985 Sch 2. In cases concerning ground 2 nuisance or other anti-social behaviour, then the notice must state that proceedings may be started immediately.

6.4 It is beyond the scope of this book to go into every ground for possession, and so we will deal with the two that come up most often for duty advisers: grounds 1 and 2. Other cases for possession including absolute grounds for possession are dealt with briefly below, but we refer readers to *Defending Possession Proceedings* (DPP) for more extensive commentary on all grounds for possession under the HA 1985.

Ground 1

Rent lawfully due from the tenant has not been paid or an obligation of the tenancy has been broken or not performed.

6.5 This is the most common ground, either on its own or in combination with other grounds. The ground is in two limbs: the first being that rent has not been paid; and the second that any other obligations of the tenancy is breached or not carried out as required.

6.6 The first limb deals straightforwardly with rent due. However, even if this ground is made out, the court must still consider it reasonable for a possession order to be made in all the circumstances.

6.7 The second limb can refer to any obligation expressed or implied in the tenancy agreement and often includes the obligation to pay charges alongside rent, such as water charges. Increasingly, we see claims where the failure to allow access for gas safety or other inspections are pleaded under ground 1. The second limb is also subject to the fact that the court must still consider it reasonable for a possession order to be made in all the circumstances.

Rent lawfully due and water charges

The obligation which makes up a claim for rent arrears is to pay rent lawfully due. The duty adviser must therefore be sure to check as far as possible that the rent claimed in the notice and in the particulars of claim is rent lawfully due.

The starting point is the tenancy agreement. After that, any purported rent increases also need to be checked for validity against the provisions of the agreement or statutory means to increase the rent.

Particularly since the COVID-19 crisis, defendants should be asked if there have been any agreements for rent-free periods or rent reductions for any reason, and what evidence they have of those agreements.

Any charges on top of net rent should be carefully checked to make sure they are (i) relevant to the premises which is the subject of the proceedings and (ii) properly chargeable as rent.

In *The Mayor & Burgesses of the Royal Borough of Kingston-Upon-Thames v Moss* (2020) EWCA Civ 1381 the Court of Appeal, by the judgment of Lewison LJ in that case, effectively confirmed that:

- around 69 council and RSLs who have agreements with Thames Water were or had been, pursuant to that agreement 'water resellers';
- therefore where they had demanded and received water charges as part of rent but did not pass on discounts to them from Thames Water, that was unlawful;
- it follows that amounts of rent arrears claimed by these borough in some cases may be wrong and that may be raised as a defence in possession proceedings.

Duty advisers will have to make enquiries in their local areas as to the types of agreements used by the local landlord and water suppliers to see if this issue affects their own practice.

More reading on this case and previous cases can be done at 'Nearly Legal: Housing Law News and Comment' on water sellers: https://nearlylegal.co.uk/2020/11/water-sellers/ as a starting point.

6.8 The date after which proceedings can be brought must be stated on the notice. The notice period before proceedings is set out at chapter 4 above and appendix 7 below, as is the date after which the notice may no longer be used.

6.9 The court can dispense with the requirement for notice. Duty advisers should always work hard to persuade the judge not to dispense with notice to the tenant.

6.10 Ground 2 is a nuisance/anti-social behaviour ground. The behaviour must be a nuisance or annoyance or be likely to cause a nuisance or annoyance to neighbours or others in the locality, and may include the landlord (ie housing officers or others) their agents or other people carrying out hosing management functions.

Ground 2

The tenant or a person residing in or visiting the dwelling-house–

(a) has been guilty of conduct causing or likely to cause a nuisance or annoyance to a person residing, visiting or otherwise engaging in a lawful activity in the locality,

(aa) has been guilty of conduct causing or likely to cause a nuisance or annoyance to the landlord of the dwelling-house, or a person employed (whether or not by the landlord) in connection with the exercise of the landlord's housing management functions, and that is directly or indirectly related to or affects those functions, or

(b) has been convicted of–
   (i) using the dwelling-house or allowing it to be used for immoral or illegal purposes, or
   (ii) an indictable offence committed in, or in the locality of, the dwelling-house.

6.11 This ground is also available to the landlord where they can show that a tenant has used the property for immoral or illegal purposes or that they have committed an indictable offence in the property or in the locality.

6.12 'Locality' is not defined, and whether nuisance or anti-social behaviour occurred in the locality of the premises is a factual issue to be decided on the evidence.

6.13 An indictable offence is an offence of a more serious type, which can be listed on an indictment and is usually tried in the Crown Court.

6.14 Proceedings may be brought immediately once a notice is served, and the notice must specify that fact.

6.15 These cases will be very fact-specific. For that reason, in many courts these cases have not traditionally been listed in the housing possession block lists. If duty advisers do have these cases in their lists, then it should be relatively straightforward in the majority of cases to argue that the factual background of the case is disputed and cannot possibly be adequately dealt with without live evidence and in the time available, so the case should be adjourned with directions which will allow the defendant to obtain legal advice.

Other discretionary grounds

6.16 Other discretionary grounds available in respect of secure tenancies are (broad descriptions):

- 2ZA – an indictable offence during and at the scene of a riot in the UK;
- 2A – a tenant or spouse or civil partner or person living together with the tenant as if they were a spouse or civil partner has left because of domestic violence and is unlikely to return leaving the perpetrator of the domestic violence in the premises;
- 3 – deterioration of the premises due to neglect or default;
- 4 – deterioration of landlord's furniture for the same reason;
- 5 – tenancy obtained by a false statement;
- 6 – a premium was paid in relation to an assignment;
- 7 – accommodation which part of or adjacent to a building used for other purposes is let pursuant to the tenant's employment and conduct by the tenant or other resident means it would not be right from them to remain in occupation having regard to the purpose of the rest of the building;
- 8 – ground for possession of a decant property where works on the original accommodation have been completed.

6.17 The remaining grounds 9, 10, 10A, 11, 12, 13, 14, 15, 15A and 16 are grounds which are contingent upon suitable alternative accommodation being available to the tenant and are so rare on duty lists as to be not worth consideration here. Again, we would advise perusal of DPP for detailed consideration of these and other grounds if required.

6.18 The notice period for each of these grounds is discussed at chapter 4 above and appendix 7 below. Again, these cases are fact-based, and advisers should be able to argue either that the issues can be resolved by agreement between the parties outside of court or that the factual background of the case is disputed and will need live evidence to resolve and therefore an adjournment with directions is appropriate.

Housing Act 1985 s84A

6.19 This is a mandatory ground for possession for anti-social behaviour, based on:

a) a conviction of a serious offence committed in the dwelling or the locality of other dwelling elsewhere and committed against the landlord or a person employed in connection with housing management functions and connected directly or indirectly to those functions; or
b) a breach of an anti-social behaviour injunction (ASBI) in or in the locality or again elsewhere where the breach is connected to nuisance or annoyance to neighbours, the landlord or persons employed in connection with housing management functions and connected directly or indirectly to those functions; or
c) a breach of a criminal behaviour order with the same location conditions as above; or
d) the premises has been made subject to a closure order and access has been prohibited for a continuous period of 48 hours or more; or
e) the tenant or resident or visitors have been convicted of an offence under Environmental Protection Act 1990 s80 in relation to a statutory nuisance under that act, being a noise nuisance.

6.20 While this is a mandatory ground for possession and the only defence available would be a public law, Equality Act (EA) 2010 or Human Rights Act (HRA) 1998 defence (see chapter 10 below), there would usually be a great deal of factual background that the claimant would need to satisfy the court of. There are also particular notice requirements under HA 1985 s83ZA, and a review process under s85ZA that the court must be satisfied of.

6.21 It follows that duty advisers consulted by tenants facing this ground should be able to argue that the factual background of the case is disputed and/or pre-litigation requirements are disputed, and will need live evidence to resolve and therefore an adjournment with directions is appropriate.

Introductory tenancies

6.22 Introductory tenancies are tenancies granted by local authorities, and were introduced by HA 1996 Part 5 Chapter 1. The local authority must have elected to grant introductory tenancies – the issue of election or not is not one we would expect to arise on a duty list.

6.23 The purpose of the introductory tenancy is for there to be a 'trial period' of one year (and possible extension) during which the landlord can assess the ability of the tenant to comply with obligations of the tenancy. If all is well, the introductory tenancy becomes a secure tenancy or flexible tenancy automatically after one year or at the end of an extension.

6.24 If there is a breach of the obligations, then the landlord may extend the period of the introductory tenancy and/or may start possession proceedings to bring the tenancy to an end.

6.25 An extension occurs where the landlord gives notice prior to the eight weeks before the expiry date of the introductory tenancy and either the tenant does not request a review of that decision or the review is not upheld.

6.26 The requirements for possession proceedings are:

- The tenancy must be a valid introductory tenancy, ie the council has elected to grant such tenancies, it was not granted to someone who was immediately prior to the grant a secure and relevant assured tenant, and the tenancy was still in the 'trial period' when the notice was served.
- A notice of possession proceedings on prescribed form under HA 1996 s128 must be served giving at least four weeks' notice of proceedings (but see variations on notice period in chapter 4 above and appendix 7 below).
- The notice must give reasons why the landlord would seek possession of the property.
- The notice must set out the tenant's right to request a review of the decision within 14 days of the date of service of the notice.
- The council must conduct the review including allowing an oral hearing if requested.
- If the council still decides to seek possession, it must write to the tenant and give reasons why.

6.27 A dispute as to any of the matters set out above may form a defence to the proceedings and so, in respect of duty desk advice, that may form the basis an application for an adjournment for a defence on that basis to be filed and served.

6.28 However, if there is no dispute as to the procedure set out above, then the only defence available to the tenant would be by way of public law arguments, human rights arguments or the EA 2010 (chapter 10 below).

6.29 A duty adviser may argue it is disputed that the procedure was followed and, further and in the alternative, that the defendant has a public law, HRA 1998 or EA 2010 defence.

6.30 The bringing of possession proceedings keeps the introductory tenancy within the trial period until the proceedings are determined.

Flexible tenancies

6.31 Since April 2012, following the coming into force of the Localism Act 2011, local authorities in England have been required to develop a 'tenancy strategy' (s150). That strategy may be drawn so as allow them, if it decides to do so in individual circumstances, to grant flexible tenancies in place of periodic secure tenancies. A flexible tenancy is a tenancy for a fixed term rather than the ongoing periodic 'lifetime' secure tenancy we describe above. Flexible tenancies were introduced by amendments to the HA 1985 to insert ss107A–107E.

6.32 Councils that have elected to grant introductory tenancies, but also have a flexible tenancy strategy, will grant tenancies that are introductory and then become flexible tenancies at the end of the 'trial period'.

6.33 Statutory directions provide that flexible tenancies should be offered for a minimum fixed-term period of five years except in exceptional circumstances when the minimum is two years.

6.34 To grant a flexible tenancy, the local authority must give notice to the prospective tenant setting out the minimum term. There is no right of review of a decision to offer a flexible tenancy rather than a periodic tenancy. The prospective tenant may request a review of the minimum term within 21 days of the offer. There is no right to appeal a decision upholding the period of the flexible tenancy. Challenges in this regard would have to be by way of complaint or judicial review.

6.35 At the end of the fixed term, the council may serve notice that they will not renew the flexible tenancy, grant a further flexible tenancy for a further fixed term, or agree to grant a period secure tenancy. If the council does nothing and is not seeking possession of the premises, then a periodic secure tenancy will result automatically.

6.36 During the fixed term of the tenancy, the council may seek possession on any of the grounds that are applicable to a periodic secure tenancy and all of the commentary above would be applicable in such a case.

6.37 To end a tenancy on the basis that the fixed term has expired, the landlord must serve two notices:

1) A notice of not less than six months of non-renewal in writing at any time up to the end of the fixed period and must set out the reasons for not granting further tenancy. The tenant has the right to a review of that decision with 21 days of receiving the notice and the request does not have to be in writing.
   The review must consider whether the decision not to renew is compatible with any policy it has in relation to renewing flexible tenancies.
   The review decision must be notified to the tenant in writing and give reasons. This notification must occur before the expiry of the relevant notice of seeking possession.
   There is no right of appeal of such a review decision and any further remedy would only be by way of formal complaint or judicial review.
2) A notice of seeking possession in writing which must be served before the expiry of the fixed term. See chapter 4 above and appendix 7 below for notice requirements.

6.38 As with introductory tenancy cases coming before the court, a dispute as to any of the matters set out above may form a defence to the proceedings and so in relation to duty desk advice that itself may form the basis of an application for an adjournment for a defence to be filed and served.

6.39 However, if there is no dispute as the procedure set out above then the only defence available to the tenant would be by way of public law arguments, human rights arguments or the EA 2010 (see chapter 10 below).

6.40 A duty adviser may argue that it is disputed that the procedure was followed and, further and in the alternative, that the defendant has a public law, HRA 1998 or EA 2010 defence.

Local authority demoted tenancies

6.41 By amendment to the HA 1985 which added s82A, the Anti-Social Behaviour Act 2003 provided that secure tenancies could be ended and replaced with a 'demoted tenancy'. This is achieved by application to the county court and the conditions for an order to create the demoted tenancy are that the tenant, other resident or visitor has engaged in or threatened to engage in anti-social behaviour as described in HA 1996 s153A or s153B, and that the court considers it is reasonable to make an order.

6.42 The effect of the making of such an order is that the tenancy is demoted for a period of one year. A demoted tenancy is subject to the possibility of the landlord obtaining possession on a mandatory ground under HA 1996 s143D(2). This is because the court on application by the landlord must make a possession order if it is satisfied that a valid notice under s143E has been served and have carried out an appropriate review if the tenant has requested one within 14 days of having served the notice.

6.43 The notice must be in writing, must give reasons why the landlord is seeking possession, must inform the tenant of the right to a review, and must usually be for a period of at least four weeks or longer if the period of the tenancy is longer. See chapter 4 above and appendix 7 below for details of extended notice period due to COVID-19.

6.44 There is no power for the court to waive the requirement for the notice.

6.45 The tenant is entitled to a review which may include an oral hearing if requested. The outcome of the review must be conveyed to the tenant before the notice of possession expires.

6.46 As with introductory and flexible tenancy cases coming before the court, a dispute as to any of the matters set out above may form a defence to the proceedings and so in relation to duty desk advice that itself may form the basis of an application for an adjournment for a defence to be filed and served.

6.47 If there is no dispute as to the procedure set out above then the only defence available to the tenant would be by way of public law arguments, human rights arguments or the EA 2010 (chapter 10 below).

6.48 A duty adviser may argue that it is disputed that the procedure was followed and, further and in the alternative, that the defendant has a public law, HRA 1998 or EA 2010 defence.

Local authority family intervention tenancies

6.49 Family intervention tenancies may be offered by local authorities to families where the tenants of a secure or assured tenancy has either been made subject to a possession order for anti-social behaviour or such an order could have been made if the tenant had such a tenancy. They may also be offered by RSLs, for which see chapter 7 below. Before a family intervention tenancy is created a notice must be served setting out the reasons why such a tenancy is to be offered.

6.50 There must be an intention to provide and accept behaviour support services in accommodation away from the original accommodation where relevant, that has been agreed in writing between the council as landlord and local authority, the family intervention project and the tenant. A tenant cannot be compelled to enter into such an agreement for a family intervention tenancy. 'Guidance on the use of Family Intervention Tenancies' (Ministry of Housing, Communities and Local Government, January 2009) can be found here: www.gov.uk/government/publications/family-intervention-tenancies.

6.51 Family intervention tenancies are described in the guidance as common law tenancies which can be ended with a 28 days' notice to quit – see chapter 4 above and appendix 7 below for details of extensions to notice periods due to COVID-19.

6.52 If a local authority wishes to bring a family intervention tenancy to an end, they must serve a 'notice of intent' to serve a notice to quit. That notice must be in writing, must set out the effect of the notice to quit that is proposed to be served, must state the reason for the decision to serve notice and when it is proposed to be served, and set out review rights to be exercised within 14 days. The review procedure is subject to regulations and allows for written and oral representations.

6.53 If no review is requested, or a review is requested but then withdrawn, or a review is conducted and the tenant is given reasons in writing as to why the decision is upheld, then the landlord may serve a notice to quit and bring proceedings.

6.54 Proceedings will almost always be brought because there has been a refusal to accept the support which is the basis of the tenancy, or the behaviour which led to the tenancy has not significantly changed.

6.55 Because, as set out above, family intervention tenancies are quite properly described in the government guidance as 'common law tenancies' which can be ended with (usually – but see chapter 10 below) 28 days' notice to quit, duty advisers may use the following section on non-secure tenancies and licences as a guide to dealing with family intervention tenancy possession cases.

Non-secure tenancies and licences

6.56 Non-secure tenancies is the name generally given to tenancies provided by local authority landlords which do not enjoy the protection of HA 1985 and other statutory protection. They are sometimes also described simply as contractual tenancies.

Conditions

6.57 There are two main ways in which non-secure tenancies come about – (i) tenancy condition for secure tenancy is not satisfied and (ii) accommodation is procided as temporary accommodation to a homless person or family (although see family intervention tenancies above).

The tenancy condition

6.58 A secure tenancy which enjoys the protection of HA 1985 is subject to a number of conditions including the tenant condition. The tenant condition is satisfied where the tenant or at least one of the joint tenants occupies the accommodation as their only or principal home. The tenancy condition can be met by a spouse or civil partner making good the absence of a tenant or joint tenant – see Family Law Act 1996 s30.

6.59 However, statutory security of tenure can be lost or indeed never gained if a tenant or none of joint tenants has resided or has ceased to reside in the accommodation as their only or principal home and their absence is not made good by a spouse or civil partner. Where there is no statutory security of tenure a tenancy still exists, but it is a contractual tenancy only and does not have the protections guaranteed in the HA 1985.

6.60 That means that such a tenancy can be brought to an end by a simple notice to quit giving four weeks' notice (see chapter 4 above and appendix 7 below for details of notice requirements). Once the notice has expired the landlord can bring possession proceedings and if the status of the tenancy as a contractual tenancy, as well as service of a valid notice is proven to the court then the judge must make an order for possession.

6.61 It is important for advisers to be aware that tenants can move in and out of the statutory protection of the HA 1985 and that might affect the outcome of possession proceedings. If a tenant moves out of the property such that the tenant condition is not fulfilled, is served a notice to quit, but returns to the property before the notice expires, then they will regain security of tenure under the secure tenancy. If they do not return before the expiry of the notice, then security will be lost and they will be a contractual tenant only and vulnerable to a mandatory possession order.

Homelessness temporary accommodation

6.62 Homeless applicants were often, and to much lesser extent still are, granted non-secure tenancies by local authorities in exercise of their homelessness duties under HA 1996 Part 7. While the landscape in the exercise and discharge of those duties has changed, non-secure tenancy cases relating to homelessness accommodation still appear regularly in possession lists.

6.63 In those cases, there are a number of underlying reasons why the local authority landlord is seeking possession of the property. This is a non-exhaustive list:

- rent arrears;
- anti-social or nuisance behaviour;
- the property is owned by someone else and leased to the council for use as homelessness accommodation, the lease has come to an end and the owner wants the property back;
- the council's homelessness duties to the tenant have come to an end.

6.64 In homelessness cases arising on duty days, the authors have never seen a case where it was possible to dispute that the tenancy lacks security, but that possibility should not be ruled out by duty advisers. What does occur, often where there is a long and sometimes complicated history to the letting, is a muddle as to the identity of the landlord as opposed to the identity of a letting agent. Claims where the claimant is a letting agent should be scrutinised carefully to check if the claimant really is the landlord.

6.65 Likewise the identity of the person or organisation serving the notice to quit and the identity and role of the person representing the claimant should be considered carefully by the duty adviser – in relation to the identity of the landlord, the person serving the notice to quit and the person at court, see chapter 4 above.

6.66 Otherwise a dispute as to the service or the validity of the notice to quit may form a defence to the proceedings and so in relation to duty desk advice that itself may form the basis of an application for an adjournment for a defence to be filed and served or even for the claim to be struck out if the tenant's case can be proven there and then.

6.67 However, if there is no dispute as to the notice then the only defence available to the tenant would be by way of public law arguments, human rights arguments or the EA 2010 (chapter 10 below).

6.68 A duty adviser may argue that it is disputed that procedure was followed and, further and in the alternative, that the defendant has a public law, HRA 1998 and/or EA 2010 defence.

6.69 Where a local authority claims possession on the basis that that the homelessness duty has come to an end, but the defendant has an outstanding review or an appeal, then it would be a viable defence in public law to say that the underlying reason for seeking possession was not yet crystallised and therefore the proceedings were unlawful. See chapter 10 below as to public law defences and how they work.

Licences

6.70 While this section refers to the concepts of licences and exclusive possession of residential accommodation, it is beyond the scope of this book to provide a fulsome analysis of the legal implications of these concepts. DPP has the detail if required, but this section deals with the basics and the most common cases that come up on duty days.

6.71 Where there is permission to occupy premises but there are no other features which would determine the arrangement as a tenancy of any kind, then the arrangement is likely to be a licence. A licence can, but does not have to, be in writing, and regardless of whether it is in writing can be a bare licence (where there is no fee or service rendered in exchange for permission to reside) or a contractual licence (where there is a fee or service rendered).

6.72 What is most often most important in local authority licence cases seen on duty is whether the occupier has exclusive possession or not.

6.73 If an occupier does have exclusive possession, then in general whether an arrangement is a licence or not is a dispute that can give rise to a defence. A duty adviser may well apply for an adjournment for that defence to be prepared, filed and served. Cases where the claimant claims a service occupancy are examples of cases of this kind.

6.74 A licence with exclusive possession will require a notice to quit and so it follows that a dispute as to the service or the validity of the notice to quit may form a defence to the proceedings.

6.75 Where the local authority has granted a licence of accommodation with exclusive possession to a person to whom they owe homelessness duties (except for hostel accommodation and interim duties under HA 1996 s188) then the situation is no different to non-secure tenancies in respect of the issues that may be raised – see above.

6.76 Hostel accommodation or a licence granted pursuant to interim homelessness duties under section 188 does not attract the protection of Protection of Eviction Act (PEA) 1977 and therefore a formal notice to quit and possession proceedings are not required to end the licence and for eviction to take place. However, if such a case is before the court on duty then there is no reason not to treat the case as if there was such protection. The alternative is to claim that the proceedings are an abuse of process, although it is hard to see how that helps the defendant in any material way.

CHAPTER 7

Registered Social Landlords

Key points

- This chapter is concerned with cases where the landlord is a housing association or other social housing landlord that is not a local authority. They are often called RSLs (short for Registered Social Landlord) and while Private Registered Provider of Social Housing (PRPSH) is the current formal name in England, we have chosen to use the more widely used RSL, which remains the formal name in Wales.
- RSL tenancies can be permanent assured tenancies or short-term assured shorthold tenancies and identifying the type of tenancy is a key starting point.
- In either case, RSL cases can be brought on mandatory or discretionary grounds or a mixture of both, so the next step is understanding that.
- Discretionary ground cases are mostly dealt with in the same way as a local authority secure tenancy cases, with the same consideration of whether it is reasonable to make a possession order or not. Welfare benefits to help with rent are often an important consideration as are other financial issues, health issues and whether there may be a counterclaim and/or set off.
- Mandatory ground cases will require careful consideration. It is essential to check the amount of rent arrears both at the date of the notice and at the hearing – both must be above the threshold required to make out the ground for possession.
- Consider the use of Equality Act 2010, Human Rights Act 1998 or public law defences, as well as possible counterclaims in mandatory ground cases.
- Duty advisers may occasionally come across accelerated possession claims on duty, both at 'substantive (S) hearings' and 'review (R) dates'.
- Mandatory grounds cases may be met with public law defences in appropriate cases.

Introduction

7.1 Much (but not all) of the information in this chapter is in relation to tenancy types common to both RSLs and private landlords. Much of the text from this chapter will therefore be repeated in chapter 8, and we have done that for the sake of ease of reference.

7.2 The main differences relevant to duty advisers can be listed as follows:

- RSLs must follow the Pre-action Protocol for Possession Claims by Social Landlords (see chapter 3 above) regardless of what sort of tenancy is the subject of the claim. That includes section 3 on mandatory grounds for possession.
- A claim for possession brought by an RSL may in the right circumstances be met with a public law defence, a Human Rights Act (HRA) 1998 defence and/or an Equality Act (EA) 2010 defence (see chapter 10 below). An RSL may, in certain circumstances, be subject to the public sector equality duty (PSED) (under EA 2010 s149).

7.3 The majority of the cases will be assured tenancies, although we are increasingly seeing assured shorthold tenancy cases with a fixed term of two or five years.

7.4 There will also be assured shorthold periodic tenancies where RSLs have granted tenancies to assist local authorities with their duties to homeless persons under Housing Act (HA) 1996 Part 7.

7.5 There are some RSL secure tenancies, but these are vanishingly rare these days.

7.6 In some cases the tenancy held by the tenant by an RSL will have started life as a secure tenancy with a local authority ie if there has been a stock transfer from the local authority to the RSL and the secure tenancy held by the tenant converted to an assured tenancy with the RSL. Generally, the RSL will show evidence of that stock transfer with their claim documents but if they don't then an adjournment should be sought for them to provide those documents.

7.7 Where a tenancy has been subject to a stock transfer a question arises as to whether it is just or fair for the RSL to rely on mandatory ground 8 in a possession claim when no such mandatory ground was available with the original tenancy. This could give rise to a defence to the mandatory ground for possession in public law but we are not aware of the point being tested.

7.8 There are cases where a tenancy may have started with one RSL but have a completely different RSL landlord at the date of the hearing. They may even have been through a number of RSL landlords as mergers and take-overs have occurred in the RSL sector. Unless the landlord can produce the original tenancy agreement to the court then they should not be allowed to rely on ground 8. This is because it was common practice in years gone by for RSLs to stipulate in the tenancy agreement the grounds for possession they would rely upon and those they would not, and many tenancy agreements said that ground 8 would not be relied upon.

7.9 It is depressing to note that latterly RSLs tend not to adopt policies restricting themselves from using mandatory grounds for possession. The availability of public law defences in appropriate cases is therefore very important.

The tenancy condition

7.10 An assured or assured shorthold tenancy which enjoys the protection of HA 1988 is subject to a number of conditions, including the tenant condition. The tenant condition is satisfied where the tenant or at least one of the joint tenants occupies the accommodation as their only or principal home. The tenancy condition can be met by a spouse or civil partner making good the absence of a tenant or joint tenant – see Family Law Act 1996 s30.

7.11 Statutory security of tenure can be lost or indeed never gained if a tenant or one of the joint tenants has resided or has ceased to reside in the accommodation as their only or principal home and their absence is not made good by a spouse or civil partner. Where there is no statutory security of tenure, a tenancy still exists, but it is a contractual tenancy only and does not have the protections guaranteed in HA 1988.

7.12 That means that such a tenancy can be brought to an end by a notice to quit giving usually at least four weeks' notice (see chapter 4 above and appendix 7 below for details of notice requirements). Once the notice has expired, the landlord can bring possession proceedings and if the status of the tenancy as a contractual tenancy, as well as service of a valid notice is proven to the court, then the judge must make an order for possession.

7.13 It is important for advisers to be aware that tenants can move in and out of the statutory protection of HA 1988 and that might affect the outcome of possession proceedings. If a tenant moves out of the property so that the tenant condition is not fulfilled, is served a notice to quit, but returns to the property before the notice expires, they will regain security of tenure under the secure tenancy. If they do not return before the expiry of the notice, then security will be lost, and they will be a contractual tenant only and vulnerable to a mandatory possession order.

Mandatory claims – rent

7.14 Ground 8 is a mandatory ground for possession. HA 1988 Sch 2 as amended provides that if the requirements of ground 8 are proven by the landlord, then the judge must make an order for possession. The judge does not have the discretion to consider whether it is reasonable for a possession order to be made. The judge is simply concerned with whether the ground is made out. If it is then the judge does not have the power to postpone the order or suspend enforcement. There is nothing in the Master of the Rolls Working Group on Possession Proceedings' 'Overall Arrangements for Possession Proceedings in England and Wales: "The Overall Arrangements"' which changes this position. COVID-19 Case Marking, for example, does not affect the judge's lack of discretion in mandatory cases and cannot prevent an outright possession order being made where the ground is made out.

7.15 The matters the judge must be satisfied of are:

- that a valid notice of seeking possession pursuant to HA 1988 s8 in the prescribed form was served on the tenant; and
- at the date of the service of the notice:
  - (a) if rent is payable weekly or fortnightly, at least eight weeks' rent is unpaid;
  - (b) if rent is payable monthly, at least two months' rent is unpaid;
  - (c) if rent is payable quarterly, at least one quarter's rent is more than three months in arrears; and
  - (d) if rent is payable yearly, at least three months' rent is more than three months in arrears;

  and for the purpose of this ground 'rent' means rent lawfully due from the tenant. [HA 1988 Sch 2]
- that at the time the matter comes before the court the tenant is still or is again in arrears of rent of those amounts or more.

7.16 Any dispute as to any of the matters set out above which cannot be easily and quickly resolved by evidence at the hearing may form a defence to the proceedings. It will be essential for the duty adviser to check the calculation of rent both at the date of the notice and at the date of hearing. If these factual matters cannot be resolved by way of duty desk advice because there is insufficient time, then that itself may form the basis of an application for an adjournment for a defence to be filed and served.

7.17 The judge cannot dispense with the requirement for notice on a mandatory ground 8 claim and so a dispute as to the service of the notice and/or the validity of the notice may be a defence to proceedings. For that very reason ground 8 is almost always pleaded along with grounds 10 and 11 dealt with below.

7.18 It is long established case-law that the judge cannot adjourn a ground 8 claim because there are outstanding housing benefit issues even if it is likely that arrears will be cleared or brought below the ground 8 threshold when the issues are resolved – *North British Housing Association Ltd v Matthews* [2004] EWCA Civ 1736, [2005] 2 All ER 667.

7.19 That said, the public law jurisdiction in the county court would allow in appropriate cases (see chapter 10 below) for a public law and or HRA 1998 defence to be filed on the basis that it was (i) perverse and contrary to the purpose of social housing policy to seek possession when arrears of rent were capable of being resolved and/or (ii) disproportionate to the aim sought for the same reasons.

7.20 There would have to be exceptional circumstances to allow an adjournment for future events to transpire – but it is possible. What might constitute a sufficient level of exceptionality has not been tested in the higher courts but is often argued in the county courts. Duty advisers learn to be creative when defendants are facing mandatory ground proceedings. *Legal Action* magazine's 'Housing: Recent Developments' update is a very useful resource for duty advisers and should be scoured monthly for useful and persuasive arguments that can be put to judges when the higher courts have not yet resolved those issues.

7.21 In mandatory cases it may be that procedural points are all the duty adviser has to try to buy the tenant more time to reduce the arrears below the threshold. The most common such point arises out of Civil Procedure Rules 1998 (CPR) Practice Direction (PD) 55B concerning Possession Claims Online (PCOL) and the rent account schedule – see chapter 3 above. Such a point will gain an adjournment to give the tenant an opportunity to bring the arrears down and can be the difference between them keeping their home or not.

7.22 A counterclaim (for example, for disrepair and housing conditions) can be set off against arrears and form the basis of a defence and counterclaim in order to prevent a possession order from being made.

7.23 In the event that the defendant discloses facts which could give rise to a counterclaim of sufficient quantum that could bring the arrears below the ground 8 threshold, then the duty adviser should make an application for an adjournment for a defence and counterclaim to be filed and served *before* evidence is taken by the court. A defendant in this situation should be advised to seek legal advice as soon as possible after the hearing to help with the defence and counterclaim.

7.24 In some cases the judge may need to be reminded that a counterclaim and set off acts as defence to the possession proceedings as well as the money claim so there can be no question of making a possession order and adjourning the money claim.

7.25 There may be cases where the arrears are so high that it is patently obvious that the counterclaim will not adequately set off the arrears and it may not be possible to prevent a possession order. The duty adviser should only concede if there is no doubt that the set off would not be enough, otherwise they should argue for an adjournment so the issue can be tried. In circumstances where the judge cannot be persuaded to adjourn, the money claim should then be adjourned even if a possession order is made.

7.26 Ground 8 mandatory claims for possession are very often pleaded alongside the two discretionary rent arrears grounds. The utility of these grounds to the landlord in conjunction with ground 8 is that they still allow a claim to proceed and the landlord to continue to ask for possession if the tenant reduces the arrears to less than the ground 8 threshold amount or even if the arrears are cleared before the hearing.

7.27 With discretionary grounds the court has the power to dispense with the requirement for the notice of seeking possession and so if there is a defect in the notice that has been served, or if there is doubt as to the service of a notice, then the discretionary grounds will allow the landlord to try to argue that notice should be dispensed with and a possession order made.

Discretionary claims – rent

7.28 HA 1988 s7(4) provides that:

> (4) If the court is satisfied that any of the grounds in Part II of Schedule 2 to this Act is established, then, subject to subsections (5A) and (6) below, the court may make an order for possession if it considers it reasonable to do so.

7.29 In rent arrears cases involving assured and assured shorthold tenancies, there are two discretionary grounds for possession available: HA 1988 Sch 2 ground 10 and ground 11.

7.30 These grounds are made out in the following circumstances:

Ground 10

Some rent lawfully due from the tenant–
(a) is unpaid on the date on which the proceedings for possession are begun; and
(b) except where subsection (1)(b) of section 8 of this Act applies, was in arrears at the date of the service of the notice under that section relating to those proceedings.

7.31 HA 1988 s(1)(b) is the provision where the court may consider it just and equitable to dispense with the requirement of such a notice.

Ground 11

Whether or not any rent is in arrears on the date on which proceedings for possession are begun, the tenant has persistently delayed paying rent which has become lawfully due.

7.32 These grounds are 'discretionary' because where they are relied upon the judge must decide whether it is reasonable in all the circumstances for a possession order to be made. If the judge considers it is reasonable to make a possession order, they will then decide whether to suspend or postpone that order – see chapter 12 below for discussion of different outcomes in possession proceedings.

7.33 Where the court has discretion to consider whether it is reasonable for a possession order to be made then there is no need for a defendant to raise public law or HRA 1998 defences.

7.34 The situation is not the same with EA 2010 defences which should be argued as such whether to meet a mandatory or discretionary claim for possession.

7.35 If it is decided that a possession order should be made the judge has the discretion to make a conditional order which will postpone or suspend enforcement of the order on terms. It is important to note that the decision as to whether it is reasonable to make a possession order must be made before any decision to postpone or suspend enforcement of the order.

Mandatory claims – Housing Act 1988 s21

7.36 There is another mandatory 'ground' for possession (although this is not one that appears in HA 1988 Sch 2 containing the grounds for possession) available by way of HA 1988 s21. This is only available where the RSL has granted an assured shorthold tenancy.

7.37 Originally designed to give landlords a quick and easy way to regain possession of residential premises once the fixed term of the tenancy has expired, this legislation has been vastly encumbered over the years by amendments to itself and by way of other legislation. There are now many issues for advisers to check when advising tenants facing proceedings brought under section 21.

7.38 Essentially, a number of housing standards and letting condition issues have been loaded on to the ability of the landlord to obtain possession without any need to establish any fault on the part of the tenant once any fixed-term has expired. These include:

- matters concerning local authority houses in multiple occupation (HMOs) and selective licensing (not applicable to RSLs);
- gas safety issues;
- the requirement for an energy performance certificate;
- the requirement to provide government information about renting;
- matters concerning the protection of tenancy deposits and the information to be provided in that regard (not always applicable in RSL cases);
- housing conditions where they have been reported to the local authority;
- prohibited payments under the Tenant Fees Act 2019 (not applicable to RSLs).

7.39 It is beyond the scope of this book to discuss all of these issues which may invalidate a notice under section 21 in detail. Readers would do well to bookmark the Nearly Legal flowchart at https://nearlylegal.co.uk/2019/09/updated-section-21-flowchart/ – and then to write to Giles Peaker of Anthony Gold Solicitors to thank him for this invaluable piece of public service.

> *Wales and section 21:* Duty advisers in Wales will be aware that where an assured shorthold tenancy in Wales is periodic from the outset, then a s21 notice will need to expire on the last day of a period of the tenancy or have a savings clauses, which is no longer the case in England.

7.40 As well as dealing with the requirements above, the flowchart also deals with the issue of the prescribed form of notice (form 6A) and the notice period required in normal times. It does not, at the time of writing, deal with special coronavirus legislation regarding notice periods – for that, see chapter 4 above and appendix 7 below.

7.41 Generally speaking, in RSL cases, the matters to be checked by duty advisers will be:

- that the claim is in relation to an assured shorthold tenancy;
- that the fixed term has expired where relevant;
- that the notice is in the prescribed form;
- that the notice was served;
- that the notice was served at the correct time (not less than four months from the start of the tenancy);
- that proceedings have been brought in time (this may depend on the notice period required for the particular notice);
- that the issues set out in the bullet points at 7.38 above do not invalidate the notice.

7.42 Any one of these issues can invalidate the notice and means the tenant would have a defence to the proceedings. There is no discretion on the judge to waive the requirement for a section 21 notice. It can be difficult for a duty adviser to check all of these complicated issues in the time available. It is perfectly legitimate to require the landlord to prove each issue to the court.

7.43 The landlord or their representative can be asked to provide their evidence for each issue prior to the court hearing. If there is any doubt as to any of the matters set out above then the duty adviser should ask the judge to adjourn the claim for a defence to be filed following which evidence can be submitted by both sides and tested at a hearing. The court must be dissuaded from trying to resolve such issues at a short initial hearing.

7.44 In some cases it is possible to prove to the court that the notice is invalid and if section 21 is the only 'ground' of possession relied upon by the landlord then a judge should be asked to dismiss the claim for possession because the landlord cannot remedy the defect.

7.45 If the landlord can prove that a valid section 21 notice has been served and the claim has been properly brought then the judge has no option but to make an outright possession order.

7.46 There is nothing preventing an RSL from pleading section 21 alongside a claim for rent arrears or other ground set out in HA 1988 Sch 2 as amended. It not unusual to see mandatory ground 8, discretionary grounds 10 and 11 and section 21 pleaded in the same claim. However, pleading section 21 alongside a rent arrears claim will mean that an N5 claim form must be used and the landlord cannot utilise the accelerated possession procedure which we set out below.

7.47 If the landlord can make out section 21 but there are any doubts as to an associated rent arrears claim then it may be of some assistance to the tenant to agree a possession order and ask the judge to stipulate that is made only pursuant to section 21 and adjourn the money claim. That may prevent any action being taken on the alleged rent arrears (often it is not worthwhile for the landlord to chase the arrears) and can be important if the tenant intends to make an application as homeless under HA 1996 Part 7. This would allow the applicant to say that the landlord obtained possession because the fixed term of the tenancy had come to an end rather than a possession order being granted based on any 'fault' on the part of the applicant.

Accelerated possession claims

7.48 Where an RSL landlord is seeking possession based solely on HA 1988 s21, it is open to them to use the accelerated possession procedure.

7.49 The accelerated possession procedure is set out at CPR Part 55 Section II; and also at CPR PD 55A Section II.

7.50 Accelerated possession proceedings are also specifically dealt with in the Overall Arrangements:

> **Accelerated Possession Claims**
>
> 60. In accordance with existing rules, in some cases (Accelerated Possession Claims) an order for possession may be made without a hearing by a Judge to whom the papers have been referred for this course to be considered.
>
> 61. Within the Overall Arrangements, Accelerated Possession Claims are however subject to the following:
>
> (a) Accelerated Possession Claims issued before 3 August 2020 will require a Reactivation Notice as with all other stayed claims.
> (b) As a guideline, Accelerated Possession Claims will be dealt with having regard to the priorities listed in the section on Prioritisation above.
> (c) Each court centre will refer Accelerated Possession Claims to a Judge at manageable frequency.
> (d) Judges will use the time freed up where Substantive (S) Hearing slots are vacated, to deal with Accelerated Possession Claims referred to them for consideration.
> (e) Where the parties agree or there is no objection, the Judge to whom an Accelerated Possession Claim has been referred for consideration may direct that a Review (R) Date be listed to enable the Defendant to receive duty scheme advice and assistance.
>
> 62. If on consideration of an Accelerated Possession Claim referred to the Judge for consideration the Judge directs a Substantive Hearing (giving any appropriate case management directions, and with the

parties to attend) that will be listed as a Substantive (S) Hearing unless otherwise directed.

7.51 The duty adviser may get accelerated possession cases at the 'review (R) date'. The task for the duty adviser will be to try to ascertain if there is a defence, and if there is, to try to persuade the landlord to drop the claim. If that is not possible, then the matter will need to progress to an S hearing and legal aid can be granted in appropriate cases for a fully pleaded defence to be filed. If that is not possible, then the defendant may seek advice again at the S hearing where their case can be put before the judge. The defence or potential defence that is identified should therefore be carefully recorded in the written advice to the defendant after the R date so that it is apparent to the duty adviser at the S hearing should that be necessary.

7.52 Broadly, the accelerated procedure enables a landlord to submit a claim form on practice form N5B with accompanying documents exhibited to that form. The purpose of the claim form and the documents is to provide to the court documentary proof that an assured shorthold tenancy has come to the end of any fixed term or the requisite period since the start of the tenancy has elapsed, a valid section 21 notice has been served and therefore the landlord is entitled to an outright possession order.

7.53 The claim form and a defence form on practice form N11B is sent to the tenant with information that they should file and serve the defence form within 14 days of receiving it. After that the claim form and the defence form (if one has been filed) are considered by the district judge without a hearing. If the landlord has made out their claim then the judge must make a possession order. If there is any doubt about the landlord's claim then the judge must list the case for a hearing.

7.54 Accelerated possession claims may come before the duty adviser in any of the following ways:

- The judge has not been satisfied on the papers that a possession order should be made and so has directed a hearing under CPR 55.16(1)(b).
- The judge decides, and there are no objections, to refer the accelerated claim to an R date for the tenant to get R advice – see Overall Arrangements para 62.
- The judge has made a possession order but the defendant has applied to set aside that order and the court has listed a hearing of that application. Either party has the right to apply to set aside an

order made in the absence of the parties (CPR 3.3(5)) and it follows that a tenant has an absolute right to apply to set aside a possession order made on the papers in accelerated possession proceedings.
- The tenant has requested in the defence form that if a possession order is made, then they are asking for it to be postponed for up to 42 days due to exceptional hardship – HA 1980 s89 and CPR 55.18.

7.55 In order to assist the defendant to prevent a possession order or have a possession order set aside, the duty adviser will need to be able to persuade the judge that there is a defence. If the matter requires evidence then, just as with a conventional first instance hearing, the duty adviser should ask the judge to adjourn the claim or application for a fully pleaded defence to be filed. The duty adviser may try to negotiate such an outcome with the claimant at the R advice stage or can put that case to the judge at the S hearing.

7.56 If it is not possible to raise a defence, the duty adviser will have to take instructions of any exceptional hardship the tenant and their household would suffer as a result of being evicted from the premises following a 14-day order. Homelessness resulting from a possession order is not usually in-and-of-itself an exceptional circumstance – but it might be argued in the midst of a pandemic crisis. The duty adviser will need to persuade the judge of matters which concern the tenant and their household. The judge can, only if persuaded of exceptional hardship, postpone the possession order for up to 42 days, but can also stipulate a period between 14 and 42 days.

7.57 Judges should be encouraged not to take into account the overall period of time that a warrant for possession might take to execute because that cannot ultimately be known. Claimants may try to persuade judges to take into account the 14 days' notice that must be given to a tenant of execution of a warrant of possession.

RSL demoted tenancies

7.58 These are tenancies that were assured tenancies, more rarely secure tenancies or fixed-term tenancies of two years or more, granted by an RSL that have been subject to a demotion order pursuant to HA 1988 s6A because of nuisance and antisocial behaviour. The tenancy is effectively converted by such an order to a weekly periodic assured shorthold tenancy which may be brought to an end by way of HA

1988 s21. The landlord may also serve a section 8 notice on a demoted tenancy citing one or more grounds for possession.

7.59 In general, the same defences to the notice as in any other section 21 notice case well as in public law, HRA 1998 and EA 2010 are available in demoted tenancy cases.

7.60 HA 1988 s20C sets out when and how a demoted tenancy will revert back to a tenancy with security of tenure and those details should be checked on RSL demoted tenancy cases.

RSL family intervention tenancies

7.61 Family intervention tenancies may be offered by RSLs as well as local authorities to families where the tenant of a secure or assured tenancy has either been made subject to a possession order for antisocial behaviour or such an order could have been made if the tenant had such a tenancy. Before a family intervention tenancy is created, a notice must be served setting out the reasons why such a tenancy is to be offered.

7.62 There must be an intention to provide and accept behaviour support services in accommodation away from the original accommodation where relevant, that has been agreed in writing between the council as landlord and local authority, the family intervention project and the tenant. A tenant cannot be compelled to enter into an agreement for a family intervention tenancy. Guidance on their use can be found here: www.gov.uk/government/publications/family-intervention-tenancies.

7.63 Family intervention tenancies are described in the guidance as common law tenancies which can be ended with a 28 days' notice to quit – see chapter 4 above and appendix 7 below for details of extensions to notice periods due to COVID-19 .

7.64 Unlike local authorities (see 6.52 above), RSLs do not have to serve a 'notice of intent' prior to serving a notice to quit, and do not have to engage in a formal review process. However the guidance referred to above makes clear that RSLs are expected 'to operate a similar termination and review procedure to that required under the Act by local authorities' (para 22). Otherwise the RSL landlord may serve a notice to quit and bring proceedings.

7.65 Proceedings will almost always be brought because there has been a refusal to accept the support which is the basis of the tenancy, or the behaviour which led to the tenancy has not significantly changed.

7.66 Because family intervention tenancies are quite properly described in the government guidance as 'common law tenancies' which can be ended with (usually – but see chapter 4 above and appendix 7 below) 28 days' notice to quit, duty advisers may use the section on non-secure tenancies and licences in the preceding chapter as a guide to dealing with family intervention tenancy possession cases.

CHAPTER 8

Private tenancies

Key points

- This chapter deals with cases where the landlord is a private individual or company.
- Nearly all the cases where there is a private landlord will be mandatory possession claims and will involve assured shorthold tenancies.
- Mandatory ground cases will require careful consideration. It is essential to check the amount of rent arrears both at the date of the notice and at the hearing – both must be above the threshold required to make out the ground for possession.
- Be alive to issues that might constitute a counter-claim and reduce the arrears below the threshold.
- Cases can be brought on both mandatory grounds and discretionary grounds at the same time. The landlord might be persuaded to agree terms on the discretionary grounds.
- A duty adviser may come across accelerated possession claims either because substantive issues are raised or because the defendant requires more time before vacating.
- There is no applicable pre-action protocol in private possession cases but compliance with Civil Procedure Rules 1998 (CPR) requirements can be key to trying to defend proceedings or buy time for a defendant.
- Public law defences cannot be raised.
- Private landlords may be in person or may have legal representation. It is important to understand the identity of the person putting the case for the landlord. An agent, for example, cannot generally represent the landlord.
- In general, private landlords want a possession order. Negotiation is only usually possible if the duty adviser can outline a defence and/or a technical problem with the claim. Even then, it is much more usual to have to argue the point before the judge in private landlord cases.
- If there are disputed facts, see whether or not the landlord or representative is in a position to prove their case evidentially, ie as to service of notices etc.
- In Wales, the case of *Jarvis v Evans and another* [2020] EWCA Civ 854 has confirmed that the failure of landlord or their agent to be licensed under Rent Smart Wales (www.rentsmart.gov.wales/en/home/) can invalidate a Housing Act (HA) 1988 s8 notice served by a landlord as well as a s21 notice.

Introduction

8.1 Much (but not all) of the information in relation to the tenancy types common to both RSL and private landlords that we set out in chapter 7 above will apply equally to this chapter. For ease of reference, we have decided to repeat relevant text rather than either keep referring back to chapter 7 or unnecessarily rewording it.

8.2 The main differences relevant to duty advisers can be listed follows:

- The representative of a private landlord at court will be the landlord themselves (an individual or member of the landlord organisation who can represent the landlord organisation) or a legal representative. No other person may represent the private landlord without permission of the court.
- There is no pre-action protocol that a private landlord must follow.
- A private landlord's claim cannot be met with a public law defence. A Human Rights Act (HRA) 1998 defence may still be available, as may be an Equality Act (EA) 2010 defence, although of course a private landlord is not subject to the public sector equality duty (PSED) (EA 2010 s149).

8.3 In the vast majority of cases, the tenancy that a duty adviser will be seeing in private landlord cases is an assured shorthold tenancy. Since 28 February 1997, nearly every new private tenancy will have been an assured shorthold (rather than an assured) tenancy. It was and is possible to create an assured tenancy from 28 February 1997, but there has been virtually no reason for any private landlord to do so.

8.4 Tenancies that started between 15 January 1989 and 28 February 1997 should be checked carefully to see whether a HA 1988 s20 notice was served prior to the commencement of the tenancy – if not the tenancy will be an assured tenant not an assured shorthold tenancy. Tenancies which started prior to 15 January 1989 may be tenancies protected by the Rent Act (RA) 1977, which are dealt with at chapter 9 below. Private landlord assured and RA tenancies will be rare now, and will become more so as time passes.

8.5 It is unusual to see a possession case involving private landlords on anything other than Housing Act (HA) 1988 s21 and/or grounds 8, 10 and 11 in HA 1988 Sch 2 (as amended). We will therefore concentrate on those in this chapter.

Mandatory claims – rent

8.6 Ground 8 is a mandatory ground for possession. HA 1988 Sch 2 as amended provides that if the requirements of ground 8 are proven by the landlord then the judge must make an order for possession. The judge does not have the discretion to consider whether it is reasonable for a possession order to be made or not. The judge is simply concerned with whether the ground is made out. If it is made out, then the judge does not have the power to postpone the order or suspend enforcement.

8.7 There is nothing in the Master of the Rolls Working Group on Possession Proceedings' 'Overall Arrangements for Possession Proceedings in England and Wales: "The Overall Arrangements"' which changes this position. COVID-19 Case Marking, for example, does not affect the judge's lack of discretion in mandatory cases and cannot prevent an outright possession order being made where the ground is made out.

8.8 The matters the judge must be satisfied of are:

- that a valid notice of seeking possession pursuant to HA 1988 s8 in the prescribed form was served on the tenant; and
- at the date of the service of the notice:

  (a) if rent is payable weekly or fortnightly, at least eight weeks' rent is unpaid;
  (b) if rent is payable monthly, at least two months' rent is unpaid;
  (c) if rent is payable quarterly, at least one quarter's rent is more than three months in arrears; and
  (d) if rent is payable yearly, at least three months' rent is more than three months in arrears;

  and for the purpose of this ground "rent" means rent lawfully due from the tenant. [HA 1988 Sch 2]
- that at the time the matter comes before the court the tenant is still or is again in arrears of rent of those amounts or more;
- in Wales, the court will need to be satisfied that the landlord or their agent is licensed with Rent Smart Wales if required.

8.9 Any dispute as to any of the matters set out above which cannot be easily and quickly resolved by evidence at the hearing may form a defence to the proceedings. It will be essential for the duty adviser to check the calculation of rent both at the date of the notice and at the date of hearing. If these factual matters cannot be resolved by way of duty desk advice because there is insufficient time, then that itself may form the basis of an application for an adjournment for a defence to be filed and served.

8.10 The judge cannot dispense with the requirement for notice on a mandatory ground 8 claim and so a dispute as to the service of the notice and/or the validity of the notice may be a defence to proceedings. For that very reason, ground 8 is almost always pleaded along with grounds 10 and 11 (dealt with below).

8.11 It is long established case-law that the judge cannot adjourn a ground 8 claim because there are outstanding housing benefit issues even if it is likely that arrears will be cleared or brought below the ground 8 threshold when the issues are resolved – *North British Housing Association v Matthews* [2005] EWCA Civ 1736, [2005] 2 All ER 667.

8.12 There would have to be very exceptional circumstances to allow an adjournment for future events to transpire. What might constitute a sufficient level of exceptionality has not been tested in the higher courts but duty advisers learn to be creative when defendants are facing mandatory ground proceedings. *Legal Action* magazine's 'Housing: Recent Developments' update is a very useful resource for duty advisers and should be scoured monthly for useful and persuasive arguments that can be put to judges when the higher courts have not yet resolved those issues.

8.13 In mandatory cases it may be that procedural points are all the duty adviser has to try to buy the tenant more time to reduce the arrears below the threshold. The most common such point arises out of Civil Procedure Rules 1998 (CPR) Practice Direction (PD) 55B concerning Possession Claims Online (PCOL) and the rent account schedule – see chapter 3 above. Such a point will gain an adjournment to give the tenant an opportunity to bring the arrears down and can be the difference between them keeping their home or not.

8.14 A counterclaim (for example, for disrepair and housing conditions) can be set off against arrears and form the basis of a defence and counterclaim in order to prevent a possession order from being made. In the event that the defendant discloses facts which could give rise to a counterclaim of sufficient quantum that could bring the arrears below the ground 8 threshold, then the duty adviser should make an application for an adjournment for a defence and counterclaim to be filed and served *before* evidence is taken by the court. A defendant in this situation should of course be advised to seek legal advice as soon as possible after the hearing to help with the defence and counterclaim.

8.15 In some cases the judge may need to be reminded that a counterclaim and set off acts as defence to the possession proceedings as well as the money claim so there can be no question of making a possession order and adjourning the money claim.

8.16 There may be cases where the arrears are so high that it is patently obvious that the counterclaim will not adequately set off the arrears and it may not be possible to prevent a possession order. The duty adviser should only concede if there is no doubt that the set off would not be enough, otherwise they should argue for an adjournment so the issue can be tried. In circumstances where the judge cannot be persuaded to adjourn, the money claim should then be adjourned even if a possession order is made.

8.17 Ground 8 mandatory claims for possession are very often pleaded alongside the two discretionary rent arrears grounds. The utility of these grounds to the landlord in conjunction with ground 8 is that they still allow a claim to proceed and the landlord to continue to ask for possession if the tenant reduces the arrears to less than the ground 8 threshold amount or even if the arrears are cleared before the hearing.

8.18 With discretionary grounds, the court has the power to dispense with the requirement for the notice of seeking possession and so if there is a defect in the notice that has been served or if there is doubt as to the service of a notice then the discretionary grounds will allow the landlord to try to argue that notice should be dispensed with and a possession order made. That may also be the case in Wales where a HA 1988 s8 notice is invalidated because of a failure to be licensed.

Discretionary claims – rent

8.19 HA 1988 s7(4) provides that:

> (4) If the court is satisfied that any of the grounds in Part II of Schedule 2 to this Act is established, then, subject to subsections (5A) and (6) below, the court may make an order for possession if it considers it reasonable to do so.

8.20 In rent arrears cases involving assured and assured shorthold tenancies there are two discretionary grounds for possession available: ground 10 and ground 11 of HA 1988 Sch 2.

8.21 These grounds are made out in the following circumstances:

> **Ground 10**
>
> Some rent lawfully due from the tenant–

(a) is unpaid on the date on which the proceedings for possession are begun; and
(b) except where subsection (1)(b) of section 8 of this Act applies, was in arrears at the date of the service of the notice under that section relating to those proceedings.

8.22 HA 1988 s8(1)(b) is the provision where the court may consider it just and equitable to dispense with the requirement of such a notice.

Ground 11

Whether or not any rent is in arrears on the date on which proceedings for possession are begun, the tenant has persistently delayed paying rent which has become lawfully due.

8.23 These grounds are 'discretionary' because where they are relied upon the judge must decide whether it is reasonable in all the circumstances for a possession order to be made. If the judge considers it is reasonable to make a possession order they will then decide whether to suspend or postpone that order – see chapter 12 below for discussion of different outcomes in possession proceedings.

8.24 The utility of these grounds to the landlord in conjunction with ground 8 is that they still allow a claim to proceed even if the tenant reduces the arrears to less than the ground 8 threshold amount or even if the arrears are cleared before the hearing.

8.25 In discretionary grounds the court has the power to dispense with the requirement for the notice of seeking possession and so if there is a defect in the notice that has been served or if there is doubt as to the service of a notice then the discretionary grounds will enable the landlord to argue that notice should be dispensed with and a possession order made.

8.26 Most private landlords will wait for ground 8 to be become available before serving a notice because it is a mandatory ground. It is therefore unusual to see discretionary grounds only in private possession claims.

8.27 With discretionary grounds the judge will decide whether it is reasonable for a possession order to be made. If it is decided that a possession order should be made the judge has the discretion to make a conditional order which will postpone the order or suspend enforcement of the order on terms. It is important to note that the decision as to whether it is reasonable to make a possession order must be made first of all before any decision to postpone the order or suspend enforcement of the order.

8.28 Arguments for the reasonableness or otherwise are in theory the same as in any other discretionary possession claim although it is the case in practice that judges are likely to find it reasonable to make a possession order in some cases where there is a private landlord where they might not for a social landlord, due to the very different roles of private and social landlords. Duty advisers may wish to remind the court that there is no such distinction in the law, and in any event increasingly private landlords are assisting local authorities to fulfil their HA 1996 Part 7 duties to homeless persons.

Mandatory claims – Housing Act 1988 s21

8.29 There is another mandatory 'ground' for possession (although this is not one that appears in HA 1988 Sch 2 containing the grounds for possession) available by way of HA 1988 s21. Originally designed to give landlords a quick and easy way to regain possession of residential premises once the fixed-term of the tenancy has expired, this legislation has been vastly encumbered over the years by amendments to itself and by way of other legislation. In some cases, it is now substantially difficult for landlords to comply with all the prerequisites of a valid section 21 notice, and there are many issues for advisers to check when advising tenants facing proceedings brought under section 21.

8.30 Essentially, what has happened to section 21 is that a number of housing standards and letting condition issues have been loaded on to the ability of the landlord to obtain possession without any need to make out fault on the part of the tenant once the fixed-term has expired. These include:

- matters concerning local authority houses in multiple occupation (HMOs) and selective licensing;
- gas safety issues (not in Wales because Deregulation Act 2015 does not apply);
- the requirement for an energy performance certificate (not in Wales);
- the requirement to provide government information about renting (not in Wales);
- matters concerning the protection of tenancy deposits and the information to be provided in that regard;
- housing conditions where they have been reported to the local authority;
- prohibited payments under the Tenant Fees Act 2019;
- in Wales, the Rent Smart licensing issues referred to above are relevant.

8.31 It is beyond the scope of this book to discuss all of these issues which may invalidate a notice under section 21 in detail. Readers would do well to bookmark the Nearly Legal flowchart at https://nearlylegal.co.uk/2019/09/updated-section-21-flowchart/ – and then to write to Giles Peaker of Anthony Gold Solicitors to thank him for this invaluable piece of public service.

8.32 As well as dealing with the requirements above, the flowchart also deals with the issue of the prescribed form of notice (form 6A) and the notice period required in normal times. It does not, at the time of writing, deal with special coronavirus legislation regarding notice periods – for that see chapter 4 above and appendix 7 below.

8.33 Generally speaking, the matters to be checked by duty advisers will be:

- that the claim is in relation to an assured shorthold tenancy;
- that the fixed-term has expired;
- that the notice is in the prescribed form;
- that the notice has been served by a person authorised to give the notice;
- that the notice was served;
- that the notice was served at the correct time (not less than four months from the start of the tenancy);
- that proceedings have been brought in time (this may depend on the notice period required for the particular notice);
- that the issues set out in the bullet points at para 8.30 above do not invalidate the notice.

8.34 Any one of these issues can invalidate the notice and means the tenant would have a defence to proceedings. There is no discretion on the judge to waive the requirement for a section 21 notice. It can be difficult for a duty adviser to check all of these complicated issues in the time available to take instructions from a tenant, but it is perfectly legitimate to require the landlord to prove each issue to the court. The landlord or their representative can be asked to provide their evidence for each issue prior to the court hearing. If there is any doubt as to any of the matter set out above, then the duty adviser should ask the judge to adjourn the claim for a defence to be filed following which evidence can be submitted by both sides and tested at a hearing. The court must be dissuaded from trying to resolve such issues at a short initial hearings.

8.35 In some cases it is possible to prove to the court that the notice is invalid and if section 21 is the only ground relied upon by the landlord, then a judge should be asked in those circumstances to dismiss the claim for possession because the landlord cannot remedy the defect.

8.36 If the landlord can prove that a valid section 21 notice has been served and the claim has been properly brought, then the judge has no option but to make an outright possession order.

8.37 There is nothing preventing a landlord from pleading section 21 alongside a claim for rent arrears or other ground set out in HA 1996 Sch 2 as amended. It not unusual to see mandatory ground 8, discretionary grounds 10 and 11 and s21 pleaded in the same claim. However, pleading section 21 alongside a rent arrears claim will mean that an N5 claim form must be used and the landlord cannot utilise the accelerated possession procedure which we set out below.

8.38 If it is the case that the landlord can make out section 21 but there are doubts as to an associated rent arrears claim, then it may be of some assistance to the tenant to agree a possession order and ask the judge to stipulate that it is made only pursuant to section 21 and adjourn the money claim. That may prevent any action being taken on the alleged rent arrears (often it is not worthwhile for the landlord to chase the arrears) and will be important if the tenant intends to make an application as homeless under HA 1996 Part 7. This would allow the applicant to say that the landlord obtained possession because the fixed-term of the tenancy had come to an end, rather than a possession order being granted based on any 'fault' on the part of the applicant.

Accelerated possession claims

8.39 Where a landlord is seeking possession based solely on HA 1988 s21, it is open to them to use the accelerated possession procedure. The accelerated possession procedure is set out at CPR Part 55 Section II; and also at CPR PD 55A Section II.

8.40 Accelerated possession proceedings are also specifically dealt with in the Overall Arrangements.

> **Accelerated Possession Claims**
>
> 60. In accordance with existing rules, in some cases (Accelerated Possession Claims) an order for possession may be made without a hearing by a Judge to whom the papers have been referred for this course to be considered.
>
> 61. Within the Overall Arrangements, Accelerated Possession Claims are however subject to the following:

(a) Accelerated Possession Claims issued before 3 August 2020 will require a Reactivation Notice as with all other stayed claims.
(b) As a guideline, Accelerated Possession Claims will be dealt with having regard to the priorities listed in the section on Prioritisation above.
(c) Each court centre will refer Accelerated Possession Claims to a Judge at manageable frequency.
(d) Judges will use the time freed up where Substantive (S) Hearing slots are vacated, to deal with Accelerated Possession Claims referred to them for consideration.
(e) Where the parties agree or there is no objection, the Judge to whom an Accelerated Possession Claim has been referred for consideration may direct that a Review (R) Date be listed to enable the Defendant to receive duty scheme advice and assistance.

62. If on consideration of an Accelerated Possession Claim referred to the Judge for consideration the Judge directs a Substantive Hearing (giving any appropriate case management directions, and with the parties to attend) that will be listed as a Substantive (S) Hearing unless otherwise directed.

8.41 In practice, few accelerated claims will come to duty advisers at 'review (R) dates' because (i) private landlords are unlikely to agree that such claim should be referred for an R date for the tenant to get duty advice and (ii) landlords and their advisers may well soon get accustomed to raising an objection to referral along with their claim form.

8.42 If the duty adviser does get an accelerated possession case at the R date, then the task for the duty adviser will be to try to ascertain if there is a defence and if there is to try to persuade the landlord to drop the claim. If that is not possible, then the matter will need to progress to a 'substantive (S) hearing' and legal aid can be granted in appropriate cases for a fully pleaded defence to be filed. Alternatively, the defendant may seek advice again at the S hearing where their case can be put before the judge. The defence or potential defence that is identified should therefore be carefully recorded in the written advice to the defendant after the R advice so that it is apparent to the duty adviser at the S hearing should that be necessary.

8.43 Broadly, the accelerated procedure is to enable a landlord to submit a claim form on practice form N5B with accompanying documents exhibited to that form. The purpose of the claim form and the documents is to provide to the court documentary proof that an assured shorthold tenancy has come to the end of its fixed term where relevant, a valid section 21 notice has been served and the landlord is entitled to an outright possession order.

8.44 The claim form and a defence form on practice form N11b is sent to the tenant with information that they should file and serve the defence form within 14 days of receiving it. After that, the claim form and the defence form if one has been filed are considered by the district judge without a hearing being listed. If the landlord has made out their claim, then the judge must make a possession order. If there is any doubt about the landlord's claim, then the judge must list the case for a hearing.

8.45 Accelerated possession claims may come before the duty adviser in any of the following ways:

- The judge has not been satisfied on the papers that a possession order should be made and so has directed a hearing under CPR 55.16(1)(b).
- The judge decides, and there are no objections, to refer the accelerated claim to an R date for the tenant to get R advice – see Overall Arrangements para 62.
- The judge has made a possession order but the defendant has applied to set aside that order and the court has listed a hearing of that application. Either party has the right to apply to set aside an order made in the absence of the parties (CPR 3.3(5)) and it follows that a tenant has an absolute right to apply to set aside a possession order made on the papers in accelerated possession proceedings.
- The tenant has requested in the defence form that if a possession order is made, then it be postponed for up to 42 days due to exceptional hardship – HA 1980 s89 and CPR 55.18.

8.46 In order to assist the defendant to prevent a possession order or have a possession order set aside, the duty adviser will need to be able to persuade the judge that there is a defence. If the matter requires evidence, then just as with a conventional first instance hearing, the duty adviser should ask the judge to adjourn the claim or application for a fully pleaded defence to be filed. The duty adviser can negotiate such an outcome with the claimant at the R advice stage or can put that case to the judge at the S hearing.

8.47 If it is not possible to raise a defence to resist a possession order being made, the duty adviser will have to take instructions of any exceptional hardship the tenant and their household would suffer as a result of being evicted from the premises following a 14-day order. Homelessness resulting from a possession order is not usually in-and-of-itself an exceptional circumstance – but it might be argued in the midst of a pandemic crisis. The duty adviser will need to persuade the judge of matters which concern the tenant and their household particularly. The judge can, only if persuaded of exceptional hardship, postpone the possession order for up to 42 days but can also stipulate a period between 14 and 42 days.

8.48 Judges should be encouraged not to take into account the overall period of time that a warrant for possession might take to execute because that cannot ultimately be known. That said, the judge almost certainly will take into account the 14 days' notice that must be given to a tenant of execution of a warrant of possession.

CHAPTER 9

Other cases

Key points

- In this chapter we will look briefly at some other forms of tenure and situations that can come before the duty adviser. These are much less common than the scenarios discussed above, but of course are no less important to the tenants seeking advice.
- Fully mutual housing association (housing co-op) cases are broadly very similar to non-secure tenancies in terms of the approach to be taken by the duty adviser.
- It will be important to carefully check notices, as it may be the only way to avoid a possession order.
- Rent Act cases will for the duty adviser almost always involve discretionary cases for possession and there will almost always be arguments to be made about why a possession order should not be made.
- Trespass cases (which will be rare) can only be dealt with under the Housing Possession Court Duty Scheme (HPCDS) if it is denied that the defendant is a trespasser, and it is important to work out which of the two types of trespasser the defendant is claimed to be.
- Succession cases are very fact-specific – the key issue of the duty adviser is to outline how the defendant might have succeeded to the tenancy by operation of law and/or whether it can be argued the landlord has dealt with the issue of statutory or non-statutory succession unfairly or in line with any policy. The duty adviser does not need to establish the facts, only the possibility of those facts being proven at a later date.

Fully mutual housing associations/co-operative housing associations

9.1 In this chapter we are dealing with the most common type of co-operative housing association being the 'par value' co-op.

9.2 Housing co-ops, as they are often called, are registered under the Industrial and Provident Societies Act 1965 and they work on the basis that all tenants are members of the co-operative. Prospective tenants can also be members. Decisions about the management of premises, including the decision to seek possession of accommodation let by a housing co-op, are taken by members.

9.3 The important issue for duty advisers to understand is that housing co-op tenancies do not attract the protection of the Rent Act (RA) 1977 or the Housing Acts (HAs) in the way that regulated, secure and introductory tenancies, and assured and assured shorthold tenancies, do. In this sense, it is helpful to consider the housing co-op regime to be similar to the non-secure or contractual tenancy regime described at chapter 6 above.

9.4 That means that such a tenancy can be brought to an end by a notice to quit giving usually at least four weeks' notice. See chapter 4 above and appendix 7 below for full details of notice requirements. Once the notice has expired the landlord can bring possession proceedings. If the status of the tenancy as a housing co-op tenancy is proven to the court then the judge must make an order for possession.

9.5 A tenant of a housing co-op should be able to rely on public law grounds to defend the claim for possession or Human Rights Act (HRA) 1998 defences and/or Equality Act (EA) 2010 defences. Broadly speaking, the decision to seek possession must have been reached by the co-op on the principles of public law and /or must be proportionate having regard to human rights law and/or must not breach the provisions of the EA 2010 (see chapter 10 below).

9.6 The duty adviser should check:

- that the tenancy is indeed a tenancy under a housing co-op;
- that the notice to quit is valid to determine the tenancy having regard to the form and notice period, the tenancy agreement and any relevant policies of the co-op;
- that the notice has been properly served;
- that the decision to seek possession is compatible with public law principles, human rights legislation and the EA 2010.

9.7 As in non-secure/contractual tenancy cases, there will be an underlying reason for seeking possession and that is usually arrears of rent or other breach of the tenancy agreement. These reasons will need to be scrutinised in relation to the matters set out above. Some tenants may argue that the co-op is run by people with improper interests, or with a prejudice against them personally. Those issues may form a defence in public law and under the EA 2010, but the threshold test for those defences must be met, for which see the relevant chapters below.

Rent Act cases

9.8 RA 1977 tenancies (properly called 'regulated tenancies') become more and more rare with each passing year. No entirely new regulated tenancy protected under the RA has been created since 15 January 1989. It is important for advisers to be aware that RA tenancies may arise very occasionally, either as possession proceedings or as warrant cases, and at least some basic knowledge is needed to be able to deal with them.

9.9 *Defending Possession Proceedings* (DPP) contains detailed information on the nature of RA tenancies and the protections afforded to tenants. In this book we simply look briefly at rent arrears cases.

9.10 Any case that comes before a duty adviser where the defendant or a family member was in occupation before 15 January 1989 need to be carefully considered to see if it has RA protection. If the proceedings have been brought on the basis that such a tenancy is an assured or an assured shorthold tenancy (and this is the most common way a duty adviser may see RA cases), then an adjournment should be sought so that this preliminary point can be ascertained. If the tenant can prove their tenancy is in fact protected by the RA, then the proceedings cannot be remedied and will have to be dismissed.

9.11 If a claim is properly brought on the basis that the tenant has the protection of the RA, then the landlord will need to make out at least one of a number of 'cases' set out in RA 1977 Sch 15.

9.12 The rent arrears case is Case 1 and is a discretionary case for possession similar to grounds 10 and 11 (HA 1988 Sch 2) in assured tenancies.

9.13 The RA has no equivalent to HA 1988 s21 that a duty adviser needs to be aware of (we are not going into protected shorthold tenancies because they are even more rare) and so again dealing with a RA case is structurally similar to dealing with assured tenancy cases brought on discretionary grounds.

9.14 Duty advisers need to be aware that rent protection is relevant to RA tenancies and so the landlord should be put to strict proof of the level of rent charged and should be required to provide the last Rent Officer determination of rent (or any previous determination if rent over time is in dispute) in order to prove the level of rent claimed. A failure to provide that evidence at the hearing should give rise to an adjournment with directions to produce it.

9.15 The notice requirements must be checked as in any possession claim. It is important as to whether the tenancy is a contractual or statutory tenancy. If it is a periodic contractual tenancy then the landlord must bring that to an end with a notice to quit. A valid notice to quit brings the contractual tenancy to an end and statutory tenancy comes into being. There is no need to serve notice to bring proceedings for possession of a statutory tenancy and so (i) if the tenancy starts as a statutory tenancy, or (ii) a contractual tenancy has validly been brought to an end by the notice to quit the landlord can proceed to issue a claim.

9.16 Because of the increasing rarity of regulated tenancies, it is fair to say (and completely understandable) that detailed knowledge as to law and procedure in respect of lawfully ending such tenancies among the judiciary and advocates is not as immediate as with other types of tenancies. It follows, therefore, that unless the landlord can completely make out their case by reference to all the relevant requirements and take the court to the relevant legislation, such that any objection by the tenant and the duty adviser is dealt with in the time available, then the matter must be adjourned to allow a proper airing of the facts of the case as against the law. These cases relate to situations where people will have occupied the property for a very long period of time as their home and the court should be slow to make an order which would mean they are evicted from their long term home.

Trespassers

9.17 Possession claims against trespassers are not covered by the Housing Possession Court Duty Scheme (HPCDS) and so if an occupier seeks duty advice and does not disagree that they are a trespasser then you cannot advise them under the HPCDS scheme.

9.18 However, if the defendant denies they are trespasser then you may provide advice to ascertain if there is an arguable case and make representations on the defence to the proceedings brought against them.

9.19 There are two types of person who may be a trespasser. The first is a person who never had any legal right to occupy the subject premises. Colloquially the word 'squatter' is often used for these occupiers. There will be little or nothing that a duty adviser can do for a person who accepts that they never had any legal right to occupy the premises, and the duty adviser cannot advise under HPCDS.

9.20 The second type of trespasser (or for our purposes, alleged trespasser) is a person who did have licence or consent to occupy the premises but that licence or permission has ended. Those people will divide into those who have the protection of Protection from Eviction Act (PEA) 1977 and those excluded occupiers who do not. These latter cases are:

- where there is a resident landlord;
- squatters with a temporary agreement with a the owner/landlord to stay;
- holiday lets;
- accommodation for asylum-seekers;
- hostel licences;
- no right-to-rent cases;
- homeless people accommodated under HA 1996 s188 or s190; and
- some rent-free accommodation (mainly family arrangements).

9.21 It follows, therefore, that a duty client may have any one of a number causes to argue that they are not an trespasser – the key is to understand whether the circumstances mean the trespasser criteria is made out or not and the following issues are important to look out for:

- any licence to occupy has not been validly determined;
- they do not have a resident landlord contrary to the claim;
- they did not enter as squatters;
- the 'no right to rent' criteria is not made out;
- housing has been, or should have been, provided under other homelessness provisions, then HA 1996 s190 or s188.

9.22 Trespass cases will turn on the facts, and as long as the assertion of the defendant to not be a trespasser is arguable, then they can be advised under HPCDS and they may have a defence to proceedings, which should give rise to an adjournment with directions for that to be pleaded.

Succession

9.23 In some cases, spouses, civil partners, those residing with a tenant as if spouse or civil partners or other family members are entitled to succeed to a tenancy on the death of the tenant. The circumstances in which succession to a statutorily protected tenancy can take place are set in legislation in the RA 1977, HA 1985, HA 1988 and HA 1996. Succession can also take place to a contractual tenancy, even if the successor tenant is not afforded much security of tenure. In each case, the succession takes place by operation of law. If the criteria to succeed are met, then the succession takes place and the landlord has no say in the matter. It is worth recording here that there are different provisions for succession in Wales than in England. It is beyond the scope of this book to go through the succession rules – DPP and other housing law texts will provide the detail.

9.24 The type of tenancy succeeded to is also set out in legislation.

9.25 In HA 1985 it is provided that a person who is not a spouse (or civil partner in England) may succeed to a tenancy, but if the premises which are the subject of that tenancy are more extensive than the person requires, then the landlord has a ground for possession under ground 15A in HA 1985 Sch 2 (ground 16 in Wales), where suitable alternative accommodation is made available to them – see DPP for a discussion as to this ground for possession.

9.26 Succession/possession cases will come before a duty adviser in one of the following ways:

- By way of a ground 15A (ground 16 in Wales) claim for possession where the defendant wishes to argue that the accommodation is not more extensive than their needs, and/or they argue that the alternative accommodation offered by the landlord is not suitable and/or it would not be reasonable for a possession order to be made and/or the notice requirements have not been met.
- Where a landlord claims that the tenant has died, there is no person entitled to succeed to the tenancy, notice has been served on the defendant and the deceased tenant's personal representatives or the public trustee, any contractual tenancy (if any) has been brought to an end, and the defendant argues they are entitled to succeed or one of the notice requirements has not been met.
- Where a surviving occupier cannot succeed but considers they may have a public law defence to possession proceedings.

9.27 In ground 15A or 16 cases it should be straightforward to argue that the duty advice is the first advice the defendant has received and they should now be given time to set out their defence. These are highly fact-driven cases, and courts should not be looking to determine them summarily at a first substantive hearing.

9.28 In other cases, the defendant must be able to make out an argument that they are entitled to succeed and that again they should be given time to file and serve a pleaded defence.

9.29 There are strict notice requirements in ground 15A cases (ground 16 in Wales) and it will be important to check if the landlord has served the notice within the correct timescale. The notice must be served more than six months after the date of the original tenant's death but no later than 12 months – see chapter 4 above.

9.30 Public law defences, HRA 1998 defences and EA 2010 defences may be available to occupiers if they do not qualify to succeed to a statutorily protected tenancy. If, for example, a local authority has a policy by which it will consider granting a non-statutory succession to a person who does not qualify to succeed in law, and they fail to consider that policy when deciding to bring possession proceedings then that may give rise to a public law defence. See chapter 10 below for discussion of those kinds of defences.

Property guardians

9.31 Increasingly we are seeing possession cases in the county court involving 'property guardians'. These concern arrangements whereby the owner of an empty building will purport to grant to property guardian agencies the right to enter into licences with prospective property guardians. The idea is that these property guardians reside in the building as their home, paying a fee which is generally much lower than a market rent. The guardians are said to be present in order to keep the building safe from squatters and vandals, usually while the owners apply for planning permission for the site or pending demolition.

9.32 Possession proceedings come before the courts where the agency serves a notice to quit to determine the purported licence agreement and seek possession form the guardians.

9.34 Some guardians have argued in the courts that the 'licence' agreement they have signed with the agency is a sham and in fact their occupation of the premises is, as a matter of law, as an assured shorthold tenant. They therefore argue that any notice to quit can be of no effect in determining their rights to occupy as an assured shorthold tenant. Other interesting issues as to liability for rates and/or council tax, licensing matters, disrepair and housing conditions, harassment, rent repayment orders and other issues can also arise – but for duty advisers the main issue will be to try to assist to preventing a possession order being made, and to that end the duty adviser will need to persuade the court that the case should be adjourned for a final defence to be filed and directions given so that evidence as to the circumstances of the defendant's occupation of the premises can be adduced.

9.35 Claimant property guardian agencies will argue that currently the leading cases on property guardians, decided in the Court of Appeal from the county court (*Camelot Guardian Management Ltd v Khoo* (2018) EWHC 2296 (QB) upheld, *in that particular*, the property guardian agency's contention that the agreement did not confer exclusive possession and was for a licence. However, the ratio in the case also makes clear that each case must turn on its own facts, particularly regarding the actual circumstances of occupation of the premises – and so the arguments around sham licences in this context are not at an end.

9.36 As with so many developing areas of law, duty advisers are strongly advised to bookmark Giles Peaker's Nearly Legal blog to follow this still developing line of case-law. The *Khoo* case and helpful analysis is here, for example: https://nearlylegal.co.uk/2018/10/property-guardians-licence-not-tenancy-in-office-building/.

CHAPTER 10

Public law, Human Rights Act and Equality Act defences

Key points

- If the case is based on discretionary grounds you will not need to worry about a public law defence, but Equality Act (EA) 2010 defences (and counterclaims) and more rarely Human Rights Act (HRA) 1998 arguments may be relevant in discretionary ground cases.
- It is important to know the basis of and differences between these types of cases, and also the threshold test so that you can prove to the judge that your case meets that test.
- While this book may be helpful as a reminder, you will need to understand the three types of defence in order to be an effective duty adviser.
- It is not your job to prove the case yourself. You are there to show the judge that such a defence (and counterclaim) should be considered by the court.
- The test for a public law defence is that it is or is capable of being seriously arguable.
- The test for an HRA 1998 defence under European Convention on Human Rights (ECHR) Art 8 (right to respect for one's private and family life, home and correspondence), is that it is or is capable of being 'seriously arguable'.
- The test for an EA 2010 defence (and counterclaim) in disability discrimination cases is not possible to sum up in two words, but it is clearly lower than the public law and human right tests above. Consult 10.44–10.45 below.

Introduction

10.1 A whole book could be written about the three types of defences that we talk about in this chapter: public law, Human Rights Act (HRA) 1998 and Equality Act (EA) 2010 defences. *Defending Possession Proceedings* (DPP) devotes three chapters to them. Those 100 or more pages are the ones to consult for a detailed analysis of the development of these jurisdictions and the line of cases that led to public law defences being available to pursue in the county court for defendants facing possession proceedings.

10.2 There can be a tendency to conceptualise the three types of defences together and think of them as being essentially the same. That would be understandable – but a mistake. For example, the terminology of 'legitimate aims' and 'proportionality' is common to European Convention on Human Rights (ECHR) Art 8 (right to respect for one's private and family life, home and correspondence) human rights defences (which the HRA 1998 incorporates into domestic UK law) and to EA 2010 defences. However, they mean different things. EA 2010 defences can look conceptually similar to public law defences in the way that the decisions of the claimant are being scrutinised, but the threshold test for a public law defence is much higher than for an EA 2010 defence, and an EA 2010 defence operates in a way more akin to statutory private law protection for tenants.

10.3 Each type of defence has to be understood on its own terms to be effectively argued. We have put these three types of defences together in one chapter precisely to elucidate the differences between them.

10.4 In this book we will look to draw out the key themes that duty advisers need to be aware of when providing duty advice in the county court. It will not be the duty adviser's job (at least not the on duty day) to set out the defendant's public law, HRA 1998 and/or EA 2010 defences as if the hearing were a trial of the matter. Instead the duty adviser's job is:

a) to identify a possible defence; and
b) to persuade the opponent, or if not, the judge that the defence meets the relevant threshold for the matter to be adjourned with directions.

10.5 The four key issues to identify in each of these three areas are:

1) the identity and sometimes the role of the landlord;
2) the ground(s) for possession relied on, or the underlying reason for seeking possession;
3) the circumstances of the tenant;
4) the threshold for the particular type of defence or defences to be relied upon.

10.6 We therefore concentrate on those four issues and will refer to them specifically in the commentary that follows.

Public law defences

Overview

10.7 The first thing to say about public law defences is that they are mostly irrelevant if the judge has the discretion to consider whether or not it is reasonable to make a possession order.

10.8 It is then important to outline what we mean by a public law defence. A public law defence may be possible where a defendant argues that the decision of a public body to take steps to recover possession of the premises breaches the principles of public law – which are:

- not to make a decision or decisions which are so unreasonable that no reasonable public authority could have made it/them;
- to take into account all relevant facts and material;
- not to take into account irrelevant facts or material;
- not to misdirect itself in law – to apply the law correctly;
- not to fetter its discretion by applying a blanket policy without considering the relevant facts or material;
- not to make decisions which put it in breach of the HRA 1998 (*important* – this is separate to the HRA 1998 defences we discuss below and where we will elucidate the difference).

10.9 These are sometimes called 'judicial review principles'. Previously, it was the case that a tenant who wished to defend on the basis of these public law principles would have to ask the county court to stay the possession proceedings while they brought a claim for judicial review in the High Court.

10.10 When the vast majority of tenants of social housing let by public bodies had security of tenure, there was little need for the public law defence (although the flagship public defence case *Wandsworth LBC v Winder (No 1)* [1985] AC 461, [1984] UKHL 2 was decided in the mid-1980s).

10.11 However, as legislation and housing policies and practice developed in such a way that more tenants either lacked the security of tenure that gave them a 'reasonableness ground' to defend proceedings, or faced mandatory grounds for possession that excluded such defences, a line of cases established the right for tenants of public bodies to rely on public law defences in the county court – mainly so that the disruption of stays and separate High Court judicial review proceedings would not be necessary.

10.12 The most recent Supreme Court collection of cases on the point is reported as *Hounslow LBC v Powell* [2011] UKSC 8, [2011] 2 AC 186 and established that:

a) the reasons for seeking possession should be communicated to the defendant before proceedings are commenced;
b) public law defences can be raised at any stage in the proceedings;
c) where a case has reached the warrant stage, a duty adviser may have to decide whether a public defence can be raised to apply to

set aside the possession order, or whether the decision to seek to enforce the possession order (which was otherwise lawfully obtained) is susceptible to a public law argument.

Defences

10.13 At 10.5 above we set out four key issues for these kinds of defences and now address them in relation to *public law defences*:

1) The identity of the landlord and in some cases the purpose and/or character of the letting

The landlord must be a public body. A local authority will obviously be a public body. An RSL will be a public body if in the context of the claim for possession it is carrying out the functions of providing social housing and/or housing to the homeless under duties held by the local authority ie the letting of the premises relates to a public function. The position where RSLs let properties at market rates and not related to eg homelessness or social services' duties is less clear, but therefore arguable for the duty adviser.

Even less clear (and again therefore arguable) is the increasingly common situation where private landlords are commissioned by local authorities to house people owed housing duties under Housing Act (HA) 1996 Part 7.

2) The ground(s) for possession relied on, or the underlying reason for seeking possession

Where a tenant cannot rely on reasonableness arguments and may have recourse to public law principles, they should be given reasons why the landlord is seeking to regain possession. If no reasons have been provided, then that can be a defence in public law itself. The Pre-Action Protocol for Possession Claims by Social Landlords Part 3, which requires social landlords to set out their reasons for seeking possession, is helpful in ascertaining any public law arguments (see chapter 3 above). A breach of the protocol can give rise to a public law defence because it would be a breach of public law principles (as well as a breach of the protocol) not to have provided reasons for seeking possession.

The protocol means that not only must the social landlord inform the tenant the reasons for seeking possession but they must show to the court how they invited and considered any representations from the defendant.

The protocol should be consulted by the duty adviser each time a potential public law defence is considered.

Where reasons have been provided, then those reasons should be considered against the public law principles set out at above, and should be considered in respect of all decisions made to proceed ie the decision to serve a notice, the decision to issue a claim, the decision to proceed with a claim, the decision to enforce a possession order. If any decision does not meet the public law criteria, then a defence may be possible.

3) The circumstances of the tenant
The defendant does not need to fall within a particular class of person to rely on public law arguments. However, their circumstances may make certain decisions made in their particular case unlawful under public law principles. In those cases there may be significant overlap between public law defence points, HRA 1998 defence points and EA 2010 defence points.

4) The threshold for the particular type of defence or defences to be relied upon
Judicial review proceedings in the High Court have a 'permission stage' where, without determining the case, a judge decides whether it has sufficient merit to proceed. There is no such stage in county court possession proceedings. The higher courts have therefore developed through the case-law a threshold test for public law defences which is higher than the test for defences where there is security of tenure. The test is that the public law defence must be 'seriously arguable'. It is important that the test we set out here is for the court to allow an adjournment for a defence to be prepared, filed and served. The Civil Procedure Rules 1998 (CPR) 55.8 test is for the case to be allocated to track and directions set which we say is a different test.

10.14 It is also important to stress that it is *the case* that must be seriously arguable. The duty adviser must set out the case in brief for the judge to assess whether it is seriously arguable. The duty adviser does not have to prove all of the facts for the judge – that will be a matter for evidence and for the trial judge. Obviously, there must be some outline of the facts that give rise to a seriously arguable defence in public law – but the determination of those facts themselves will be for another time.

Human Rights Act 1998 defences

Overview

10.15 We said in the public law defence section above that one of the public law criteria for public authority decision-making is that the decision in question must not breach the rights guaranteed by the HRA 1998. Where a decision to bring or pursue possession proceedings breaches any of those rights, then that may give rise to a defence in public law.

10.16 However, a separate type of defence relies on the rights guaranteed by the HRA 1998 in a different way. These defences are not predicated on an unlawful decision being made by the landlord – but instead focus on the effect of seeking to regain possession from the defendant. It can be broadly helpful (but only to an extent) to think of public law defences as being primarily about *process* (decisions) and HRA defences as being substantially about *outcome* (effect). That said, there is a great deal of blurring between those two boundaries, and ECHR Arts 6 (right to a fair trial) and 8 (right to respect for one's private and family life, home and correspondence) human rights defences in particular can include procedural matters.

10.17 Human rights points are mostly irrelevant if the judge has the discretion to consider whether or not it is reasonable to make a possession order.

10.18 Again, similarly as with modern iterations of public law defences, it has taken a line of case-law to establish the parameters of the right to raise human rights defences – consult DPP for an account of that.

10.19 In this book we concentrate on Article 8 defences, which are by far the most common of potential cases faced by duty advisers. DPP may be consulted to understand how ECHR Arts 6, 9, 10, 11, 14 and Article 1 of the First Protocol may work in this context, along with commentary as to the human rights challenges as to the law underlying claimants' rights to seek possession of residential premises.

10.20 The HRA 1998 incorporates the ECHR into domestic UK law. Essentially that means that it is unlawful for any public authority to act in a way that is incompatible with convention rights. The court is a public authority, and therefore must not act in way incompatible with convention rights. If a defendant can show that their eviction would be incompatible with one or more convention rights, then they may argue the court must not take steps which would lead to them being evicted.

10.21 The human rights defence mostly does not attack a *decision by a landlord*, but instead directs itself to the *duty of the court* to not contravene the HRA 1998. For our purposes, Article 8 is by far the most important of the rights guaranteed by the HRA 1998. Key to the concept of the Article 8 human rights defence is 'proportionality', and human rights defences are often called 'proportionality defences'. The reason for this, without going into a long discussion of the human rights jurisdiction in UK law, is that it can be said that evicting anyone for whatever reason is an interference with, for example, the Article 8 right to respect for one's 'home'. Therefore, interference with a human right is *not unlawful* if it is 'necessary' (as expressed in the Act) in the sense of being *proportionate to achieve a legitimate aim*. That legitimate aim can be as simple as the orderly management of housing stock, but the eviction of a tenant must be proportionate to that legitimate aim.

10.22 An HRA 1998 defence, in order to succeed, must show that the consequences of eviction for the defendant means that the eviction is not proportionate to the aims, however legitimate, of the landlord. Again, it is not the decision of the landlord to seek possession per se that is attacked. Instead, the court is urged to see what the outcome of the eviction would be for the defendant and find that it is not proportionate to the legitimate aim of seeking possession for the reasons claimed by the landlord.

10.23 If an HRA 1998 point appears to be seriously arguable on a warrant suspension/set aside application, and there has been a change in circumstances since the possession order giving rise to the point, then there is nothing that prevents human rights arguments being deployed at that stage. The position if the HRA 1998 point could have been raised at an earlier stage is less clear but duty advisers have nothing to lose (and their clients potentially have much to gain) by arguing the point.

Defences

10.24 At 10.5 above we set out four key issues for these kinds of defences and now address them in relation to *HRA 1998 defences*:

1) The identity of the landlord and in some cases the purpose and/or character of the letting

Following *McDonald v McDonald and others* [2016] UKSC 28 (also European Court of Human Rights (ECtHR) – *FJM v UK*, App No 76202/16, 29 November 2018), and although the human rights defence focuses on the court's role as public authority rather than the decision of the landlord, such a defence can only be brought where the claimant is a public authority, and in the case of RSLs, the letting is of a public nature.

2) The ground(s) for possession relied on, or the underlying reason for seeking possession

The reason why the landlord has sought possession will form part of the equation as to whether the outcome of eviction for the tenant is proportionate. The landlord may seek to counter an HRA 1998 defence by arguing that the reasons why they are seeking possession means they are *pursuing a legitimate aim* and that the tenant's eviction is *proportionate.*

3) The circumstances of the tenant

The circumstances of the tenant if evicted is the other side of the proportionality equation. While physical and/or mental disability, learning disabilities and many other vulnerabilities will be the most common circumstances which may give rise to HRA 1998 defences, the courts have been careful not to define the circumstances which would give rise to such a defence and, on the other hand, these conditions in and of themselves will not give rise to a defence. Exceptionality of circumstances is not a requisite for such a defence, but the significance of the interference with the rights is.

4) The threshold for the particular type of defence or defences to be relied upon

First, the HRA 1998 defence must be raised – it is not for the court to conduct an inquiry in each case. The court may consider the argument summarily, meaning for our purposes that at a first instance hearing the court will consider the duty adviser's outline of what the pleaded HRA 1998 defence would be. The assessment for the judge is whether the defence is 'seriously arguable' – *Hounslow LBC v Powell and others* [2011] UKSC 8 at para 33.

We repeat what we said about public law defences and the factual background to the cases – it is important to stress that it is the case that must be seriously arguable. The duty adviser must set out the case in brief to for the judge to assess whether it is seriously arguable. The duty adviser does not have to prove all of the facts for the judge – that will be a matter for evidence and for the trial judge. Obviously, there must be some prospect of being able to establish facts that give rise to a seriously arguable proportionality defence – but the determination of those facts themselves will be for another time.

Equality Act 2010 defences

Meaning

10.25 Unlike public law and HRA 1998 defences (broadly speaking), EA 2010 defences may often be found alongside all or any of the other types of defences to possession proceedings. The availability of reasonableness defences does not override or obviate the purpose of an EA 2010 defence.

10.26 Concepts key to defences under the EA 2010 are 'protected characteristics' and discrimination. In the context of possession claims, EA 2010 s35(1) is important where it provides:

> **35 Management**
>
> (1) A person (A) who manages premises must not discriminate against a person (B) who occupies the premises–
> (a) in the way in which A allows B, or by not allowing B, to make use of a benefit or facility;
> (b) by evicting B (or taking steps for the purpose of securing B's eviction);
> (c) by subjecting B to any other detriment.

Section 4 sets out the protected characteristics:

> **4 The protected characteristics**
>
> The following characteristics are protected characteristics–
> - age;
> - disability;
> - gender reassignment;
> - marriage and civil partnership;
> - pregnancy and maternity;
> - race;
> - religion or belief;
> - sex;
> - sexual orientation.

Disability discrimination and the Equality Act 2010

10.27 In this book we focus solely on the EA 2010's protected characteristic of disability discrimination because that is where the case-law lies in relation to defending possession proceedings. It seems likely that other protected characteristics may start to figure in possession claim defences in the future – the important work on sex discrimination in the 'no DSS' cases is just one example that leads us to think this – and we will look to include such cases in future updates.

10.28 Of the protected characteristics in the Act, disability discrimination is considered differently to the others. A disabled person may need to be treated differently than a non-disabled person in order that they receive equal treatment – *Akerman-Livingstone v Aster Communities Ltd(formerly Flourish Homes Ltd)* [2015] UKSC 15.

10.29 In relation to disability, EA 2010 s15 is relevant:

> **15 Discrimination arising from disability**
> (1) A person (A) discriminates against a disabled person (B) if–
> (a) A treats B unfavourably because of something arising in consequence of B's disability, and
> (b) A cannot show that the treatment is a proportionate means of achieving a legitimate aim.
> (2) Subsection (1) does not apply if A shows that A did not know, and could not reasonably have been expected to know, that B had the disability.

10.30 Putting the two sections together, if the reason for the eviction is something arising in consequence of a defendant's disability, and the eviction cannot be shown to be proportionate in pursuit of a legitimate aim, then the EA 2010 may provide a defence to proceedings.

10.31 While the language of section 15 reminds us of Article 8 human rights defences outlined above, it would be wrong to consider the strength of protection to be the same under both headings:

- Importantly, by way of EA 2010 s136, it is for a landlord to prove that their actions were not discriminatory.
- EA 2010 defences apply to both public authorities and private landlords.
- In disability discrimination cases, the different treatment requirements outlined above is relevant.

10.32 In looking at the approach the court is to take when considering the possibility of the EA 2010 defence it, is worth having to hand para 31 of Lady Hale's judgment from *Akerman-Livingstone*:

> 31. No landlord is allowed to evict a disabled tenant because of something arising in consequence of the disability, unless he can show eviction to be a proportionate means of achieving a legitimate aim. He is thus obliged to be more considerate towards a disabled tenant than he is towards a non-disabled one. The structured approach to proportionality asks whether there is any lesser measure which might achieve the landlord's aims. It also requires a balance to be struck between the seriousness of the impact upon the tenant and the importance of the landlord's aims.

10.33 DPP outlines this 'structured approach' taking into account the case-law Lady Hale had recourse to, and we gratefully reproduce this outline here with kind permission of the authors:

- What are the claimant's aims or objectives in taking steps for the purpose of securing the defendant's eviction?
- Is there a rational connection between the claimant's objectives and the defendant's eviction?
- Is the eviction of the defendant no more than is necessary to accomplish those objectives?
- Is the eviction proportionate in the wider sense, or, in other words, does the eviction strike a fair balance between the claimant's need to accomplish its objectives and the disadvantages thereby caused to the defendant as a disabled person?

Duty to make reasonable adjustments

10.34 The duty to make reasonable adjustments is set out at EA 2010 s20 and is another example of how the protected characteristic of disability is different to the other protected characteristics. A landlord or owner of accommodation is obliged to take steps to avoid disadvantages to disabled tenants or occupants, and that may include the provision of aids for that purpose. Advisers should familiarise themselves with the provision including those which do and do not apply to landlords or those involved letting of premises. See, for example, the exemption from adjustments in relation to physical features of premises.

10.35 Where a duty is identified and relates to the bringing of possession proceedings, then that may form the basis of an EA 2010 defence. An obvious example (but by no means the only one) would be a landlord who, knowing of a disability of the tenant related to managing finances, bringing possession proceedings based on rent arrears without offering some form of reasonable assistance that may help to prevent or alleviate the arrears.

Public sector equality duty

10.36 The public sector equality duty (PSED) is set out at EA 2010 s149. It applies to public authorities and those exercising public functions only. It places enhanced positive duties on those authorities to eliminate discrimination, advance equality of opportunity and foster good relations between those with protected characteristics and those without. The duty to take account of disabilities is expressly set out at subsection (4), and subsection (6) iterates the possible need to treat people with all protected characteristics differently ie more favourably.

10.37 The PSED must be taken into account when making any decision about seeking possession from a disabled person (or people with other protected characteristics) and if it hasn't then that may form the basis for an EA 2010 defence.

10.38 While the following passage of Lady Hale's judgment in *Hotak and others v Southwark LB and another* [2015] UKSC 30 para 78 is directed to homelessness reviews, it is right that the sharp focus referred to applies equally in PSED decisions about possession proceedings:

> It is therefore appropriate to emphasise that the equality duty, in the context of an exercise such as a section 202 review, does require the reviewing officer to focus very sharply on (i) whether the applicant is under a disability (or has another relevant protected characteristic), (ii) the extent of such disability, (iii) the likely effect of the disability, when taken together with any other features, on the applicant if and when homeless, and (iv) whether the applicant is as a result 'vulnerable'.

10.39 A breach of the PSED may form the basis of a defence under EA 2010.

Counterclaims

10.40 Breaches of the EA 2010 committed by landlords or owners can give rise to a claim for damages. It follows, therefore, that such a claim can be expressed as a counterclaim within possession proceedings and could therefore be raised as a set off against any rent arrears found due. Such a counterclaim may be particularly important to eliminate any mandatory ground 8 claim for possession on the basis of rent arrears but any rent arrears claim may be very usefully met by a counterclaim. See chapter 5 above for discussion of counterclaims generally.

10.41 While it is beyond the scope of this book to go into great detail about quantum of damages on EA 2010 claims and counterclaims, advisers should be aware that damages for injury to feelings are to be assessed generally on the three banded Vento scales arising from the case of *Vento v Chief Constable of West Yorkshire Police* [2002] EWCA Civ 1871:

- The lower band applies to 'less serious cases' where the act of discrimination is a one-off or isolated occurrence.

- The middle band applies to serious cases that do not fall within the higher band.
- The higher band applies to the most serious cases, for example, where there has been a lengthy campaign of discrimination and/or harassment.

10.42 At the time of writing, the Vento bands from April 2020 were:

- lower band of £900 to £9,000;
- middle band of £9,000 to £27,000;
- upper band of £27,000 to £45,000 with the most exceptional cases capable of exceeding £45,000.

10.43 These are updated annually (next April 2021) and so advisers should make themselves aware of the current guidance. It can be seen that even lower-band awards can have a serious impact on rent arrears cases and so judges may need to be made aware of the banding.

Defences

10.44 At 10.5 above we set out four key issues for these kinds of defences and now address them in relation to *EA 2010 defences*:

1) The identity of the landlord and in some cases the purpose and/or character of the letting
An EA 2010 defence may be raised in actions by any landlord or owner. However only public authorities and those exercising public functions are subject to the PSED.

2) The ground(s) for possession relied on, or the underlying reason for seeking possession
The reason why the landlord has sought possession will form part of the equation as to whether seeking possession is a 'proportionate means of achieving a legitimate aim' (EA 2010 s15); *Akerman-Livingstone*). The landlord may seek to counter an EA 2010 defence by arguing that the reasons why they are seeking possession mean they are pursuing legitimate aim and that the tenant's eviction is proportionate. It will be for the duty adviser to argue to the contrary, perhaps by suggesting other potentially effective remedies available to the claimant which fall sort of requiring the defendant to leave the premises.

3) The circumstances of the tenant
The circumstances of the tenant if evicted is the other side of the proportionality equation. In a passage in which the Supreme Court

sought to outline the differences between proportionality for the purpose of Article 8 and the HRA 1998 and proportionality in the context of the EA 2010, Lady Hale in *Akerman-Livingstone* said:

> 34. I am prepared to accept that, in possession actions brought by social landlords against tenants who otherwise have no right to remain in the property, it can generally be taken for granted that the landlord is acting in pursuance of the twin aims; and further that those twin aims are entitled to weigh heavily in a proportionality exercise. However, as already explained, that is not by itself enough to counter a discrimination defence. Once facts are established that could give rise to a discrimination claim, the burden shifts to the landlord to prove otherwise. This will depend upon the particular type of discrimination alleged. If it is a claim (or defence) of direct discrimination, for example that a disabled person has been evicted when a non-disabled person in the same or similar circumstances has not, then the landlord would have to show that the disability was not the reason for the difference in treatment. If it is a claim of indirect discrimination, for example that the landlord has imposed a requirement upon its tenants which puts disabled tenants at a particular disadvantage, then the landlord would have to show that there was a good independent reason for the requirement. If it is a claim of disability discrimination under section 15, then the landlord would have to show that there was no less drastic means of solving the problem and that the effect upon the occupier was outweighed by the advantages. The express burden of proof provisions in the Equality Act cannot simply be ignored because there are some elements in the proportionality exercise which can be taken for granted.

4) The threshold for the particular type of defence or defences to be relied upon

Again, in this section we have found it helpful to quote Lady Hale from *Akerman-Livingstone*:

> 58. . . . Provided that a defendant establishes that the landlord is (or at a summary stage, may well be) seeking to evict him 'because of something arising in consequence of [his] disability', the landlord faces a significantly more difficult task in having to establish proportionality than does a landlord who faces an Article 8 defence.
>
> . . .
>
> 60. The problem for a landlord seeking summary judgment for possession in such a case would not be one of principle, but one of practice. Each of the three types of issue referred to . . . [above] would often give rise to disputed facts or assessments, eg whether the defendant suffers from a physical or mental disability, whether it has led to the possession claim, and where the proportionality balance comes down. Summary judgment is not normally a sensible or

> adequate procedure to deal with such disputes, which normally require disclosure of documents, and oral and/or expert evidence tested by cross-examination. There will no doubt be cases where a landlord facing a section 35(1)(b) defence may be well advised to seek summary judgment, but they would, I suspect, be relatively rare.

10.45 These passages make it clear that if disability is in play and the eviction would arise in consequence of it then (i) the threshold test is much lower than in Article 8 cases and (ii) the need to establish the facts will mean that judges must be very slow indeed to deal with such a case at a first instance hearing. The fact that it is held that summary judgment against a defence would be rare means that at a first hearing where it is argued that there may be an EA 2010 defence, it should be even more rare for a possession order to be made.

CHAPTER 11

Mortgage possession proceedings and charging orders

Key points

Types of cases

- In this chapter we are concerned with mortgages and other charges. Put at its simplest (and at an acknowledged risk of oversimplification), these relate to sums of money owed which are secured by agreement or by legal action against property such that the creditor can seek possession of the property if amounts due are not paid.
- Mortgages come in two main types:
  1) *Repayment* where the monthly payment consists of payments towards the capital amount borrowed and interest payments, and are calculated to pay off everything owed by the end of the term of the mortgage.
  2) *Interest-only* where the monthly payments are only towards the interest and nothing is being paid to the capital amount. Borrowers will either have some other means to pay off the capital, usually an investment type product such as an endowment policy, or they stand at risk of losing their home at the end of the term if they cannot pay off the capital and time has run out.
- Duty advice and representation can only be provided if the claim involves the defendant's home. Duty advice is not available for buy-to-let mortgage actions.
- In most cases encountered on duty, the mortgage relates to the amount borrowed to purchase the home. However, there are also cases involving re-mortgages and second charges for loans for home improvements, car purchase or any other purposes.
- These can include 'all money charges' and Consumer Credit Act 1974 loans which are charged agent the borrower's home.
- There are also *charging orders*. This is where a creditor has obtained judgment for a debt and has successfully applied to the court for the debt to be charged against the defendant's home. These cases will come to the duty adviser as application for an order for sale and applications to stay, set aside or suspend an order for sale.
- Tenants of borrowers have some protection where their landlord is facing possession proceedings and these cases may be seen by the duty adviser.

Mortgages and the law protecting borrowers

- Mortgage cases are distinctly different from rented accommodation cases in that the main focus is whether the defendant can meet payments of the monthly instalment and towards the arrears, so that a suspended possession order can be made, or to avoid an outright order. It is almost always as stark as that.

- Prior to 2014, mortgages cases which were not Consumer Credit Act (CCA) 1974 cases were dealt with on the basis of determining whether the defendant would be able pay off all the arrears within the remaining term of the mortgage in accordance with the guidance set out in *Cheltenham & Gloucester Building Society v Norgan* [1995] EWCA Civ 11. If not, then an outright possession order would generally be made.
- Changes brought about in 2014 and in 2016 mean that (i) the power available under CCA 1974 Part 9 to alter the terms of the loan agreement apply to all regulated mortgage contracts (RMCs) and (ii) nearly all residential mortgages became RMCs.
- Duty advisers can assume that all mortgage cases may benefit from CCA 1974 Part 9 including the application of time orders. Consequently, the guidance of the Court of Appeal concerning time orders in *Southern and District Finance plc v Barnes* (1995) 27 HLR 691 is relevant and we set that out in the text.
- If there is an argument that the mortgage in question is not an RMC, then that rather complicated issue should not be decided summarily and would require an adjournment to another hearing.

Introduction

11.1 In this book, where we have mainly been talking about rented accommodation we have stressed the need for the duty adviser to work hard to prevent the making of a conditional possession order and particularly a suspended possession order. The situation is a little different in mortgage cases.

11.2 Mortgage cases do not involve considerations of whether it is reasonable to make an order. The criteria of reasonableness that the court applies in rented accommodation cases does not apply here. Mortgage cases are primarily about the figures – specifically the figures as to whether the borrower can pay the mortgage and the arrears.

11.3 It follows that negotiations with lenders' representatives will be mostly on the issues of finances and come down to how persuasive the adviser and their client can be that they can meet the payments they propose. While that may seem rather harsh and calculating, it does mean that mortgage duty work can be more straightforward to conduct. For example, because it is almost a given that the best outcome for the defendant is that a suspended possession order will be made, then it is also straightforward and helpful to the defendant's case to remind the judge that the lender has nothing to lose from such an order. If the borrower does not make the payments, the lender can enforce.

11.4 Readers are strongly advised to read this chapter in conjunction with the mortgage pre-action protocol section of chapter 3, as well as the protocol itself. The protocol is extremely useful in outlining the critical issues in mortgage possession cases.

11.5 Following the Legal Aid, Sentencing and Punishment of Offenders Act 2012 (LASPO), mortgage cases were moved into the legal aid debt category and subject to the mandatory 'telephone gateway'. The result was that most advice and representation work for mortgage borrowers dried up and it is now mainly the duty adviser who will have experience of these cases. A lot of advisers shy away from mortgage work, but, at least in duty work, it is relatively straightforward. We set out below the statutory law and case-law you will need on a duty day. For the full analysis we recommend *Defending Possession Proceedings* (DPP) which runs to more than 160 pages just on mortgages.

11.6 With mortgage cases, the lender (mortgagee) already has the right to possession but will not usually seek to enforce it unless there has been a breach. The court has statutory powers to consider this right and postpone possession.

Types of mortgage

11.7 There are two main types of mortgage – repayment and interest only:

- *Repayment mortgage* – based on one monthly repayment towards the capital amount that has been borrowed and ongoing interest on the loan. The idea is that these monthly payments result in the mortgage being completely paid off at the end of the term.
- *Interest only mortgage* – a monthly repayment of just the interest on the capital borrowed often (but not always) with a separate payment to an insurance company or other investment vehicle which should grow enough funds to pay off the capital repayment at the end of the term. Problems can arise if there are no separate

arrangements to pay off the capital at the end of the term, or the arrangements are not sufficient to pay off the capital in full.

Possession proceedings and the courts' powers

11.8 The lender must comply with the Pre-action Protocol for Possession Claims Based on Mortgage or Home Purchase Plan Arrears in Respect of Residential Property before commencing possession proceedings. The claimant must bring the protocol checklist (form N123) to the hearing. Duty advisers should request a copy of the checklist, and if not, available this should be grounds to apply for an adjournment. Details of the protocol are outlined in chapter 3 above, and also see appendix 5.

11.9 Where a lender seeks a possession order of residential premises against a borrower (mortgagor), the court has powers to adjourn, postpone or suspend an order for possession for a reasonable period.

> A borrower may have more than one mortgage or loan secured against their home and the proceedings may not be in relation to the main mortgage.
>
> The checklists provided by appendix 1 below include the facility to record more than one mortgage or loan. This is important because the position with each loan will determine whether there is a prospect of the borrower making good the account on the mortgage or loan that is before the court.
>
> It is not unknown for duty clients to be facing multiple proceedings in respect of different loans. While that may appear to be a daunting prospect for an adviser, in fact it is simply a case of working out the overall financial position of the defendant and ascertaining whether they can meet obligations under all loans in order to save their home.
>
> It may be necessary to apply for an adjournment to work that out, but the adviser will need to show some prospect that payments can be made.

11.10 The courts' powers to restrict a lender's right to possession are contained within:

- Administration of Justice Act (AJA) 1970 s36(1);
- Administration of Justice Act (AJA) 1973 s8(2);
- Consumer Credit Act (CCA) 1974 Part 9.

Administration of Justice Acts 1970 and 1973

Overview

11.11 AJA 1970 s36 provides (emphasis added):

> **36 Additional powers of court in action by mortgagee for possession of dwelling-house**
>
> (1) Where the mortgagee under a mortgage of land which consists of or includes a dwelling-house brings an action in which he claims possession of the mortgaged property, not being an action for foreclosure in which a claim for possession of the mortgaged property is also made, the court may exercise any of the powers conferred on it by subsection (2) below if it appears to the court that in the event of its exercising the power the mortgagor is **likely** to be able within a **reasonable period** to pay any **sums due** under the mortgage or to remedy a default consisting of a breach of any other obligation arising under or by virtue of the mortgage.
>
> (2) The court –
>
> (a) may adjourn the proceedings, or
>
> (b) on giving judgement, or making an order, for delivery of possession of the mortgaged property, or at any time before the execution of such judgment or order, may:
>
> (i) stay or suspend execution of the judgment or order, or
>
> (ii) postpone the date for delivery of possession,
>
> for such period or periods as the court thinks reasonable.
>
> (3) Any such adjournment, stay, suspension or postponement as is referred to in subsection (2) above may be made subject to such conditions with regard to payment by the mortgagor of any sums secured by the mortgage or the remedying of any default as the court thinks fit.
>
> (4) The court may from time to time vary or revoke any condition imposed by virtue of this section.

And AJA 1973 s8 provides (emphasis added):

> **8 Extension of powers of court in action by mortgagee of dwelling-house**
>
> (1) Where by a mortgage of land which consists of or includes a dwelling-house, or by any agreement between the mortgagee under such a mortgage and the mortgagor, the mortgagor is entitled or is to be permitted to pay the principal sum secured by instalments or otherwise to defer payment of it in whole or in part, but provision is also made for earlier payment in the event of any default by the mortgagor or of a demand by the mortgagee or otherwise, then for purposes of section 36 of the Administration of Justice Act 1970 (under which a court has power to delay giving a mortgagee possession of the mortgaged property so as to allow the mortgagor a reas-

onable time to pay any **sums due** under the mortgage) a court may treat as due under the mortgage on account of the principal sum secured and of interest on it only such amounts as the mortgagor would have expected to be required to pay if there had been no such provision for earlier payment.

(2) A court shall not exercise by virtue of subsection (1) above the powers conferred by section 36 of the Administration of Justice Act 1970 unless it appears to the court not only that the mortgagor is **likely** to be able within **a reasonable period** to pay any amounts regarded (in accordance with subsection (1) above) as due on account of the principal sum secured, together with the interest on those amounts, but also that he is likely to be able by the end of that period to pay any further amounts that he would have expected to be required to pay by then on account of that sum and of interest on it if there had been no such provision as is referred to in subsection (1) above for earlier payment.

11.12 AJA 1973 s8(1) ensures that, where the mortgage agreement is for monthly instalments or other deferred payments, borrowers retain the protection of AJA 1970 s36 even if there is a term in the agreement that all sums become due if the borrower defaults on those monthly instalments or deferred payments. However there needs to be a contractual provision for the amount due to be payable by monthly instalments or other deferral. Where deferral is not part of the contractual agreement then that is sometimes described as an 'all monies charge' and s8(1) does not apply.

Terms

11.13 Some of the terms in AJA 1970 s36 and AJA 1973 s8 which we have highlighted in bold above warrant some definition and analysis:

'Sums due'

11.14 While 'sums due' could technically be the whole amount of the outstanding mortgage, AJA 1973 s8(1) and (2) assists the borrower by allowing payment of the monthly amount to be made and a lump sum off the arrears within a reasonable amount of time. The borrower must show that they can afford to keep up the current monthly instalment plus an amount off the arrears.

'Likely'

11.15 What is 'likely' is a matter of evidence for the judge. Often the borrower seeking advice from the duty adviser does not bring any evidence of ability to pay to the court, but the court can still take into account the evidence from the borrower on the day. If this issue is raised by the lender's representative, you can rely on the case of *Cheltenham & Gloucester Building Society v Grant* (1994) 24 HLR 703, CA at p707 which provides:

> ... it must be possible for [judges] to act without evidence, especially where, as here, the mortgagor was present in court and available to be questioned and no objection to the reception of informal material is made by the mortgagee.

11.16 It must appear to the court that the borrower can both pay the missed payments within a reasonable period and the current monthly instalment as it falls due. There does have to be a prospect that the borrower can reduce the arrears for the court to consider a suspension of the order (*Abbey National Mortgages v Bernard* (1996) 71 PCR 257, CA).

'Reasonable period'

11.17 In discussing the term 'reasonable period' in AJA 1970 s36(1), we need to have regard to the well-known case of *Cheltenham & Gloucester Building Society v Norgan* [1995] EWCA Civ 11. While *Norgan* remains good law, it is also the case that since 2016 virtually all mortgage cases have been susceptible to applications for a time order under Consumer Credit Act (CCA) 1974 Part 9, which we discuss below. Consequently, what follows is not the last word on what a defendant might argue in order to try to save their home in mortgage possession proceedings. Instead, it should be seen as a starting point before considering whether an application for a time order is appropriate.

11.18 What is a reasonable period is set out in *Norgan*. In determining what is the reasonable period:

> ... the court should take as its starting point the full term of the mortgage and pose at the outset the question: would it be possible for the mortgagor to maintain payment-off of the arrears by instalments over that period? (Waite LJ at 458).

The lender's representative will often work out the 'Norgan' figure and use this as a minimum figure in negotiations.

11.19 At its simplest, the 'Norgan' figure is *arrears* divided by *the number of months left on the mortgage term*. That is not to say that every case will be settled by payments of the monthly instalment plus 'Norgan'. 'Norgan' was until relatively recently the minimum amount on which a judge could postpone the making or enforcement of a possession order. A judge can decide in appropriate cases that a reasonable period means that a borrower should pay more than 'Norgan'.

11.20 The relevant factors in determining a reasonable period were set out in the case by Evans LJ (357–358):

(a) How much can the borrower reasonably afford to pay, both now and in the future?
(b) If the borrower has a temporary difficulty in meeting his obligations, how long is the difficulty likely to last?
(c) What was the reason for the arrears which have accumulated?
(d) How much remains of the original term?
(e) What are relevant contractual terms, and what type of mortgage is it i.e. when is the principal due to be repaid?
(f) Is it a case where the court should exercise its power to disregard accelerated payment provisions (section 8 of the 1973 Act)?
(g) Is it reasonable to expect the lender, in the circumstances of the particular case, to recoup the arrears of interest (1) over the whole of the original term, or (2) within a shorter period, or even (3) within a longer period, i.e. by extending the repayment period? Is it reasonable to expect the lender to capitalise the interest, or not?
(h) Are there any reasons affecting the security which should influence the length of the period for payment?

In the light of the answers to the above, the court can proceed to exercise its overall discretion, also taking into account any further factors which may arise in the particular case.

Mortgage possession – the changed legal landscape

- Prior to 2014, mortgage cases which were not CCA 1974 cases were dealt with on the basis of determining whether the defendant would be able, within a reasonable period, to pay any sums due under the mortgage (in accordance with the guidance set out in *Cheltenham & Gloucester Building Society v Norgan* [1995] EWCA Civ 11 – that is, pay off all the arrears within the remaining term of the mortgage). If not, then an outright possession order would generally be made.
- Changes brought about in 2014 and in 2016 mean that (i) the power available under CCA 1974 Part 9 to alter the terms of the loan agreement itself (time order) applies to all regulated mortgage contracts (RMCs) and (ii) nearly all residential mortgages contracts become RMCs.

- A time order can be made if the loan is a Regulated Credit Agreement or an RMC. From 21 March 2016, the majority of residential mortgages were brought within the scope of regulation (and became RMCs) under the Financial Services and Markets Act (FSMA) 2000 regardless of when they were granted by virtue of Financial Services and Markets Act 2000 (Regulated Activities) Order (FSMA(RA)O) 2001 SI No 544 art 61, as amended by Mortgage Credit Directive Order 2015 SI No 910 Sch 1 para 4(21), implementing EU Directive 2014/17/EU (known as the Mortgage Credit Directive).
- Consequently, the position prior to 2014 no longer applies. Duty advisers can assume that all mortgage cases that come before them may benefit from the provision of CCA 1974 Part 9 including the application of time orders. The guidance of the Court of Appeal concerning time orders in *Southern and District Finance plc v Barnes* (1995) 27 HLR 691 is relevant, and we set that out in the text.
- If there is an argument that the mortgage in question is not an RMC, then that would require an adjournment to another hearing to work out that issue which could not be decided summarily.
- While it is important for the duty adviser and the court to be aware of the power to vary the terms of the mortgage agreement, including extending the term of payments, that does not mean that the court will necessarily exercise that power.
- If a borrower's case can be brought on the basis that they will pay the monthly instalment and in addition at least meet the 'Norgan' amount to pay the arrears off by the end of the term, then that should be the starting point for negotiations and/or submissions to the court. These are submissions the court is well used to dealing with.
- Only if that is not possible should the possibility of asking the court to vary the terms of the mortgage be raised – and in that case it may well be that the duty adviser will need to ask for an adjournment to allow time the proposal to be formulated and put before the court in a structured and fully argued case, preferably with the assistance of legal aid.
- Because of the dramatic drop in mortgage work, and despite the length of time since they were introduced, it is unclear how familiar the courts are with the new powers across all mortgages to vary terms. See the article by D Clarke, D McConnell and S Mullings, 'Mortgage possession claims: the changed legal

landscape', LAG (at www.lag.org.uk/article/204910/mortgage-possession-claims—the-changed-legal-landscape) for further discussion – and having a copy of that article may be useful to show to judges to (a) indicate the range of the powers available and (b) to persuade them that an adjournment is necessary so that the legal framework and the defendant's proposal can be set out in sufficient detail for the court to give proper consideration.

Consumer Credit Act 1974 Part 9

Overview

11.21 On 1 April 2014, the powers under CCA 1974 Part 9 were extended to RMCs that were entered into after 31 October 2004. Prior to that date, the two regimes were distinct. This was significant for borrowers in mortgage possession claims as the court now had a wide discretion. It was no longer bound by the requirement that the arrears be paid within a reasonable period and in any event by the end of the term of the mortgage, and had the power to make a time order and thereby amend the terms of the mortgage.

Time orders

11.22 CCA 1974 s129(1) gives the court the power to make a time order 'if it appears to the court just to do so'. CCA 1974 s129(2) provides:

> (2) A time order shall provide for one or both of the following, as the court considers just–
> (a) the payment by the debtor or hirer or any surety of any sum owed under a regulated agreement or a security by such instalments, payable at such times, as the court, having regard to the means of the debtor or hirer and any surety, considers reasonable;
> (b) the remedying by the debtor or hirer of any breach of a regulated agreement (other than non-payment of money) within such period as the court may specify.

11.23 CCA 1974 s135(1) provides:

> (1) If it considers it just to do so, the court may in an order made by it in relation to a regulated agreement include provisions –
> (a) making the operation of any term of the order conditional on the doing of specified acts by any party to the proceedings;

(b) suspending the operation of any term of the order either –
  (i) until such time as the court subsequently directs, or
  (ii) until the occurrence of a specified act or omission.

11.24 This provision gives the court powers to suspend an order for possession and impose conditions of payment of instalments.

11.25 CCA 1974 s136 gives the court powers to vary the agreement and it is important to note that those powers necessarily have an effect on all three of: (i) the amount of the monthly instalment; (ii) the term of the agreement; and (iii) the interest being paid. In *Southern and District Finance plc v Barnes* (1995) 27 HLR 691 the Court of Appeal held (at 693):

> (1) When a time order is applied for . . . the court must first consider whether it is just to make a time order; that will involve consideration of all the circumstances of the case, and of the position of the creditor as well as the debtor;
>
> (2) When a time order is made, it should normally be made for a stipulated period on account of temporary financial difficulty;. . . .
>
> (3) When a time order is made relating to the non-payment of money:
> (a) The 'sum owed' means every sum which is due and owing under the agreement, but where possession proceedings have been brought by the creditor that will normally comprise the total indebtedness; and
> (b) The court must consider what instalments would be reasonable both as to amount and timing, having regard to the debtor's means;
>
> (4) The court may include in a time order any amendment of the agreement which it considers just to both parties, and which is a consequence of a term of the order; if the rate of interest is amended, it is relevant that smaller instalments will result both in a liability to pay interest on accumulated arrears, and, on the other hand, in an extended period of repayment; . . .
>
> (5) If a time order is made when the sum owed is the whole of the outstanding balance due under the loan, there will inevitably be consequences for the term of the loan or the rate of interest or both;
>
> (6) If justice requires the making of a time order, the court should suspend any possession order that it also makes, so long as the terms of the time order are complied with;
>
> . . .

11.26 From 21 March 2016, the majority of residential mortgages (regardless of when they were granted) were brought within the scope of regulation under the FSMA 2000 and subject to the Financial Conduct Authority (FCA)'s Mortgage Conduct of Business Rules (MCOB) (see www.handbook.fca.org.uk/handbook/MCOB/1/?view=chapter). Essentially this gives the court the broader powers set out in CCA 1974 Part 9, as well as the inherent powers under the AJA 1970 and 1973.

11.27 The extended powers available to the court are of real benefit to borrowers with regulated agreements. The court is no longer bound by the borrower's ability to clear the arrears within a 'reasonable period' and in any event by the end of the term of the mortgage, but can now make 'time orders' and has the power to vary agreements.

Taking instructions and applying the law

11.28 In general, the duty adviser should first look to make out a case that the defendant can pay the current monthly instalment plus amounts such that the arrears can be cleared within a reasonable period of time ie within *Norgan*. If that case cannot be established, then the adviser needs to consider whether an application for a time order is appropriate. Either way, it is for the defendant to establish the facts that give rise to either case.

11.29 When you first meet with your client, it is essential to ascertain: what term is left on the mortgage; the balance outstanding; the type of mortgage (repayment or interest-only); the monthly instalment; the value of the property; the last payment made; the reason for the arrears; the 'Norgan figure'; and what the borrower can afford to pay monthly towards the arrears. The checklist at appendix 1 will be of use in this regard.

11.30 The key considerations are:

- *Income maximisation* – What can the borrower afford to pay? Do they have evidence of their ability to pay, a new job due to be starting or a payment due from another source? Alternatively, if they are not working, have they applied for a loan from the Department for Work and Pensions (DWP) to pay the mortgage instalments (from 6 April 2018 repayable loans replaced benefit support for mortgage interest). The new Support for Mortgage Interest (SMI) loans will result in a charge on the property and will attract interest until the loan is paid off.
- *Mortgages and coronavirus* – The FCA produced guidance in June 2020 to firms which provided for a three-month deferral on mortgage payments for borrowers. This was updated in September 2020 suggesting a tailored response to supporting borrowers.

This related solely to arrears caused by COVID-19. (See 'Finalised guidance: Mortgages and coronavirus: additional guidance for firms' at www.fca.org.uk/publication/finalised-guidance/mortgages-coronavirus-additional-guidance-for-firms.pdf.)

- *Reducing mortgage costs or extending the term of the mortgage* – Is this possible? If the mortgage has a high interest rate or there is a short term left, it may be worth considering these options. It may be that this is not possible in the short time available at court and may need an adjournment to consider these options and put forward an application to the court.
- *Time for the borrower to sell* – If the borrower is not in a position to make payment on the mortgage and pay off the arrears within a reasonable time and there is no prospect of their circumstances changing, then they can apply for time to sell the property. This will put the borrower in control and is more likely to result in the borrower maintaining more of the outstanding equity. This is more likely if there is sufficient equity in the property and supported by a valuation.

If the mortgage has ended

CCA 1974 s129 can be relied upon even if the mortgage term has expired but there is still an amount left outstanding on the mortgage. The borrower can ask the court to make a time order to reschedule the amount due which will extend the period to pay the remaining sum and also reduce the amount of interest if appropriate.

A time order will only be possible if the borrower has the means to pay the balance within the suggested period. In making a decision, the court must weigh up the borrower's circumstances with that of the lenders interest. If the court makes a time order it will specify the new term.

As we set out above, a time order can be made if the loan is a Regulated Credit Agreement or an RMC. From 21 March 2016, the majority of residential mortgages were brought within the scope of regulation (and became RMCs) under the FSMA 2000 regardless of when they were granted.

If the borrower would like to apply for a time order, an adjournment should be requested at the hearing in order to file a full defence.

If the borrower cannot pay the outstanding sum, then an application could be made for time for the borrower to sell the property or to obtain alternative funding to discharge the mortgage. Usually in these circumstances the judge will make a possession order but postpone the date it takes effect to allow the defendant time to sell or make substantial progress with a sale.

Costs

11.31 In the majority of mortgage cases, the lender is contractually entitled to their costs, charges and expenses reasonably and properly incurred in preserving the security or recovering the mortgage debt. This means the costs of the proceedings will be added to the security. For this reason, lenders' representatives rarely have to trouble the court for a costs order. If the lender does ask for a costs order at court, Civil Procedure Rules 1998 (CPR) 44.5 applies to those costs and provides that the costs must be reasonably incurred and reasonable in amount. In some cases it might be appropriate to ask the judge to give an indication in the order if there are costs that were not reasonably incurred, or are not reasonable in amount if being summarily assessed.

Amount of costs where costs are payable under a contract

44.5

(1) Subject to paragraphs (2) and (3), where the court assesses (whether by summary or detailed assessment) costs which are payable by the paying party to the receiving party under the terms of a contract, the costs payable under those terms are, unless the contract expressly provides otherwise, to be presumed to be costs which–

(a) have been reasonably incurred; and

(b) are reasonable in amount,

and the court will assess them accordingly.

(2) The presumptions in paragraph (1) are rebuttable. Practice Direction 44 – General rules about costs sets out circumstances where the court may order otherwise.

(3) Paragraph (1) does not apply where the contract is between a solicitor and client.

Relationship breakdown

11.32 Duty advisers will see mortgage cases where there is a joint mortgage but there has been a relationship breakdown between the parties. It may even be that both parties are at court. The duty adviser may need to make it clear that they can only advise and represent one of these parties.

11.33 In other cases, the estranged spouse or civil partner of a mortgagor may be at court where they remain in occupation but the mortgagor has left. In addition, there may be occupiers who have equitable interests in the premises.

11.34 In these cases, the client will need to be referred to family law advice if possible. However, in terms of trying to save the person's home, it is necessary to make out the same arguments as in any other mortgage case. The court will need to be persuaded that immediately or reasonably imminently, the person seeking to prevent a possession order being made can sustain the monthly instalments due and make payments to any arrears that are due. If the client is not the mortgagor, then the court will need to be told that this person intends to assert their statutory rights under the Family Law Act 1996 or be informed of the nature of the person's equitable interest. This may be a case where a court should be asked to adjourn proceedings rather suspended order be made.

11.35 As always, DPP has the details on these matters.

Undue influence

11.36 Undue influence may occur in relation to actions of the lender, or may occur thought actions of the principal debtor where the person seeking to save their home stood as surety for the debts. Where the misconduct is on the part of the lender, that can invalidate the legal charge by which the lender seeks possession. Where the misconduct is on the part of a principal debtor, the same applies, but the debt as against the principal debtor remains a matter between the lender and the principal debtor.

11.37 Lender misconduct may be argued where a borrower asserts that the lender misrepresented the nature of the agreement leading to the legal charge on the property or the borrower was pressured into the agreement.

11.38 Principal debtor misconduct mostly involves cases where a lender is deemed to be on notice that one joint mortgagor is pressured or misled in relation to a second mortgage on a matrimonial home by the other joint mortgagor. In the case-law, and we think in cases generally, this form of undue influence arises mostly between joint mortgagors who are spouses, civil partners and cohabitants – but other forms of relationships can be involved in undue influence cases where one person stands as surety for another's debts.

11.39 Although these cases are much more rare than they used to be, duty advisers should be aware of the principles in case the issue arises – and for more details they should consult DPP.

Warrants in mortgage cases

11.40 Duty advisers will see cases where a borrower has applied to suspend a warrant for eviction. These will be cases where an outright possession order has been made in the first place, or there has been a breach of a suspended possession order. Essentially the arguments that a duty adviser will wish to negotiate on and/or deploy in court are the same, and the court has all the same powers as set out above, but of course the court will need to know why any breach of a suspended order occurred and why the situation has changed. In outright order cases the court will generally want to see good evidence of a change in circumstances to justify the suspension of the warrant.

11.41 A borrower facing eviction may still apply to stay that eviction pending sale of the property, but they will need to show good evidence of progress with a sale for such an application to have any prospect of success.

Charging orders and orders for sale

11.42 Where a creditor brings a claim against a debtor and obtains judgment for the amount owed, the creditor/claimant has a range of options to try to enforce the order they have obtained and secure the money they are owed. These options include an application for a charging order and CPR Part 73 and the accompanying practice direction (PD) deal with these. For our purposes, the relevant rule is CPR 73.10C:

> **Enforcement of charging order by sale**
>
> **73.10C**
>
> (1) Subject to the provisions of any enactment, the court may, upon a claim by a person who has obtained a charging order over an

interest in property, order the sale of the property to enforce the charging order.

(2) Where the charging order was made at the County Court Money Claims Centre a claim for an order for sale under this rule must be made to the judgment debtor's home court.

(3) Subject to paragraph (2) a claim for an order for sale under this rule should be made to the court which made the charging order, unless that court does not have jurisdiction to make an order for sale.

(4) The claimant must use the Part 8 procedure.

(5) A copy of the charging order must be filed with the claim form.

11.43 CPR PD 73 para 4.3 sets out the information that the claimant must provide in their claim, which is a useful checklist for a duty adviser:

> **4.3** The written evidence in support of a claim under rule 73.10C must–
> (1) identify the charging order and the property sought to be sold;
> (2) state the amount in respect of which the charge was imposed and the amount due at the date of issue of the claim;
> (3) verify, so far as known, the debtor's title to the property charged;
> (4) state, so far as the claimant is able to identify–
> (a) the names and addresses of any other creditors who have a prior charge or other security over the property; and
> (b) the amount owed to each such creditor; and
> (5) give an estimate of the price which would be obtained on sale of the property;
> (6) if the claim relates to land, give details of every person who to the best of the claimant's knowledge is in possession of the property; and
> (7) if the claim relates to residential property–
> (a) state whether–
> (i) a land charge of Class F; or
> (ii) a notice under section 31(10) of the Family Law Act 1996, or under any provision of an Act which preceded that section,
> has been registered; and
> (b) if so, state–
> (i) on whose behalf the land charge or notice has been registered; and
> (ii) that the claimant will serve notice of the claim on that person.
>
> **4.4** The claimant must take all reasonable steps to obtain the information required by paragraph 4.3(4) before issuing the claim.

11.44 A creditor who wishes to enforce a charging order applies under CPR Part 8 for an order for sale – essentially, they will bring possession proceedings and seek a possession order based on the charge.

The matter may, then, come to the duty adviser at the first or adjourned hearing of such proceedings. The list of proceedings set out in the Housing Possession Court Duty Scheme (HPCDS) contract guidance ('Housing Possession Court Duty Scheme: Guidance for Service Providers', Legal Aid Agency, 30 September 2020; www.gov.uk/government/publications/housing-possession-court-duty-schemes-hpcds) includes (at para 2.3(e)):

> Clients with charging orders relating to property whereby the client is at immediate risk of losing their home through a forced sale.

11.45 If there is an arguable case as to whether a charging order and order for sale should have been made, then the duty adviser will almost always need to apply for an adjournment for evidence to be filed and served to make out that case which will be too complicated to be dealt with summarily.

11.46 Otherwise, the advice to be given to the defendant, and the means of trying to prevent the defendant losing their home is the same as defending mortgage proceedings. The default position is that the creditor is entitled to possession in order to secure the debt by way of sale of the property, but the court has the power to suspend the giving up of possession on terms. The defendant will need to be able to persuade the court that they can clear the debt which will include the costs incurred in the proceedings within a reasonable period of time.

Orders for sale

An order for sale can be suspended or postponed giving the defendant time to pay off the debt and keep their home. It is worth reminding the court that the lender already has the protection of the charging order.

The court will balance the interests of all the family members as against the rights of the claimant. Some issues to consider:

- Check who owns the property. If the debt is only with one owner and the property is jointly owned an order for sale might be more difficult to obtain, especially if the joint owner was not aware of the debt.
- Is there sufficient equity in the property to discharge the debt? If not, it may not be worth the lender forcing the sale.

- Who lives in the household? If there are children or members of the family with disabilities residing in the property then this may influence the judge's decision to suspend an order for sale.
- Is there an alternative way the defendant can pay off the debt? Are they able to raise funds through other means?

11.47 Charging order cases may also come before the duty adviser in the form of an application made by the defendant to suspend a warrant obtained to enforce an order for sale. Again, the principles are the same as seeking to suspend a warrant to enforce a mortgage possession order.

Tenants of borrowers

11.48 Tenancies granted before the date of the mortgage are binding on the lender – even if the grant of the tenancy breached the terms of the mortgage.

11.49 Tenancies granted after the date of the mortgage will not be binding on the lender.

11.50 Pursuant to Mortgage Repossessions (Protection of Tenants etc) Act 2010, a tenant has the right to apply to the court for a postponement of the possession order for up to two months. If no application has been made to postpone the possession order, a tenant can apply at the warrant stage to postpone the warrant for possession for the same period. Section 1 is worth setting out here for reference should it be needed.

> **1 Power of court to postpone giving of possession**
>
> (1) This section applies if–
>
> (a) the mortgagee under a mortgage of land which consists of or includes a dwelling-house brings an action (other than an action for foreclosure) in which the mortgagee claims possession of the mortgaged property, and
>
> (b) there is an unauthorised tenancy of all or part of the property.
>
> (2) When making an order for delivery of possession of the property, the court may, on the application of the tenant, postpone the date for delivery of possession for a period not exceeding two months.
>
> (3) Subsection (4) applies where an order for delivery of possession of the property has been made but not executed.
>
> (4) The court may, on the application of the tenant ('the applicant'), stay or suspend execution of the order for a period not exceeding two months if–

(a) the court did not exercise its powers under subsection (2) when making the order or, if it did, the applicant was not the tenant when it exercised those powers,
(b) the applicant has asked the mortgagee to give an undertaking in writing not to enforce the order for two months beginning with the date the undertaking is given, and
(c) the mortgagee has not given such an undertaking.

(5) When considering whether to exercise its powers under this section, the court must have regard to–
(a) the circumstances of the tenant, and
(b) if there is an outstanding breach by the tenant of a term of the unauthorised tenancy–
(i) the nature of that breach, and
(ii) whether the tenant might reasonably be expected to have avoided breaching that term or to have remedied the breach.

(6) The court may make any postponement, stay or suspension under this section conditional on the making of payments to the mortgagee in respect of the occupation of the property (or part of the property) during the period of the postponement, stay or suspension.

(7) The making of any payment pursuant to–
(a) a condition of an undertaking of a kind mentioned in subsection (4)(c), or
(b) a condition imposed by virtue of subsection (6),
is not to be regarded as creating (or as evidence of the creation of) any tenancy or other right to occupy the property.

(8) For the purposes of this section there is an 'unauthorised tenancy' if–
(a) an agreement has been made which, as between the parties to it (or their successors in title), is or gives rise to–
(i) an assured tenancy (within the meaning of the Housing Act 1988), or
(ii) a protected or statutory tenancy (within the meaning of the Rent Act 1977), and
(b) the mortgagee's interest in the property is not subject to the tenancy.

(9) In this section 'the tenant', in relation to an unauthorised tenancy, means the person who is, as between the parties to the agreement in question (or their successors in title), the tenant under the unauthorised tenancy (or, if there is more than one tenant, any of them).

11.51 Duty advisers will see these cases where tenants of borrowers have applied under subsections 1(2) and/or (4). Subsections 1(5) and (6) set out the criteria that the court will apply when considering whether to grant the tenant/applicant's application, and so provide an indication of the instructions that the adviser will need from the tenant/applicant.

CHAPTER 12

Outcomes

Key points

- The best possible outcome for the defendant (in nearly all circumstances) is for the claim for possession to be struck out. There will need to be irremediable defects in the claim for the court to make such an order.
- Otherwise, the duty adviser is most often trying to get the claim adjourned generally.
- Other times, it may be necessary to ask the court to adjourn proceedings to allow for events to clarify the issues in the claim – such as welfare benefits, employment, medical or other issues.
- If it is not possible to achieve an adjournment, then a conditional possession order may have to be made. We set out below the two types of conditional possession order. Duty advisers should not agree any kind of possession order unless there is no prospect at all of the case being adjourned.
- Usually with adjournments, and on all conditional orders, it will be necessary to agree terms. The duty adviser needs to be very careful to make sure agreed terms are realistic and sustainable for the defendant to comply with.
- The duty adviser should consider whether direct payments from a defendant's benefits would be helpful or not. It can be very unhelpful in universal credit cases (see 12.49 et seq).
- There is still useful advice a duty adviser can give even if an outright possession order is made.
- The duty adviser may need to try to resist an application for enforcement to be transferred to the High Court.

Introduction

12.1 There are seven possible outcomes at a first instance substantive possession hearing ('S hearing'):

- strike out;
- adjournment – general/on terms;
- adjournment – fixed date;
- directions;
- postponed possession order;
- suspended possession order;
- outright possession order;

and there is a further possible outcome if an enforceable possession order is made:

- transfer to High Court for enforcement.

These range in the levels of jeopardy for the defendant from zero, with the landlord's claim being struck out; to the worst possible outcome, with an outright possession order being made. If an outright order is made, the landlord can apply for enforcement (the actual eviction) to be transferred to the High Court.

Strike out

12.2 For the court to strike out a landlord's claim for possession, there generally has to be (i) no arguable case that the landlord can make out and (ii) no reasonable means for the landlord to rectify any defects in the possession claim in a way that is fair to the tenant. Given the court's wide-ranging powers to take evidence at almost any stage in proceedings, it is not common for the court to strike out a claim for possession.

12.3 Nevertheless, advisers should be alert to the possibility of persuading a judge that the landlord's case is hopeless and could not be remedied without prejudice to the tenant and so should be struck out. For example, if a pre-action protocol has not been followed and that has put the defendant at a major disadvantage, it can be argued that this is a defence in *these* proceedings which cannot be remedied after issue.

12.4 If a landlord does not attend the court hearing, then the court should be asked to strike out the proceedings as the landlord's evidence in support of their claim cannot be challenged by the tenant or their adviser in the court. However, judges are sometimes more inclined to adjourn proceedings in those circumstances to give the landlord another chance to present their case. It is still possible to ask the judge to adjourn proceedings generally with provision to allow the landlord an opportunity to restore proceedings by a certain date. If they are not restored by that date, then they should be struck out.

Unless orders

Duty advisers should be alert to the possibility of the court applying an 'unless order' to any direction it gives to a party to do something by a certain time.

An 'unless order' works like this. If, for example, a claimant is directed to amend their claim because of a defect it may be possible to ask the court to make that subject to an 'unless order' so that if the claimant does not comply with the direction by the time stipulated then, for example, their claim would be struck out.

If the landlord does not show up to the S hearing but the court is not prepared to strike out the case, then an 'unless order' may be appropriate.

Duty advisers also need to be aware that defendants can of course also be made subject to 'unless order' and must therefore advise clearly what the defendant has been told to do and by what date and what the consequences of not doing so will be (usually that they are debarred from defending the proceedings).

12.5 Under the Master of the Rolls Working Group on Possession Proceedings' 'Overall Arrangements for Possession Proceedings in England and Wales: "The Overall Arrangements"', it appears to be possible for a judge to strike out proceedings at the 'review (R) date', but of course the duty adviser will not have any influence over that and is entirely a matter for the judge.

Adjournment – general/on terms

12.6 In as many cases as possible, the adviser will be looking to get a claim adjourned generally. The adjournment is often conditional upon terms for the tenant to comply with, such as payment of weekly or monthly rent. As long as the tenant complies with the order, the matter will not come back to court.

12.7 A general adjournment is always, whether expressed in the order or not, subject to the fact that either party can apply to the court to restore the proceedings – referred to as 'liberty to restore'.

12.8 In the case of a general adjournment, whether or not on terms, the court will often put an end date by which, if proceedings have not been restored then they shall stand dismissed. This is to ensure claims are not extant on the court system for no reason. If the judge does not do this of their own accord, it is good practice to suggest that they do so, and most judges are grateful to be reminded.

12.9 'Terms' are conditions set for the claim to remain adjourned and therefore keeping the possession claim from coming back to court. If the terms are breached then the claimant can lodge an application for the claim to be restored which would then trigger a new hearing. Notice of the hearing will be sent to the defendant.

12.10 It is important, therefore, that terms agreed with the landlord are realistic and achievable. On a busy possession court day there are often great pressures from landlords or even the court for the tenant to agree to terms which might be beyond their means or abilities. Tenants and borrowers, understandably frightened of losing their home and keen to get away from the court, can sometimes be persuaded to agree to terms which they either know they cannot keep to or are not sure that they can keep to. This should be resisted and so duty advisers must make sure they obtain sufficient instructions from the defendant as to their financial position now, and in the near future, that will allow the adviser to negotiate affordable terms.

12.11 A defendant who does not keep to the terms of an adjournment is at a much greater risk of some form of possession order being made at a further hearing. Judges in these situations often take the view that a tenant has been given a chance which they failed to comply with the terms of and therefore a more draconian measure is required next time around. It is crucial therefore that if terms are to be set for an adjournment that the terms are affordable and achievable by the tenant.

12.12 Sometimes a tenant's representative will ask the court to award the landlord their costs. This should be resisted on the basis that the court has not made any findings in the case and so is not in any reasonable position to decide where the costs should lie under the usual court costs principles. It is not always possible to prevent costs orders in this way, but they should always be resisted.

Adjournment – fixed date

12.13 In this section we are dealing with adjournments to a fixed date prior to any directions to file a defence and or counterclaim.

12.14 On many occasions the defendant will want to argue or have their adviser argue that the court does not yet have all the information required to decide the case. This might be because of an outstanding benefit claim, backdated or otherwise, which will help improve the situation with the rent account. There may be the prospect of employment which will mean that the rent or mortgage can be paid and arrears cleared but time is needed to see if the job is offered or what the salary will be. Medical issues may fall to be resolved before the facts of the defendant's position can be fully appreciated by the court.

The defendant is essentially saying that it is not reasonable for a possession order to be made in these circumstances and so the case should be adjourned.

12.15 In these circumstances, the duty adviser should ask the court to adjourn the proceedings to a fixed date in the future so that these issues can be crystallised, and the court can make a proper informed decisions with the benefit of all the relevant facts. The length of the adjournment can be anything from a day (or even to later the same day) to a number of months depending on the circumstances. A judge may adjourn to a hearing the next day if the tenant has promised they can pay off arrears later the same day. A long adjournment may be ordered if, for example, there is a benefits appeal in train which is not likely to come to a conclusion for several weeks or even months.

12.16 Again, there will be pressure to agree to a short adjournment rather than a long one. Advisers should always try to be realistic with the court about how long it will take to get matters resolved. There is no benefit to either party, or the court, in the case coming back only to have to be adjourned again, no matter how much the claimant may wish to get the case back before a judge quickly.

12.17 A claimant may seek conditions for the adjournment if the period of the adjournment is long. If the defendant can comply with the terms then in most cases it will be in their interests to agree such terms. They can then have clarity about what they must do during the period of the adjournment and can show a commitment to clearing the arrears. However, as above, only terms that can be complied with should be agreed, and otherwise they should be resisted with reasons.

12.18 Sometimes it is essential that no terms are agreed. For example, if housing-related benefits are not being paid then in most cases the defendant will not be able to promise to pay the rent plus an amount against the arrears while the benefit is being sorted out. The duty adviser should resist an order that provides for rent plus an amount against the arrears. However, the adviser may well advise the defendant to agree to pay an amount as a contribution to the rent while the benefit is being sorted out. Care should be taken to make sure the judge records that sort of condition in such a way that there can be no suggestion that the defendant had to pay rent plus the amount. This will usually involve recording the benefit issue in the preamble to the order and in the order itself, wording similar to:

> The claim shall be adjourned [generally/to the first open date after . . .] on terms that the defendant do pay £xx.xx per week as a contribution towards rent and any arrears.

12.19 A claim for possession may also be adjourned to a new date to allow the landlord to rectify a defect in their claim and/or produce evidence that the court deems necessary. Such an adjournment may give a tenant an opportunity to improve their position before the next hearing.

12.20 If they do not do so of their own accord, either in a preamble or in formal directions, the judge should be asked to record the reasons for the adjournment on the order so that the next judge to deal with the case has that guidance.

Directions

12.21 Where a defence and/or counterclaim is identified and can be summarised for the judge, then the adviser will ask for directions to file and serve the defence. This will be in the form of a date on which (by 4pm) the tenant's pleading is to be filed and served. Further directions may then be agreed. At the very least, there would usually be a direction for the claimant to file a reply to defence and if appropriate defence to counterclaim, and there then be either allocations questionnaires issued or an allocation hearing.

12.22 It is rare for directions to be made that would take a matter to a trial at this stage, but practice may vary from court to court and region to region.

12.23 Some judges may make orders which provide for a defence (and counterclaim) to be filed and served by a certain date, in default of which the case will be relisted for a further short hearing. The purpose of that type of order is to allow the claimant a quick opportunity to ask once again for a possession order at a short hearing in the event the tenant fails to file and serve their defence.

12.24 As with adjournments to a new date, it is incumbent upon advisers to be realistic with the court about how long it will take for a defence (and counterclaim) to be filed and served. Judges may not be aware how long complicated means assessments can take for legal aid, and so it is the adviser's job to inform them.

Postponed possession order

12.25 We are using the term *postponed possession order* in two senses, both of which are distinct from a 'suspended possession order'. The wording we are using is in general use (which is why we adopt it here), but we concede is imprecise. The suspension referred to in a 'suspended possession order' is in fact suspension of enforcement, not of the order itself.

12.26 The first type of postponed possession order is where an outright possession order is made (execution is not suspended) but the court decides to extend the date for when possession is to be given up which it may do for up to 42 days (Housing Act (HA) 1980 s89). In this book we call this an 'outright postponed possession order'.

12.27 The second type, which we call simply a 'postponed possession order' and which is found on practice form N28A, is somewhat akin to a suspended possession order, but is not as common. In this type of order, a possession order is made, but the date for giving up possession is postponed generally on terms to be complied with by the tenant. If the tenant breaches the terms, there is a mechanism in the order for the landlord to ask the court, to apply on written notice to the tenant, to fix the date for possession which would then make the order into an outright possession order.

12.28 That gives the defendant the opportunity to reply to the claimant and the court to explain any breach or refute any alleged breach. In this sense, the postponed possession order offers slightly more protection for defendants than the suspended possession order (see below) and while the postponed possession order is often thought to have been used to deal with the now defunct issue of tolerated trespass, such orders can be a useful 'halfway house' order for tenants where an adjournment is not on the cards but a suspended order puts the tenant at too great a risk of eviction through circumstances, perhaps beyond their control.

12.29 The protection for the defendant is that the claimant must write to the court on notice to the defendant for the date for possession to be fixed, giving the defendant an opportunity to intervene and explain the situation. Duty advisers wishing to argue for this protection will need to set out what circumstances might lead to an inadvertent or unavoidable breach of the conditions of the order.

12.30 An explanation as to the need for this kind of order can be found in *Defending Possession Proceedings* (DPP).

Suspended possession order

Overview

12.31 A *suspended possession order* is an order where possession is ordered to be given up by a certain date, usually within 28 days, but execution of that order is suspended, on terms that the defendant must meet. Those terms are usually concerning payment of rent/mortgage and amounts towards the arrears. There is a form used by judges to make suspended possession orders which is practice form N28.

12.32 The mechanics of a suspended possession order are as follows. As long as the tenant complies with the terms set out in the order to the letter, then the landlord cannot take any steps to evict the tenant by enforcing the order. However, if the defendant misses a payment they are obliged to make under the terms by, for example, even just one day, or is short in the amount they must pay, by even just £1, then strictly speaking the claimant is entitled to apply for a warrant for the tenant's eviction. While the defendant may still have an opportunity to apply to the court in respect of the warrant (see chapter 15 below), breaching the terms of a suspended possession order is to be avoided virtually at all costs.

12.33 One of the biggest pressures a duty adviser faces in a busy possession court duty day is to agree suspended possession orders with the claimant or their representatives. Social landlords and lenders in particular are keen to achieve suspended orders even if they don't really want to evict the defendant. They see the suspended order as a means of (i) holding a severe penalty against the defendant if the rent/mortgage is not paid and arrears not cleared and (ii) a quick way of being able to evict if they feel they need to.

12.34 In rented accommodation cases in particular, the duty adviser must push back against the pressure to agree suspended possession orders outside court and try to persuade judges not to make suspended possession orders inside court:

- A suspended possession order must *never* be agreed where there is no reasonable and secure prospect of the tenant complying with terms. To agree a suspended possession order in these circumstances is tantamount to agreeing an outright order and praying for a miracle. Landlord/lender representatives sometimes ask for terms which are clearly not feasible for a defendant. It is important to resist that, because accepting such terms puts the defendant at very high risk of a breach and therefore losing their home.
- Even if it appears that terms could be complied with, it must still be 'reasonable for a possession order to be made' and in hard times the financial future of tenants can never be certain. Given the severe outcomes, if there were even a small blip in payments judges should be reminded that possession orders of any kind

should only be made in the very last resort, even if they are to be suspended.

- A housing/income officer or landlord representative may say in all good faith that they do not have any intention of enforcing the suspended possession order for minor breaches but they just want to hold the tenant to an agreement. For all their good faith, they may not be dealing with the case the next time around and their colleague may take a different view.
- The landlord will almost certainly be awarded their costs if a suspended possession order is made, adding to the tenant's indebtedness to the rent account, albeit the costs will almost always be suspended on payments under the same terms as the arrears.

12.35 There are cases where arrears are very high and/or there have been numerous broken agreements in the past, where it may be necessary to agree a suspended possession order. On rare occasions it may be in the tenant's interests to agree a suspended possession order if an adjournment to a new date is likely to increase the costs incurred by the landlord and which the landlord is likely to seek and be granted as against the tenant in the end. However, such a calculation must be carefully weighed against the potential risk to a tenant of a suspended possession order.

12.36 In mandatory possession cases, some tenant representatives will (rarely) offer a suspended possession order if they think their mandatory order might be in danger of some technical challenge. It is not permissible for the court to make a suspended order on a mandatory claim for possession but subject to their duties to the court, no tenant's adviser would prevent the court from doing so if that avoided the certain making of a mandatory possession order. Technically, it is to be supposed, the judge could be asked not to make a finding on the amount of arrears as at the date of the notice and so make a suspended order on an alternative ground to ground 8, such as ground 10 or ground 11 (of HA 1988 Sch 2).

Terms in rented accommodation cases, 'the usual amount' and third party deductions

Terms

12.37 The terms set for an adjournment or conditional order in a rent arrears claim will usually be set out similar the following:

> . . . on terms that the defendant do pay current rent plus £xx.xx per towards rent and arrears of £xx.xx.

12.38 The amount to be paid is entirely in the discretion of the judge and it is for the parties or their representatives to make submissions as to what the amount should be. It is important to be able to provide the judge with the defendant's current and near future financial position so as to justify the amount that the defendant is proposing.

'Usual amount'

12.39 In respect of defendants on the lowest forms of state benefits, or otherwise for whatever reason on a very low income, there has developed a 'standard' minimum amount which the courts will order a defendant to pay. Judges and experienced representatives will often refer to 'the usual amount'. We have put the word 'standard' in quotes because in fact this so-called 'standard' can vary.

12.40 It is very likely that the basis for the 'usual amount' has historically been the amount that is prescribed for the Department for Work and Pensions (DWP) to pay from various income-related benefits when the department is asked to pay directly to a landlord from a tenant's income benefits – third party deductions (TPDs).

12.41 In Social Security (Claims and Payments) Regulations 1987 SI No 1968 Sch 9, the amount that could be deducted from income support for rent arrears was restricted to five per cent of the standard applicable amount for a person aged 25 or over (Sch 9 para 5(6)).

12.42 The five per cent restriction was retained as benefits such as jobseeker's allowance (JSA), employment and support allowance (ESA) and pension credit (PC) were introduced. It became adopted colloquially at court as 'the usual amount' when making orders for payments towards rent arrears against benefit-claimant tenants, whether or not the payments are made by TPDs. However, what appears to have happened over time is that claimant representatives and/or the courts have increased this amount from year to year in line with some notional idea of inflation when benefit amounts have not increased until very recently.

12.43 Claimant representatives will often tell duty advisers that the 'usual amount' is now £3.85, £3.90 or even £4 to allow for 'inflation'.

12.44 The amount is in fact currently **£3.75** weekly, and amounts are recorded by the DWP in 'Benefit and pension rates 2020 to 2021' at www.gov.uk/government/publications/benefit-and-pension-rates-2020-to-2021/benefit-and-pension-rates-2020-to-2021.

12.45 However, duty advisers should be alert to the fact that in some cases people are not in receipt of JSA, ESA, income support (IS) or

PC but still be on an income low enough to persuade a judge that 'the usual amount' is appropriate.

Third party deductions

12.46 Where defendants are in receipt of JSA, ESA, IS or PC it is a useful tool for duty advisers to (i) advise the claimant and the court that the defendant will agree TPDs being made to cover the amount against the arrears and/or (ii) criticise social landlord claimants for not looking to request TPDs in advance of bringing proceedings as is the right of landlords to do. If there is any doubt as to the claimant's right to apply unilaterally, they may be referred to the government's 'A guide for landlords – rent arrears and service charges' (www.gov.uk/government/publications/how-to-request-deductions-from-benefit-a-guide-for-creditors/third-party-deductions-from-benefits-a-guide-for-landlords-rent-arrears-and-service-charges).

12.47 It may be argued, therefore, that a failure to request TPDs, especially in but not limited to cases of vulnerability, is a breach of the spirit and letter of the pre-action protocol, or a public law matter or Equality Act (EA) 2010 matter.

12.48 This must be considered with great caution in respect of cases of universal credit (UC) because of the following.

Third party deductions and universal credit

12.49 With TPDs and UC, the same rules as to the minimum amount to deduct do not apply. Universal Credit and Miscellaneous Amendments (No 2) Regulations 2014 SI No 2888 reg 6(2)(c) changed the figure in Universal Credit, Personal Independence Payment, Jobseeker's Allowance and Employment and Support Allowance (Claims and Payments) Regulations 2013 SI No 380 Sch 6 para 7(5) – instead of five per cent, the amount is now 'no less than 10% and no more than 20%'.

12.50 Effectively, that means that direct deductions made from UC cannot be less than 10 per cent of the standard allowance nor more than 20 per cent. So, where the amount had previously been maintained at five per cent (currently £3.75 per week), deductions *must* for a single person now be no less than £7.90 per week and can be up to £18.92 per week. Different rates apply depending on whether the claimant is under 25 or not, and also there are different rates for couples. The amounts are all set out as monthly amounts in the DWP's 'Benefit and pension rates 2020 to 2021' (www.gov.uk/

government/publications/benefit-and-pension-rates-2020-to-2021/benefit-and-pension-rates-2020-to-2021).

12.51 Unfortunately, a useful tool to assist tenants with managing payment towards rent arrears in order to keep their home has become, to those who subsist entirely or mostly on UC, an unaffordable repayment burden.

12.52 There is a need, therefore, (i) to persuade the judge that the amounts are too much for a tenant to be able to afford and (ii) to suggest a way to the judge to ensure that the council did not have recourse to TPDs from UC so as not to leave the tenant destitute and unable to manage. We suggest that the duty adviser try to negotiate the following form of preamble to the order if they can:

> **UPON** the claimant agreeing not to ask the Department of Work and Pensions to make direct payments from the defendant's universal credit towards the arrears because the minimum that could be paid that way is £7.90 per week (10% of the standard weekly allowance), leaving the defendant at risk of destitution.
>
> **AND UPON** the parties agreeing that it would be more appropriate for the court to order that the defendant pay towards the arrears 5% of the standard allowance, currently £3.75 per week.

12.53 The judge cannot, in the normal run of proceedings, restrain the claimant from making an application for third party deductions. This form of order, if it can be successfully negotiated, records the claimant's agreement not to apply for third party deductions.

Outright possession order

12.54 An *outright order for possession* is the worst outcome for the tenant who wishes to stay in their home. An outright order states that possession is to be given up on a certain date which may be from 'forthwith' up to 42 days. A forthwith order is unusual, and most orders are made as 14-day orders.

12.55 Tenants will need to be advised that this is not the date that they will be removed from their home. While the order will record that they are obliged to leave on that date, in fact that date records the date on or after which the landlord may apply for enforcement of the order by way of a warrant of eviction. The practicalities are that the landlord applies for a warrant, the court bailiffs in the county court or High Court Enforcement Officers in the High Court set a date of the eviction to take place and give at least 14 days' notice to the tenant (see Civil Procedure Rules 1998 (CPR) 83.8A). That date which is notified to the tenant is the date by which they may be removed from the premises.

12.56 The landlord will usually be granted a money judgment for any arrears of rent they have proven, and they will also be awarded the costs of the proceedings.

12.57 In cases where the order is not made on mandatory grounds, the tenant may apply to suspend or set aside the warrant but good reasons will need to be shown to prevent an eviction from taking place based on an outright possession order. In mandatory cases there is no such right.

12.58 A possession order made on mandatory grounds must be stated on the face of the order to be made on mandatory grounds, otherwise it is not a mandatory order – *Diab v Countrywide Rentals 1 plc* October 2001 *Legal Action* 15; (2001) *Independent* 5 November; 10 July 2001, unreported, ChD.

12.59 For these reasons, an outright possession order is of course to be avoided whenever possible.

The position with the enforcement of possession orders as at January 2021

In England on 17 November 2020 the Public Health (Coronavirus) (Protection from Eviction and Taking Control of Goods) (England) Regulations 2020 SI No 1290 came into force, essentially banning any eviction (with exceptions for illegal occupation, false statement, anti-social behaviour, eviction of perpetrators of domestic abuse in the social sector where the victim is housed elsewhere, where a property is unoccupied following death of a tenant and serious rent arrears) from residential accommodation in England between 17 November 2020 and 11 January 2021. That was replaced from 11 January 2021 by the Public Health (Coronavirus) (Protection from Eviction) (England) Regulations 2021 SI No 15 which extended the ban to 21 February 2021 and then The Public Health (Coronavirus) (Protection from Eviction) (England) (No. 2) Regulations 2021 SI No 164 has extended the ban further to 31 March 2021. Unfortunately in the last two regulations the protection for renters was significantly watered down in that the exceptions included cases with arrears of rent of six months or more (down from nine months), whether at the time of the possession order or not. and whether all or any of those arrears are coronavirus related or not.

In Wales, the equivalent regulation is Public Health (Protection from Eviction) (Wales) (Coronavirus) Regulations 2021 No 12

(W.5). Subject to a periodic three-week review, bailiffs are not allowed to enforce evictions until 31 March 2021, except in cases relating to illegal occupation, anti-social behaviour, eviction of perpetrators of domestic abuse in the social sector where the victim is housed elsewhere and where the property is unoccupied following the death of a tenant. The exceptions in Wales do not include any rent arrears grounds.

In either jurisdiction an application under CPR Part 23 will need to be made if a landlord wishes to seek an eviction under these exceptions.

By the time you are reading this, the residential eviction part of the regulations will be soon to be or more likely are defunct, but we have included this section in case the effect of the regulations is extended and in case the historical record of what happened with evictions is helpful.

Transfer to High Court for enforcement

12.60 Where an outright order for possession is made, many representatives of private landlords will be instructed to ask for transfer of the case to the High Court for enforcement.

12.61 The motivation for the landlord is that enforcement has traditionally been quicker in the High Court. Enforcement is carried out by commercial operators who have an interest in providing a quicker service than the court bailiffs who undertake enforcement in the county court.

12.62 Until recently there was no provision for notice to be given to the tenant of the date on which the warrant or writ was going to be executed. In the county court it was standard practice that tenants received a notice of eviction. Not so in the High Court, where people could find enforcement officers turning up to evict them without having any notice of them coming.

12.63 Changes to CPR Part 83 have now brought both procedural codes into alignment and tenants must have at least 14 days' notice of the date on which bailiffs or sheriffs will attend to execute the warrant or writ. These amendments to CPR Part 83 have significantly changed the situation as regards the benefits to claimants of enforcing in the High Court. The changes brought about by the amendment are:

- defendants must by virtue of CPR 83.8A now be given at least 14 days' notice of the eviction date on form N54 – previously no such notice was required;

- while permission to transfer proceedings to the High Court for enforcement is still required, permission to issue a writ of possession is not.

12.64 Duty advisers will still need to try to resist applications for permission to transfer proceedings to the High Court when a possession order is made. What is not known is whether it will still be sufficiently quicker to enforce in the High Court and therefore whether applications to transfer will be as common as they used to be. At the time of writing, we have not seen these procedures in action.

12.65 The previous position (with the lack of requirement for notice to the defendant) used to be a staple argument to resist the application for permission. The fact that notice was not given to tenants meant that many judges would not grant permission for the transfer, especially in cases where there were children or vulnerabilities in the household. That argument is not available now. Duty advisers will need to argue that the speed of enforcement (if that remains a factor) and the costs of enforcement (which the claimant may seek to recover from the defendant) mean that it would not be just to allow the transfer.

12.66 This issue is discussed further below, where we set out the advice to be given to a defendant where permission has been given for transfer to the High Court.

12.67 At the time of writing, the Public Health (Coronavirus) (Protection from Eviction) (England) Regulations 2021 SI No 15 have been brought into force essentially banning any eviction (with exceptions) from residential accommodation in England between 17 November 2020 and 21 February 2021. Government guidance and legislation is rapidly changing in this area. At the time of writing, the country is in lockdown and there may be changes to possession cases and evictions.

Advice to defendant when a possession order is made

Advice where a conditional possession order is made

12.68 Where a conditional possession order is made, then the defendant is not facing an immediate threat of a warrant or writ for eviction being issued because if they keep to the conditions of the order then the claimant may not apply for eviction. A defendant in that position should still be advised as to the possibility of a warrant or writ being issued if they breach the terms of the order, and what that means.

12.69 In essence that will involve advising the defendant that if they breach the terms of the order – even if, for example, only by being £1 short or being one day late with a payment – then the claimant has the absolute right to apply for a warrant without any further notice to the defendant and, in rent arrears cases, without needing any permission from the court.

12.70 A balance needs to be drawn in advice between stressing the importance of complying with the conditions strictly, but also indicating to the defendant that if there are minor breaches then keeping in contact with their landlord may well mean that minor breaches will be overlooked. The ability and judgement to be able to effectively draw that balance is something that a duty adviser gains with experience.

12.71 Permission is required if the possession was made on anti-social behaviour grounds or the possession order was made more than six years prior. A warrant itself is valid for 12 months, and may be renewed by the court after 12 months.

12.72 The defendant can be advised that they may be able to apply to suspend or set aside the writ or warrant and the procedure for doing so. However, it is also very important to urge the defendant to do one or more of the following if they anticipate breaching the order or find that they have breached the order, or just have difficulties in meeting the terms of the order:

- Speak to the landlord as soon as possible, explain the situation and see if the landlord will agree to new terms or not to enforce the possession order – the defendant should make a note of the time and date and content of any such conversation.
- Try to make good the breach of the order as soon as possible – stay in contact with the landlord and let them know that has been done.
- If necessary, apply to the court to vary the conditional order, if for example the payment terms become unaffordable but affordable payments terms can be suggested in their place – the court will generally give a defendant credit for being proactive and explaining their situation on an application to vary a conditional order over a defendant who is applying to suspend a warrant or writ. See chapter 13 below.

Advice where an outright possession order is made

12.73 There is nothing to prevent a defendant from continuing to keep in contact with their landlord to try to persuade them not to enforce an outright possession order, and defendants should be advised to do so.

12.74 If an outright possession order is made on discretionary grounds, then the defendant has an unqualified right to apply to set aside or suspend the possession order. While a change in circumstances is not necessary to get a hearing on such an application, it will of course vastly improve the prospect of the application if the defendant can show a change of circumstances since the possession order was made to justify preventing the landlord from enforcing their order. There is no reason why the order itself should not be the subject of an application to vary to a conditional order but it will be for the judge to decide the outcome.

12.75 If an outright order is made on mandatory grounds, then while there are circumstances in which the court may say it does not have the jurisdiction to stay, set aside or suspend a warrant or writ (see HA 1980 s89) in practice if the defendant lodges an application then the court will have to list and hear it.

High Court writs

12.76 Claimants who are awarded an outright possession order in the county court may apply for permission to transfer the claim to the High Court for enforcement. Claimants have generally applied for such permission, despite the higher costs of enforcement in the High Court, because it has traditionally been much quicker to enforce by way of a writ of possession executed by High Court Enforcement Officers than by a county court bailiff's warrant.

12.77 Where permission is granted, duty advisers will need to advise defendants that they must look out for the notice of execution of a writ which will give them 14 days' notice of the date that High Court Enforcement Officers will attend, and will set out their right to apply to the court. The defendant should be advised that an application to stay or suspend the writ for possession must be made to the High Court. Housing Possession Court Duty Scheme (HPCDS) duty advisers will not see those cases on duty.

CHAPTER 13

Set aside and variation applications

Key points

- The duty list may include the hearings of applications made by the claimant or the defendant in ongoing proceedings.
- In this chapter we deal with applications that the defendant may have made and application defendants may want to make in the future, if their circumstances change.
- It is important to advise defendants who have any kind of conditional order made against them that if in the future they are struggling to meet the terms of the order, they have the right to make and should strongly consider making an application to vary the terms.
- If there are disputed facts, it will be important to see whether or not the landlord or representative is in a position to prove their case evidentially, ie as to service of notices etc.

Introduction

13.1 Where a possession order has been made (outright, postponed or suspended), it is possible in appropriate cases to apply to set aside the order or to vary the order. Such applications may come up on duty lists for the duty adviser to assist with but the duty adviser must also be ready to provide advice to defendants on their right to apply in certain circumstances, particularly if they struggle to meet the terms of a conditional order and need to vary the amount to be paid.

13.2 In relation to set aside applications, it is important to note that such an application can only be made in certain circumstances. Broadly speaking, if the tenant was present at the hearing and disagrees with the outcome, then their remedy is to appeal the decision (see chapter 14) rather than apply to set aside the order (but also see 13.13 below).

Set aside – accelerated possession proceedings

13.3 Where a possession order has been made on the papers in accelerated possession proceedings, the tenant may apply to set aside the order as of right. This is because the order has been made without a hearing. Civil Procedure Rules 1998 (CPR) 3.3(5) provides that where an order is made without a hearing a party may apply to set it aside as of right.

13.4 A tenant in such a position may apply on practice form N244 to set aside the order within 14 days of receiving the order and the court must list the case for a hearing (CPR 55.19). Such a hearing is likely to be listed alongside possession cases covered by the Housing Possession Court Duty Scheme (HPCDS) in accordance with the Master of the Rolls Working Group on Possession Proceedings' 'Overall Arrangements for Possession Proceedings in England and Wales: "The Overall Arrangements" '.

13.5 For the duty adviser, the task is the same as if the matter was before the court for the first time. If there is an arguable defence then the adviser will either seek to set out that defence and invite the judge to summarily dismiss the claim because the defence is unanswerable or direct that a fully pleaded defence is filed and served within an appropriate time-frame.

Set aside – other proceedings

13.6 In other possession cases where a possession order has been made and the tenant has applied to set aside the possession order, the first question for a duty adviser is whether the possession order was made at a trial of the claim (ie a hearing following directions and allocations to track) or at a hearing before trial.

13.7 If the order was made at trial, then the three-stage test set out at CPR 39.3(5) applies. The question is whether the tenant:

a) acted promptly when they found out that the court had made an order against them;
b) had a good reason for not attending the trial; and
c) has a reasonable prospect of success at a trial.

13.8 All three requirements must be in place for such an application to be granted.

13.9 If the order was not made at trial, then the court has a much wider discretion to set aside the order.

13.10 In either case, if the requirements are made out, the task for the duty adviser is to either seek to set out the defence and invite the judge to summarily dismiss the claim or to allow the application on the basis that there is an arguable case and to direct that a fully pleaded defence is filed and served within an appropriate time-frame.

13.11 There is nothing in the making of mandatory orders which prevents an application to set aside if the requirements are made out.

It is the prospect of success that is often the problem in mandatory cases.

Varying a possession order – outright order

13.12 An application to vary an outright possession order can only be made if the order was made on discretionary grounds. The purpose is to convert an outright order into a suspended or a postponed possession order.

13.13 An application of this kind will usually be made in one of two possible sets of circumstances:

1) The tenant did not attend the first possession hearing, an outright order was made and the tenant now wants the judge to exercise its discretion under Rent Act (RA) 1977 s100(2), Housing Act (HA) 1985 s85(2) or HA 1988 s9(2).
2) The tenant was present when an outright order was made but now has a change of circumstances and they want the court to consider their proposal for terms under which the order might be suspended or postponed or execution of the order suspended, again relying on the court's discretion under RA 1977 s100(2), HA 1985 s85(2) or HA 1988 s9(2).

13.14 In the first case, the duty adviser will need instructions as to what, if any, reason the tenant had for not attending the hearing where the possession order was made. Good reason is not a requirement as such, but judges will want to know in order to consider whether to exercise their discretion. After that, the considerations are the same as if it were a first hearing.

13.15 In the second example, it will be incumbent on the duty adviser to outline to the court the change in circumstances which now justifies the exercise of the court's discretion in contrast to the last occasion where the court declined to do so, but again once that is done the considerations and tactics are the same.

Varying the terms of a suspended or postponed possession order

13.16 It is an important right held by tenants and borrowers, who are subject to suspended or postponed possession orders, to be able to apply to the court to ask for the terms of the suspension of enforcement or postponing of the date or possession to be varied.

13.17 The terms may have been set when a tenant, borrower or other household member was working but that work may have come to an end. Entitlement to benefit may have reduced, leaving the household with less income than when the order was made.

13.18 In these circumstances, and if the terms of the order are not possible to comply with without significant hardship, then a tenant or borrower is strongly advised to apply to vary the terms to avoid any breach and enforcement action by the landlord. Judges are often impressed by a tenant or borrower who takes matter into their own hands in this way – and also often bemoan the fact that they don't if the matter comes before them as an application to suspend a warrant.

13.19 On such an application to vary the terms of an order, the job of the duty adviser is to:

- identify the change or changes in circumstances;
- work out an affordable payment plan; and
- try to negotiate that with the claimant.

When arguing the case before the judge, the basis of the court's discretion is the same as usual.

CHAPTER 14

Appeals

Key points

- Appeals against possession orders or other orders made in possession cases will not come up on duty lists.
- However, the duty adviser needs to be ready to recognise the possibility of an appeal and the right to an appeal so that they can advise defendants.
- The court records the hearing – so make representations as fully as possible as the transcript will be available for the appeal court.
- The duty adviser may wish to ask the judge to give permission to appeal, although it is always possible, and arguably better to apply for permission to appeal at a later date but within 21 days of the order being made.
- When asking for permission to appeal or advising a defendant on the possibility of an appeal, the duty adviser should first consider what it is that would be appealed – the decision not to adjourn the case, or a making of a possession order, or both.

Introduction

14.1 In some cases it will be necessary for the duty adviser to consider whether to advise the tenant that they might appeal the judge's decision. Generally, if the tenant was present at the hearing and disagrees with the outcome, then their remedy is to appeal the decision. The tenant will need to argue that the judge made an error of law or of procedure in making the possession order.

14.2 If the duty adviser considers that there has been an error in law or procedure in the making of an order, then they may ask the judge for permission to appeal at the hearing. It is also always possible to apply for permission to appeal at a later date but within 21 days of the order being made.

14.3 While this is a rare occurrence, the duty adviser needs to be alert to the possibility of an appeal in an appropriate case so that the tenant can be advised promptly. The time limits for an appeal are strict, and generally the tenant will need legal advice and if appropriate representation under legal aid in order to bring an appeal.

14.4 This means that if a tenant is going to appeal the outcome, then they will need to act quickly after the hearing. At the same time, a tenant needs to know as best as can be advised what the prospects of success on an appeal are going to be. A tenant would not be well advised to pursue an appeal that had no realistic prospects of success.

14.5 It is beyond the scope of this book to deal with appeals in possession proceedings and appeal procedure in great detail. We seek here to give an overview of some of the issues that duty advisers should be aware of when considering appeals.

The rules

14.6 Appeals in general are dealt with in Civil Procedure Rules 1998 (CPR) Part 52 and in the relevant practice directions (PDs) 52A and 52B.

14.7 CPR 52.3 and PD 52A 4.1 confirm that permission to appeal is required, but that permission may be sought from the court making the decision (ie from the judge at the hearing) or from the appeal court. In most cases there will be little point in seeking permission from the judge making the order. The only exception might be where it is clear that the court accepts there is some ambiguity in the law which may need resolving by way of further argument on appeal. It should also be said that there is really little to lose in asking for permission and being refused.

14.8 CPR 52.6 sets out the test for permission being granted, requiring that:

a) the court considers that the appeal would have a real prospect of success; or
b) there is some other compelling reason for the appeal to be heard.

14.9 CPR 52.12 sets the time for an appeal to be lodged at 21 days unless directed by the lower court. The tenant needs to be advised of the deadline date as soon and as clearly as possible. The tenant should also be advised per CPR 52.16 that an appeal does not in-and-of-itself stop an order from being enforced and so an application to stay proceedings or otherwise stop the order from taking effect needs to be made alongside the appeal.

14.10 PD 52A Section III sets out the destinations of appeals. Appeals from a deputy district judge or district judge are to the circuit judge – see PD 52A 3.5 Table 1.

14.11 PD 52B is mostly concerned with the procedure for the appeal, but for our purposes it contains (at the end of the PD) a table setting out where an appeal must be issued.

14.12 Defendants being advised that they may consider an appeal must also be advised, as in any litigation, that there are costs risks associated with an appeal. Those costs risks may be mitigated if the tenant is able to get legal aid, but the risks must still be explained to the tenant.

14.13 County Courts Act 1984 s77(6) provides that the tenant may not appeal on an issue of fact if proceedings are based on discretionary grounds for possession, but an appeal may be brought regarding the exercise of that discretion. It is difficult to appeal such a decision, however, precisely because it involves the exercise of a discretion.

Potential grounds for an appeal

14.14 There follows a non-exhaustive list of the potential grounds for appeal:

- failure to properly apply CPR 55.8 and whether the claim is 'genuinely disputed on grounds that appear to be substantial'; in so doing, a failure to consider the nature and strength of any potential defence;
- failure to properly exercise the discretion to adjourn and/or grant directions;
- failure to take into account relevant factors/material evidence or, conversely, taking into account irrelevant factors, in the exercise of the court's discretion;
- failure to apply the CPR rules and/or PDs;
- failure to apply the primary legislation (eg obvious error in granting a possession order on ground 8 (Housing Act (HA) 1988 Sch 2) when it is accepted the arrears are one month's rent);
- failure to give reasons for a possession order.

CHAPTER 15

Warrants for possession

Key points

- Applications to suspend warrants for possession will arise on duty lists and are usually listed at the last moment – they often will appear on the list at the start of the day.
- It is important to remember that it is the defendant's application, and so it is for the duty adviser to commence the hearing and set out the defendant's case.
- We deal here with warrants because an application to suspend or set aside a writ of possession will be in the High Court or District Registry and therefore not on a duty list. Nevertheless, for the purposes of advising defendants the same principles apply.
- It is important to meet and speak with the claimant or their representative as soon as possible to help understand the case and to obtain the current position with, for example, arrears or perhaps whether there have been any anti-social behaviour complaints recently.
- In general, negotiation is only usually possible if the duty adviser can outline a seriously good argument for the warrant to be suspended, such as the arrears having been cleared. Usually a claimant will want to let the judge decide.
- If there are disputed facts, see whether or not the landlord or representative is in a position to prove their case evidentially.
- It is for the defendant to prove their case, as it is their application.
- It is possible to ask the court to adjourn an application to set aside or suspend a warrant in order to allow time for something to happen or for evidence to be obtained or persuade the court. However, the warrant application is often called by judges 'the last chance saloon'. You must use all your skills to be persuasive to get an adjournment.

Introduction

15.1 In the event an outright possession order is made, the duty adviser will need to advise the defendant that although the judge will have ordered that they are to give possession on a certain date, that is not the date they will be forced to leave the accommodation. The court has ordered that they must leave and if they can leave by that date they should. However, if they are not able to leave because they do not have anywhere else to go, or even that they simply will not leave, then they cannot be forced to leave on that day.

15.2 If they do not leave, then the landlord may apply to the court for an eviction warrant once the specified date for giving up possession has passed. For example, if the court makes a possession order in 14 days, the landlord can apply for a warrant on or after the 15th day by filing (but there is no need to serve the defendant) form N325 and paying the relevant fee. A date for eviction will then be set, and that is the date on which the defendant will be forced to leave the premises.

15.3 In some circumstances it may still be possible to apply to the court to stop the eviction and save the tenant's home. In this chapter we set out how to approach cases which come before the duty adviser, and also the advice that a duty adviser should give when a possession order is made. Advice about applications to set aside and vary orders as well as appeals appears at chapters 13 and 14 above.

Applications to stay, suspend and set aside warrants for possession

15.4 An application for suspension or stay of a warrant will usually be listed when the court has time – often before the main duty list. Under the Master of the Rolls Working Group on Possession Proceedings' 'Overall Arrangements for Possession Proceedings in England and Wales: "The Overall Arrangements" ', these applications will be listed either side of the 10 substantive hearings in the duty day or in the slots of substantive hearings that have been vacated by settlements.

15.5 Applications may be listed a few days before execution of the warrant or right up to the morning that the warrant was to be executed – with the bailiffs being told to hold until the outcome of the defendant's application. Occasionally the court will list after the date for execution of the warrant, stay the warrant in the meantime, and the landlord will need to re-apply if the tenant is not successful in their application.

15.6 'Stay' means to stop the execution of the warrant for a period of time or until further order of the court. A stay is sometimes necessary where the factual matrix of the case is in flux and the warrant needs to be stopped from being executed to see what happens. This may be the case where a benefits decision is expected or a job prospect is imminent.

15.7 'Suspend' means roughly the same as where a possession order is suspended. The warrant is suspended on certain conditions being fulfilled. If those conditions are adhered to then the warrant remains suspended, but if there is a breach then the claimant is entitled to apply for a new date for the warrant to be executed (which in turn the defendant could apply to stay, suspend or set aside).

15.8 'Set aside' means roughly the same as when a possession order is set aside. The warrant no longer has any force and the claimant would have to apply for a new warrant if they felt they were still entitled to enforce the possession order. Setting aside a warrant will generally only be possible if there was procedural irregularity of some kind in the issuing of the warrant.

15.9 Ideally an application will formally include an application to suspend the warrant on terms and an application for a stay pending the final outcome of the application. Then if the matter cannot be resolved at the first hearing, the court can be asked to adjourn the application and stay the warrant until the next hearing, usually where some intervening event needs to take place so that the court can properly consider the position of the defendant. Courts are used to dealing with less than complete application notices and working out what is intended by the application.

15.10 The application is made on practice form N244 which gives the basic details of the case and includes a box for the defendant to set out their reasons for applying. On duty, the information provided in the application may be extensive and might even be set out in a separate statement and exhibits. On the other hand, the information may only extend to a line stating that the defendant wishes to stop the eviction.

15.11 Either way, the duty adviser must obtain quite a lot of information very quickly in order to ascertain the reasons as to why the landlord might be persuaded to agree the application (rare even with social landlords, but not unknown) or the court might be persuaded to stay, suspend or set aside the warrant.

15.12 As always with duty advice, a checklist is helpful and a form for warrant cases is provided in appendix 1.

15.13 The sorts of issues that a duty adviser may need to ascertain are not different from ones raised to prevent a possession order being made but the emphasis may need to be on what has changed since the making of the possession order or the breach of the conditional order. It will be important to show: (i) the effect of eviction on the defendant and their household and/or (ii) the defendant's ability to maintain their tenancy in the future if given an opportunity.

15.14 If it is not possible to get all the information required to make the case fully to suspend the warrant, then it is possible to ask for the application to be adjourned. It will usually be necessary to give an idea of what the position is likely to be on the next occasion and to point to some prospect of success on the application. It helps a great deal (and in many cases may be essential) if the defendant can offer to make relevant payments or other commitments during the period of the adjournment.

Statutory basis on which the court may stop an eviction from taking place

15.15 It is worth setting out here the statutory basis of the discretion of the court to stop an eviction from taking place.

15.16 In the case of Rent Act (RA) tenancies, the relevant legislation providing discretion to the court to suspend a warrant and to set conditions on the suspension is set out in RA 1977 s100(2):

> **100 Extended discretion of court in claims for possession of certain dwelling-houses.**
>
> (1) Subject to subsection (5) below, a court may adjourn for such period or periods as it thinks fit, proceedings for possession of a dwelling-house which is let on a protected tenancy or subject to a statutory tenancy.
>
> (2) On the making of an order for possession of such a dwelling-house, or at any time before the execution of such an order (whether made before or after the commencement of this Act), the court, subject to subsection (5) below, may–
> (a) stay or suspend execution of the order, or
> (b) postpone the date of possession,
> for such period or periods as the court thinks fit.
>
> (3) On any such adjournment as is referred to in subsection (1) above or any such stay, suspension or postponement as is referred to in subsection (2) above, the court shall, unless it considers that to do so would cause exceptional hardship to the tenant or would otherwise be unreasonable, impose conditions with regard to payment by the tenant of arrears of rent (if any) and rent or payments in respect of occupation after termination of the tenancy (mesne profits) and may impose such other conditions as it thinks fit.

15.17 In the case of secure tenancies, the relevant legislation providing discretion to the court to suspend a warrant and to set conditions on the suspension is set out in Housing Act (HA) 1985 s85(2):

> **85 Extended discretion of court in certain proceedings for possession.**
>
> (1) Where proceedings are brought for possession of a dwelling-house let under a secure tenancy on any of the grounds set out in Part I or Part III of Schedule 2 (grounds 1 to 8 and 12 to 16: cases in which the court must be satisfied that it is reasonable to make a possession order), the court may adjourn the proceedings for such period or periods as it thinks fit.
>
> (2) On the making of an order for possession of such a dwelling-house on any of those grounds, or at any time before the execution of the order, the court may–
>
> (a) stay or suspend the execution of the order, or
>
> (b) postpone the date of possession,
>
> for such period or periods as the court thinks fit.
>
> (3) On such an adjournment, stay, suspension or postponement the court–
>
> (a) shall impose conditions with respect to the payment by the tenant of arrears of rent (if any) and rent unless it considers that to do so would cause exceptional hardship to the tenant or would otherwise be unreasonable, and
>
> (b) may impose such other conditions as it thinks fit.

15.18 In the case of assured tenancies the relevant legislation providing discretion to the court to suspend a warrant to set conditions on the suspension is set out a HA 1988 s9(2):

> **9 Extended discretion of court in possession claims.**
>
> (1) Subject to subsection (6) below, the court may adjourn for such period or periods as it thinks fit proceedings for possession of a dwelling-house let on an assured tenancy.
>
> (2) On the making of an order for possession of a dwelling-house let on an assured tenancy or at any time before the execution of such an order, the court, subject to subsection (6) below, may–
>
> (a) stay or suspend execution of the order, or
>
> (b) postpone the date of possession,
>
> for such period or periods as the court thinks just.
>
> (3) On any such adjournment as is referred to in subsection (1) above or on any such stay, suspension or postponement as is referred to in subsection (2) above, the court, unless it considers that to do so would cause exceptional hardship to the tenant or would otherwise be unreasonable, shall impose conditions with regard to payment by the tenant of arrears of rent (if any) and rent and may impose such other conditions as it thinks fit.

(4) If any such conditions as are referred to in subsection (3) above are complied with, the court may, if it thinks fit, discharge or rescind any such order as is referred to in subsection (2) above.

(5) . . .

(5A) . . .

(6) This section does not apply if the court is satisfied that the landlord is entitled to possession of the dwelling-house–

(a) on any of the grounds in Part I of Schedule 2 to this Act; or

(b) by virtue of subsection (1) or subsection (4) of section 21 below.

15.19 It will be seen that the provision does not extend to cases where the possession order was granted pursuant to grounds other than where it had to be reasonable for a possession order to be made (discretionary cases). In relation to possession orders made or apparently made on mandatory grounds see 15.26 below.

Further issues at the warrant stage

15.20 In relevant cases, however, the discretion to stay or suspend the warrant is wide. A counterclaim can be raised as a reason to stay or suspend a warrant and there is no limit to the number of applications to suspend a warrant that can be made.

15.21 This means that if the court dismisses an application to suspend a warrant it is still possible for the defendant to make a further application, but this will only be advisable if there is a change of circumstances after the first dismissal. Sometimes a court will try to guard against multiple unmeritorious applications to suspend a warrant by putting a condition that any subsequent application must be subject to permission of the court. In practice, this makes little difference because the court would still have to consider a subsequent application for permission which would include all the same material as the application to suspend or stay itself.

15.22 It should also be borne in mind that the Court of Appeal in *Sheffield City Council v Hopkins* [2001] EWCA Civ 1023 decided that additional issues to those which made up the ground for possession could be raised where the defendant applies to suspend or stay the warrant. It follows that anti-social behaviour issues, for example, could be raised by the claimant as a reason not to suspend a warrant, even if the possession order was made only on the basis of rent arrears, or vice versa. The new issue may be dealt with summarily at the hearing of the defendant's application.

15.23 The defendant should have had notice of the allegations to be raised, and if they haven't, then that should at least give rise to an adjournment. Care also needs to be taken in this regard where there is potentially an Equality Act (EA) 2010 defence to the new material and in those circumstances it may be argued that the summary approach set out in *Sheffield* is not appropriate because EA 2010 defences have an element of complexity and the burden of proof can be reversed in some considerations of such a defence (see chapter 10 above).

Public law and human rights at the warrant/writ stage

15.24 Where the tenure or type of proceedings means that the discretion set out in RA 1977 s100, HA 1985 s85 or HA 1988 s9 is not available to the court then the defendants will need to rely on public law, Human Rights Act (HRA) 1998 and/or EA 2010 grounds to apply to set aside, stay or suspend the warrant.

15.25 The primary position arising from HA 1980 s89 is that outside of the statutory discretion set out above and in cases of mandatory possession orders then a defendant cannot apply to stay or suspend the warrant except to delay the possession order by no more than six weeks:

> **89 Restriction on discretion of court in making orders for possession of land.**
>
> (1) Where a court makes an order for the possession of any land in a case not falling within the exceptions mentioned in subsection (2) below, the giving up of possession shall not be postponed (whether by the order or any variation, suspension or stay of execution) to a date later than fourteen days after the making of the order, unless it appears to the court that exceptional hardship would be caused by requiring possession to be given up by that date; and shall not in any event be postponed to a date later than six weeks after the making of the order.

15.26 It is important to the check the wording of the possession order. For a possession order to be a mandatory possession order, the fact of it being made on mandatory grounds must be stated on the face of the order, otherwise it should be assumed to not be mandatory order – *Diab v Countrywide Rentals 1 plc* October 2001 *Legal Action* 15, (2001) *Independent* 5 November; 10 July 2001, unreported, ChD.

15.27 A decision to issue a warrant is the sort of decision that may be susceptible to a public law challenge. If the possibility of public law and/or human rights arguments arise at the hearing of an application to stay/suspend/set aside a warrant, then the duty adviser's job is to get time for the defendant to get legal advice. It therefore follows that where is a lack of clarity the duty adviser should set out what the public law and/or human rights point would look like and seek time for advice to be obtained and a fully argued case put before the court, with a stay of the warrant being ordered in the meantime.

15.28 The EA 2010 may be relevant in cases where the discretion to stay or suspend is present. In cases where that discretion is absent, the guidance we have is from the case of *Paragon Asra Housing Ltd v Neville* [2018] EWCA Civ 1712. Where the EA 2010 points were raised at trial and dealt with, then absent a material change in circumstances relevant to an EA 2010 proportionality assessment (see chapter 10 above), then those points cannot be argued again at the warrant stage. That of course leaves open the possibility to argue such points if they were not raised when the possession order was made or if there is a relevant material change in circumstances.

15.29 The key is to make the point that such an argument is possible and therefore the court should stay the warrant and adjourn to allow time for the defendant to get legal advice leading to a fully argued case. For all applications of this kind it is right and proper to argue that such an application needs more consideration than that allowed by a short hearing.

Applications for re-entry

15.30 We have seen from HA 1985 s85 and HA 1988 s9 set out above that the discretion to stay or suspend the warrant only exists up to the point at which the warrant is executed.

15.31 Once a possession order has been enforced by execution of the warrant, there are only two circumstances in which the defendant can apply to get back in to the property – where:

1) the defendant has an application which to set aside the possession order; or
2) there has been oppression or abuse of process in the execution of the warrant or the warrant was obtained by fraud.

15.32 The range of situations where there may be oppression or abuse of process are wide. The conduct amounting to oppression may be that of the court and court staff, as well as by the landlord and agents. Many cases where oppression or abuse of process has been made out concern the claimant's lack of communication to the tenant. Examples include where information to the defendant that the warrant was being applied for or an eviction proceeded with, when the claimant knew the defendant was not aware, or was under the impression, that the eviction was not proceeding. The decision to proceed with eviction, even once arrears are cleared, has been found to be oppressive.

15.33 An eviction was found to be oppressive when the defendant had written to the court in a simple letter saying she did not believe she should be evicted but the court staff had not referred this to the judge because it was not on or with an application notice.

15.34 Fraud cases will be rare, but they do occur, and duty advisers should be alert to the possibility.

CHAPTER 16

Housing Possession Court Duty Scheme and legal aid

Outline

16.1 The Housing Possession Court Duty Scheme (HPCDS) is emergency on-the-day assistance and advocacy to anyone who is at risk of losing their home. There are 105 schemes in the county court across England and Wales which are funded by the Legal Aid Agency (LAA). There are eight independent schemes not funded by legal aid – this chapter does not apply to those independent schemes.

16.2 The HPCDS provides for free legal advice and representation for anyone who is facing possession proceedings regardless of their finances. The assistance has to be given on the day of the 'review (R) date' or the 'substantive (S) hearing' for a claim for payment to be made.

16.3 To undertake work and receive payment within the scheme you must:

- hold a Standard Civil Contract (which governs the provision of face-to-face legal aid services) in the Housing and Debt categories (www.gov.uk/government/publications/standard-civil-contract-2018);
- hold an exclusive schedule under the terms of a 2013 Standard Civil Contract (as amended) for your scheme; and
- staff the scheme with appropriate advisers who conduct a minimum of 12 hours' casework per week.

16.4 The schedule sets out the allocated volume of acts of assistance for each court and provides for a 10 per cent buffer if you go over your allocation. If the limit is exceeded beyond the 10 per cent buffer, the LAA have confirmed that they will pay for all allowable work that is claimed so HPCDS is available to anyone who requires it.

16.5 All HPCDS contracts issued in 2018 are currently extended to 30 September 2021.

New guidance

16.6 On 20 September 2020, revised guidance from the LAA came into effect to reflect the new Master of the Rolls Working Group on Possession Proceedings' 'Overall Arrangements for Possession Proceedings in England and Wales: "The Overall Arrangements"' as a result of the COVID-19 pandemic: 'Housing Possession Court Duty Scheme: Guidance for Service Providers'. (The Overall Arrangements are available here: www.judiciary.uk/wp-content/uploads/2020/09/Possession-Proceedings-Overall-Arrangements-Version-1.0-17.09.20.pdf; and the guidance is available here: https://assets.publishing.service.gov.uk/

government/uploads/system/uploads/attachment_data/file/923187/Housing_Possession_Court_Duty_Scheme_Provider_Guidance_-_for_use_from_20th_September_2020_v5.pdf.)

16.7 The guidance must be read alongside the Overall Arrangements for how possession cases will operate. Details of the Overall Arrangements as at the time of writing are also set out in appendix 9, but you are required to be familiar with any updates which are likely to be available here: www.judiciary.uk/announcements/resumption-of-possession-cases/.

16.8 There is also a revised 'HPCDS client monitoring form' and a 'HPCDS contract report form (v1.6)' to be used from 20 September 2020. Both forms are available here: www.gov.uk/government/publications/housing-possession-court-duty-schemes-hpcds and the client monitoring form appears at appendix 2 below. Note: there is now no requirement to complete a proxy means test (prior to 20 September 2020 providers had to complete a means test for each client although the scheme was not means tested).

Operation of the scheme

16.9 As duty adviser you will be on duty during the times when the court schedules the possession list. This can be by attendance at the court or remotely by video or telephone hearing. From 20 September 2020, the court will list each possession case for a 'review (R) date' and, if required a 'substantive (S) hearing' date. Each court will have its own arrangements for listing possession cases. It is for the contract holder/provider to communicate regularly with the court to ensure attendance and facilitate the smooth running of the scheme.

16.10 On the day of the hearing, whether in person or remotely, you must offer the following services to all clients:

- advice before and after the hearing;
- advocacy;
- liaising with third parties – negotiating with landlords and lenders and assisting with negotiations of any payment plans if appropriate;
- making referrals for any follow-up work;
- sending an advice letter after the hearing.

Types of proceedings covered

16.11 The HPCDS covers:

- private rented proceedings;
- public/Registered Social Landlord (RSL) rented possession proceedings;
- mortgage possession proceedings;
- applications to stay or suspend execution of warrants of possession;
- charging orders on property where the client is at immediate risk of losing their home though a forced sale.

16.12 The fee is contained in the Civil Legal Aid (Remuneration) Regulations 2013 SI No 422 Sch 1 Table 6 – and is at the time of writing £75.60 plus VAT in London and £71.55 plus VAT outside of London.

16.13 You can advise and represent the same client at more than one hearing and receive payment for each – ie at the R date and S hearing and any subsequent adjournments. You will, however, not get paid for advising the client before a hearing date or in between the R date and S hearing or any subsequent hearings.

16.14 If the client has a substantive defence, then this should where possible be funded as certificated work and an appointment made to see the client at your offices or other remote location. If you sign the client up to the Legal Help Scheme within three months of the listed hearing, then you will not be able to claim for the HPCDS work at court (see 16.20 below). Any substantive work should be progressed by way of emergency legal aid under delegated functions if directions need to be complied with urgently.

Agents

16.15 Your HPCDS schedule sets out whether you can use agents in the delivery of the service. Please check Table 4 in your schedule. If the use of agents is permitted, those agents must fulfil the essential experience requirement of 12 hours of casework per week.

16.16 The LAA, recognising some of the challenges of the new arrangements, has said it would look to be permissive about new agency arrangements where applied for and that should be done through the organisation's contract manager.

Forms

16.17 For every client you represent at court – for both R date and S hearings – you must fill out a HPCDS monitoring form (see appendix 2 below) and send an advice letter confirming the outcome of the hearing. Both documents must be retained on file. Your LAA contract manager may ask for copies of these documents at your annual audit meeting.

Making a claim for payment

16.18 In order to make a claim for payment from the LAA, you must complete the HPCDS reporting spreadsheet: HPCDS Contract Report Form (currently v1.6).

16.19 The form has been amended to reflect the changes brought about by the Overall Arrangements. To report and claim payment for each client, all fields must be completed. Only one claim can be made where more than one client is being advised in relation to a single issue (joint tenants etc). Where no client was seen at a session, only one claim for payment can be made.

16.20 You cannot claim a duty fee and a fee for Legal Help if the client is seen and signs a Legal Help form within three months of the court representation. If you know the client has received Legal Help prior to submitting the HPCDS claim, you must indicate this on the spreadsheet. If you make a claim and subsequently advise the client under the Legal Help scheme within three months of the hearing claimed for, then you should notify the LAA of the need to amend the report by emailing: HousingPossessionCourtDuty@justice.gov.uk. The Provider Assurance team at the LAA will amend the report and recoup the fee.

16.21 If you progress the case by way of Legal Help then, although you can't claim the duty fee, you can claim for the time spent at court towards the Legal Help case and the time will count towards the escape fee threshold.

16.22 You can make a claim for disbursements, but these are limited to the cost of making a call to the client ie at the R date. The guidance states you cannot claim for travel costs or the cost of purchasing a mobile phone or a Zoom subscription to facilitate the R date contact with the client, but the LAA has made one-off payments to contract holders to assist with telephony costs due to the new Overall Arrangements.

16.23 If you do not see a client at the duty session (ie no clients want help or don't show up) a claim for a 'nil session' can be made. The guidance provides that with the new arrangements there can be multiple claims if more than one adviser was available on the duty date – ie one duty adviser for the R date and one for the S hearing. If the court splits the day into two sessions, as is usual for most courts, and the contracted organisation deploys two advisers for the R date and the S hearing, then in appropriate circumstances a total of four 'nil shows' can be claimed: two in the morning and two in the afternoon.

16.24 The guidance suggests that the report (which triggers the claim) should be submitted electronically to the LAA by the 10th of each following month to: HousingPossessionCourtDuty@legalservices.gsi.gov.uk. Although this is not an absolute deadline, the guidance suggests that the report must be submitted in a timely manner, with a cut-off period of six months from the date of the listed hearing. It will be important for the duty adviser to be up-to-date with their paperwork in order to ensure a prompt claim is made. Payment is usually received (if you make the claim by the 10th) before the end of the month.

APPENDICES[1]

1 The appendices contain material that is ©Crown Copyright and is up to date to February 2021. Readers are encouraged to check gov.uk to ensure they are referring to the latest versions of the material.

APPENDIX 1

Checklists

TENANT – POSSESSION DUTY DESK QUESTIONNAIRE	**R date:** **S date:**
Name:	Date of birth:
Address:	Disability ☐ Y ☐ N ☐ U/N Ethnicity: NINO:
Cohabitants, dates of birth and relationship:	
Landlord:	

Tenancy type:					
	Secure ☐	Demoted ☐	Notes
	Introductory ☐	Family intervention ☐	
	Non-secure ☐	Licence ☐	
	Assured ☐	Shorthold ☐	

Benefits/income			
	IS/JSA/PCG ☐	Working ☐	Notes
	ESA ☐	Self-employed ☐	
	PIP/DLA/AA ☐	Full-time ☐	
	WTC/CTC ☐	Part-time ☐	
	CB ☐	Zero hours ☐	
	UC ☐	Furlough ☐	

Rent:	Housing benefit/element	Shortfall
Arrears: As at notice	As at particulars of claim	Current

Notice received		
NOSP ☐	Yes ☐	Date served
NTQ ☐	No ☐	
NRP ☐	Unknown ☐	Date expired
NOPP ☐	Grounds	

Date proceedings issued	**Any agreements made**

Health problems/COVID-19 effects (health and financial)

Disrepair/housing conditions/other issue

OUTCOME			
Adjourned generally ☐	Date by which to restore:	Adjourned on terms ☐	Dismissed ☐
Adjourned to first open date ☐	Date for possession:	Suspended possession order ☐	Postponed possession order ☐
Outright possession order ☐		Terms	First payment:
Judgment for arrears £	Costs £	Current rent plus £ per week/month	And thereafter:

TENANT – WARRANT DUTY DESK QUESTIONNAIRE	**Date:**
Name:	Date of birth:
Address:	Disability | Y | N | U/N
	Ethnicity
	NINO

Cohabitants, dates of birth and relationship:
Landlord:

Tenancy type:	Secure ☐ Introductory ☐ Non-secure ☐ Assured ☐	Demoted ☐ Family intervention ☐ Licence ☐ Shorthold ☐	Notes
Benefits/income	IS/JSA/PCG ☐ ESA ☐ PIP/DLA/AA ☐ WTC/CTC ☐ CB ☐ UC ☐	Working ☐ Self-employed ☐ Full-time ☐ Part-time ☐ Zero hours ☐ Furlough ☐	Notes

Health problems/COVID-19 effects (health and financial)
Disrepair/housing conditions/other issue

	Date	**Arrears**	**Terms**
Possession claim issued		£	£ per
Possession order		£	£ per
Application 1		£	£ per
Application 2		£	£ per
Application 3		£	£ per
Application 4		£	£ per
Application 5		£	£ per

OUTCOME

Adjourned to first open date:		Warrant suspended	Warrant set aside
Application dismissed		Terms £ per week/month	First payment:

MORTGAGE – POSSESSION DUTY DESK QUESTIONNAIRE				**R date:** **S date:**
Name:				Date of birth:
Address:				Disability | Y | N | U/N Ethnicity NINO
Cohabitants, dates of birth and relationship:		**COVID-19 effects (health and financial)**		
Employed?		Housing costs?		
Partner		Other regular expenses:		
About the loan				
Lender:				
Mortgage type:	*Repayment / Endowment / All monies charge / Interest-only / CCA / don't know* *1st charge / 2nd charge / re-mortgage / home-improvement / other*			
Amount borrowed: £		CMI: £		
Balance outstanding: £		Arrears: £		
Value of property: £		Remaining term:		
Norgan: £				
About other charges	**Loan 1**	**Loan 2**	**Loan 3**	
Lender and type:				
Amount:				
CMI:				
Any arrears:				
Remaining term:				
Outcome				
Adjourned to first open date:		**Suspended possession order**	**Dismissed**	
Outright possession order	**Date for possession** **First payment:**	**Terms**	**First payment:**	
Judgment for arrears **£**	**Costs**	**£ per month**	**And thereafter**	

<table>
<tr><td colspan="4">MORTGAGE – WARRANT DUTY DESK QUESTIONNAIRE</td><td colspan="4">Date:</td></tr>
<tr><td colspan="4">Name:</td><td colspan="4">Date of birth:</td></tr>
<tr><td colspan="4" rowspan="3">Address:</td><td>Disability</td><td>Y</td><td>N</td><td>U/N</td></tr>
<tr><td colspan="4">Ethnicity</td></tr>
<tr><td colspan="4">NINO</td></tr>
<tr><td colspan="4">Cohabitants, dates of birth and relationship:

Employed?</td><td colspan="4">COVID-19 effects (health and financial)

Housing costs?</td></tr>
<tr><td colspan="4">Partner</td><td colspan="4">Other regular expenses:</td></tr>
<tr><td colspan="8">About the loan</td></tr>
<tr><td colspan="8">Lender:</td></tr>
<tr><td colspan="2" rowspan="2">Mortgage Type:</td><td colspan="6">Repayment / Endowment / All monies charge / Interest-only / CCA / don't know</td></tr>
<tr><td colspan="6">1st charge / 2nd charge / re-mortgage / buy-to-let/ home-improvement / other</td></tr>
<tr><td colspan="4">Amount borrowed: £</td><td colspan="4">CMI: £</td></tr>
<tr><td colspan="4">Balance outstanding: £</td><td colspan="4">Arrears: £</td></tr>
<tr><td colspan="4">Value of property: £</td><td colspan="4">Remaining term:</td></tr>
<tr><td colspan="4">Norgan: £</td><td colspan="4"></td></tr>
<tr><td colspan="2">About other charges</td><td colspan="2">Loan 1</td><td colspan="2">Loan 2</td><td colspan="2">Loan 3</td></tr>
<tr><td colspan="8">Lender and type:</td></tr>
<tr><td colspan="8">Amount:</td></tr>
<tr><td colspan="8">CMI:</td></tr>
<tr><td colspan="8">Any arrears:</td></tr>
<tr><td colspan="8">Remaining term:</td></tr>
<tr><td colspan="2"></td><td colspan="2">Date</td><td colspan="2">Arrears</td><td colspan="2">Terms</td></tr>
<tr><td colspan="2">Possession claim issued</td><td colspan="2"></td><td colspan="2">£</td><td colspan="2">£ per</td></tr>
<tr><td colspan="2">Possession order</td><td colspan="2"></td><td colspan="2">£</td><td colspan="2">£ per</td></tr>
<tr><td colspan="2">Application 1</td><td colspan="2"></td><td colspan="2">£</td><td colspan="2">£ per</td></tr>
<tr><td colspan="2">Application 2</td><td colspan="2"></td><td colspan="2">£</td><td colspan="2">£ per</td></tr>
<tr><td colspan="2">Application 3</td><td colspan="2"></td><td colspan="2">£</td><td colspan="2">£ per</td></tr>
<tr><td colspan="8">OUTCOME</td></tr>
<tr><td colspan="3">Adjourned to first open date:</td><td colspan="3">Warrant suspended</td><td colspan="2">Warrant set aside</td></tr>
<tr><td colspan="2">Application dismissed</td><td></td><td colspan="3">Terms

£ per ....</td><td colspan="2">First payment:</td></tr>
</table>

APPENDIX 2

Housing Possession Court Duty Scheme – client monitoring form

HPCDS client monitoring form, Version 8, 20 September 2020, Legal Aid Agency; available from: www.gov.uk/government/publications/housing-possession-court-duty-schemes-hpcds.

HOUSING POSSESSION COURT DUTY SCHEME – CLIENT MONITORING FORM

Case Information

Listing County Court:			Organisation giving advice:	
Court room number (where multiple courts are in use. Select 'R' for Review hearing):			Name of individual giving advice:	
Alternative Hearing Venue (including any off site location and Nightingale Court):			Agent or Third Party (Y/N):	
Date of Session:			Case reference:	
Type of listing – Review or Substantive:			Time spent on this case:	
Session duration	Morning		Afternoon	
Advice method – in person or remote				
Disbursements (please specify the amount and nature for each individual disbursement. Inclusive of VAT):	1. 2.			

Client information

Forename		Surname		Date of Birth	
National Insurance Number					

(NB. If the client does not have their national insurance number then please leave this field blank.)

Equal Opportunities Monitoring

Please tick the boxes which your client would describe themselves as being:

Gender

Male		Female		Prefer not to say	

Ethnic Monitoring

White	British		Asian or Asian British	Indian	
	Irish			Pakistani	
	Other White background			Bangladeshi	
Mixed	White and Black Caribbean			Other Asian background	
	White and Black African		Black or Black British	Caribbean	
	White and Asian			African	
	Other Mixed background			Other Black background	
Chinese			Other		
Gypsy/Traveller			Prefer not to say		

Disability Monitoring

The Disability Discrimination Act defines disability as: a physical or mental impairment which has a substantial and long-term adverse effect on a persons ability to carry out normal day-to-day activities.

Not considered disabled	

If a client considers himself or herself to have a disability please select the most appropriate definition. If the client has multiple disabilities please select the definition that reflects the predominant disability.

Mental Health Condition		Visually Impaired	
Mobility Impairment		Blind	
Learning Disability/Difficulty		Long-standing Illness/Health condition	
Deaf		Other	
Hearing Impaired		Unknown	
		Prefer not to say	

Completion of this section is voluntary. This will be treated in the strictest confidence and will be used purely for statistical monitoring and research.

Type of proceedings *(Please tick one proceedings type)*

Possession Proceedings	
Warrant Applications	
Orders for Sale	

Tenure *(Please tick one type of tenure)*

Tenant – Local Authority		Tenant – Private	
Tenant – Social Landlord		Mortgage	

Outcome of listed hearing (whether review or substantive)

Please tick the option that best describes the outcome of the case for the client.

<table>
<tr><td rowspan="10">Possession Proceedings</td><td>Withdrawn by claimant</td><td></td><td rowspan="4">Applications to stay or suspend warrants of eviction</td><td>Dismissed</td><td></td></tr>
<tr><td>Dismissed</td><td></td><td>Stayed/suspended</td><td></td></tr>
<tr><td>Adjourned on terms</td><td></td><td>Adjourned</td><td></td></tr>
<tr><td>Adjourned – fixed period</td><td></td><td>Moved from Review to Substantive</td><td></td></tr>
<tr><td>Postponed possession order</td><td></td><td></td><td>Other</td><td></td></tr>
<tr><td>Suspended possession order</td><td></td><td rowspan="3">Orders for Sale</td><td>Granted</td><td></td></tr>
<tr><td>Outright Order</td><td></td><td>Refused</td><td></td></tr>
<tr><td>Time order</td><td></td><td>Moved from Review to Substantive</td><td></td></tr>
<tr><td>Moved from Review to Substantive</td><td></td><td></td><td>Other</td><td></td></tr>
<tr><td>Other</td><td></td><td></td><td></td><td></td></tr>
</table>

Did your organisation progress this case to Legal Help?

Yes		No	

APPENDIX 3

Consent order – R date

Consent order
('R' date)

In the County Court at …………………	
Claim No.	……………………
Claimant (including ref.)	………………………
Defendant (including ref.)	……………………

Before [Deputy] District Judge ………………… sitting at …………………County Court,

UPON the Defendant having received advice on the 'R' date from the duty adviser.

AND UPON the judge having considered the papers on the 'R' date

AND BY CONSENT of the parties it is hereby ORDERED that

1 The claim shall be adjourned to the first open date after ………………… days/weeks with a time estimate of ……….. minutes

2 [In the meantime the defendant shall pay current rent plus £………………. per week/month to the rent account, the first payment being due on …… ……………………………]

3 The 'S' hearing listed for …………………… shall be vacated

4 No order as to costs/costs in claim

Dated:

Signed:

For the Claimant [or confirmation of agreement to be provided by separate email]	For the Defendant [or confirmation of agreement to be provided by separate email]
……………………………………………………	……………………………………………………

Consent order
('R' date)

In the County Court at	
Claim No.	....
Claimant (including ref.)	....
Defendant (including ref.)	....

Before [Deputy] District Judge .... sitting at ....County Court,

UPON the Defendant having received advice on the 'R' date from the duty adviser.

AND UPON the judge having considered the papers on the 'R' date

AND BY CONSENT of the parties it is hereby ORDERED that

1 The defendant shall file and serve their Defence [and Counterclaim] by no later than 4 pm ....

2 The claimant shall if so advised file and serve their Reply to Defence [and Defence to Counterclaim] by no later than 4 pm ....

3 Directions Questions shall be sent to any unrepresented party and the parties shall file and serve Directions Questionnaires by no later than 4 pm ....

4 The 'S' hearing listed for .... shall be vacated

5 No order as to costs/costs in claim

Dated :

Signed:

For the Claimant
[or confirmation of agreement to be provided by separate email]

....

For the Defendant
[or confirmation of agreement to be provided by separate email]

....

Consent order
('R' date)

In the County Court at	
Claim No.	....
Claimant (including ref.)	....
Defendant (including ref.)	....

Before [Deputy] District Judge .... sitting at ....County Court,

UPON the Defendant having received advice on the 'R' date from the duty adviser.

AND UPON the judge having considered the papers on the 'R' date

AND BY CONSENT of the parties it is hereby ORDERED that

1. The claim shall be adjourned generally with permission to restore on terms that the defendant do pay current rent plus £.................... per week/month to the rent account, the first payment being due on .... [and thereafter on ....]
2. The 'S' hearing listed for .... shall be vacated
3. No order as to costs

Dated :

Signed:

For the Claimant [or confirmation of agreement to be provided by separate email]	For the Defendant [or confirmation of agreement to be provided by separate email]
....	....

APPENDIX 4

Specimen letters

Tenancy instructions – S hearing

I write further to your attendance on....................at....................County Court and write to confirm the outcome of your case.

I am aware that you obtained/did not obtain advice on the R date of this claim for possession.

Your instructions

I confirm your instructions that you have had a....................tenancy with....................since....................

You live with

You are employed earning around £

You are claiming

Your rent is £....................per week/month

You receive housing benefit/housing element of universal credit of £....................leaving a shortfall of £....................

You received/denied receiving/were unsure whether you received a notice ....dated....................when there were arrears of rent of £

As at the date of the particulars of claim there were arrears of rent of £

As at the date of the hearing the arrears stood at £

[The [other] reason the landlord is claiming possession is....................]

In relation to health problems you told me

In relation to conditions in your home you told me

The arrears of rent arose because

[The case had been in court before. This hearing was the [second/third] hearing of your application to suspend a warrant for eviction.]

Mortgage instructions – S hearing

I write further to your attendance on....................at....................County Court and write to confirm the outcome of your case.

I am aware that you obtained/did not obtain advice on the R date of this claim for possession.

Your instructions

I confirm your instructions that you have had a mortgage with....................since ....

I can confirm that:

1. You borrowed: £....................
2. The balance outstanding is: £....................
3. The current monthly instalment is: £....................
4. You have arrears of: £....................
5. You believe the property is valued at: £....................

I am not aware of any other loans secured against your property. / You have another loan/other loans secured against your home with....................and to which you pay £....................per month

You live with

You are employed earning around £....................per month net

Your partner is employed earning £....................per month net

You have a combined household income of around £....................per month net

You are claiming

You are also claiming Support for Mortgage Interest/Help with mortgage interest through universal credit and you receive payments of £.................... leaving a monthly shortfall of £....................

The mortgage arrears developed because

Tenancy outcomes – Adjourned generally

The outcome of the hearing

An order for possession was not made but rather your case has been adjourned generally. The landlord has permission to restore the proceedings, if for example the arrears go up again, but if they do not restore the proceedings by....................then the proceedings will be struck out.

What happens next?

Your case has been adjourned generally. This means that as long as you continue to pay the rent and abide by the terms of the tenancy agreement the case should not return to court.

If you receive help of any kind with your rent you must ensure that remains in payment and if there is any shortfall between your help with the rent and the rent you have to pay, you must make up the difference.

It is sensible to remain in regular contact with your landlord to ensure that your rent account is in good order.

Tenancy outcomes – Adjourned on terms

The outcome of the hearing

Your case has been adjourned generally on terms. The landlord has permission to restore the proceedings, if for example the arrears go up again, but if they do not restore the proceedings by...................then the proceedings will be struck out.

What happens next?

The court has ordered that you must pay £...................against the arrears every week/month and that you must also pay your rent every week/month.

The first payment is to be made on or by...................and each................... after that.

Your case has been adjourned generally on these terms. This means that as long as you keep to the terms the case should not return to court.

If you were to breach the terms of the adjournment, even if only once or by a small amount then your opponent would be entitled to apply to the court for a new hearing date at which the claim for possession would be considered again. You would receive notice of this hearing, but I strongly recommend that you keep to the terms and avoid the matter coming back to court.

If you receive help of any kind with your rent you must ensure that remains in payment and if there is any shortfall between your help with the rent and the rent you have to pay, you must make up the difference.

You may wish to seek help with that from ....

It is sensible to remain in regular contact with your landlord to ensure that your rent account is in good order.

If it becomes difficult to keep to the terms for the order and you want to propose different terms, you should talk to your landlord, and as long as you have sensible alternative proposals it would be preferable to make an application to the court to vary the terms rather than waiting for things to go wrong.

Tenancy outcomes – Adjourned on terms to a new date

The outcome of the hearing

I negotiated with the landlord/representative who attended on behalf of your landlord. They were prepared to adjourn the proceedings to the first open date after...........days but only on terms that you pay your rent plus £.......each week/month off the arrears. I advised you that in the circumstances the offer to adjourn was reasonable and I advised you to accept the terms.

The adjournment is to allow time for you to

You agreed to accept the terms.

As the matter was agreed the judge was happy to make that order.

Your case has been adjourned to the first open date after....................on terms that you pay your rent plus £....................per week.

What happens next?

The court has ordered that you must pay £....................against the arrears every week/month and that you must also pay your rent every week/month.

The first payment is to be made on or by...........and each...........after that.

If you receive help of any kind with your rent you must ensure that remains in payment and if there is any shortfall between your help with the rent and the rent you have to pay, you must make up the difference.

Your case has been adjourned to the first open date as indicated above. The court will find the first available date in which your case can be listed. The court will write to you and let you know the time and the date of the next hearing.

The case has been adjourned in order that any outstanding issues regarding .... can be resolved. This is so that the court can properly assess your case on the next occasion. It is therefore essential that you make all possible efforts to resolve the outstanding issues in your case. You must at least be in a position to tell the court what efforts you have made to resolve these issues by the time of the next hearing. Keep a note of what you are doing to resolve things

You may wish to seek help with that from

It is sensible to remain in regular contact with your landlord to ensure that they know of the efforts you are making and they may be able to help you with that.

If it becomes difficult to keep to the terms for the order and you want to propose different terms you should talk to your landlord and as long as you have sensible alternative proposals it would be preferable to make an application to the court to vary the terms rather than waiting for things to go wrong.

Tenancy outcomes – Suspended possession order

The outcome of the hearing

An order for possession has been made but it has been suspended on terms that you pay your rent plus £..............per week/month.

The first payment is to be made on or by..............and each..............after that.

A money judgment for the arrears of £..............and an order for the landlord's court costs of £..............have also been suspended on the same terms.

What happens next?

The court has ordered that in order to stay in your home you must pay £...................against the arrears every week/month and that you must also pay your rent every week/month.

If you do not keep to this order it is likely that your landlord will apply to the court for you to be evicted.

If you were to miss even one week then the landlord would be entitled to ask the bailiffs to issue a warrant for eviction with no further notice to yourself. It is therefore very important that you make your payments weekly/monthly and strictly on time.

Important – Clearly it is in your best interests to keep to the terms of the order as your home will be at serious risk if you do not. If you were to miss even one payment then the landlord would be entitled to write to you and then apply to the court.

If for reasons outside of your control you are not able to make a payment you should make contact with your landlord to explain why and keep a record of having contacted them.

If you receive help of any kind with your rent you must ensure that remains in payment and if there is any shortfall between your help with the rent and the rent you have to pay, you must make up the difference.

You may wish to seek help with that from

It is sensible to remain in regular contact with your landlord to ensure that your rent account is in good order. If there is any problem then it is still sensible to keep in touch with your landlord to explain what the problem is. Your landlord may be able to help and/or may hold off taking action if they know you are trying to sort things out.

If it becomes difficult to keep to the terms for the order and you want to propose different terms you should talk to your landlord and as long as you have sensible alternative proposals it would be preferable to make an application to the court to vary the terms rather than waiting for things to go wrong.

Tenancy outcomes – Postponed possession order

The outcome of the hearing

An order for possession has been made but it has been postponed on terms that you pay your rent plus £....................per week/month.

The first payment is to be made on or by....................and each.................... after that.

A money judgment for the arrears of £...............and an order for the landlord's court costs of £...............have also been suspended on the same terms.

What happens next?

The court has ordered that you must pay £....................against the arrears every week/month and that you must also pay your rent every week/month.

Once you have paid off all of the rent arrears the order will cease to be enforceable.

If you do not keep to this order, your landlord is likely to write to you giving notice that you have breached the terms of the order and that they intend to apply to the court for an order fixing the date for possession and asking you to reply to the letter.

The landlord can then make that application to the court not less than 14 days and not more than 3 months after writing to you. You would have notice of that application. Normally the court will consider the landlord's application without a hearing but a hearing can be fixed if the court believes it is necessary. You would need to make it necessary by letting the court know you oppose the application and why.

If the landlord writes to you in this way you can apply to the court for a further postponement of the date the date for possession or to stay or suspend enforcement of the possession order. You would need to either dispute that you have breached the terms of the order or explain why the order has been breached.

If the court intends to fix the date for possession it will fix the date as the next working day. Your tenancy will end on that date. Once the date for possession has been fixed, your landlord can then request that the court bailiffs evict you from your home.

Important – Clearly it is in your best interests to keep to the terms of the order as your home will be at serious risk if you do not. If you were to miss even one payment, then the landlord would be entitled to write to you and then apply to the court.

If for reasons outside of your control you are not able to make a payment, you should make contact with your landlord to explain why and keep a record of having contacted them.

If you receive help of any kind with your rent, you must ensure that remains in payment and if there is any shortfall between your help with the rent and the rent you have to pay, you must make up the difference.

You may wish to seek help with that from

It is sensible to remain in regular contact with your landlord to ensure that your rent account is in good order. If there is any problem then it is still sensible to keep in touch with your landlord to explain what the problem is. Your landlord may be able to help and/or may hold off taking action if they know you are trying to sort things out.

If it becomes difficult to keep to the terms for the order and you want to propose different terms, you should talk to your landlord, and as long as you have sensible alternative proposals it would be preferable to make an application to the court to vary the terms rather than waiting for things to go wrong.

Tenancy outcomes – Outright possession order

I am sorry but we were not able to persuade the judge to refrain from making an outright possession order.

The outcome of the hearing

An order for possession has been made. The order takes effect on. That is *not* the date you will be forced to leave the premises.

A money judgment for the arrears of £....................and an order for the landlord's court costs of £....................have also been made.

What happens next?

Once the possession order takes effect on....................the landlord can ask the court bailiffs to issue a warrant for eviction with no further notice to you.

The court bailiffs will write to you with at least 14 days' notice of the date when the eviction is set to take place. Unless you move out beforehand or apply to suspend the warrant, that is the date you will be evicted.

In some, but not all cases, you can apply for the eviction to be suspended, although such an application is only likely to be successful if there has been some change in circumstances since the possession hearing, for example clearing or significantly reducing the arrears and having proposals to bring or keep the rent account in order. That application would be made in the same county court, and details will be on the notice of the eviction date.

[The court ordered that enforcement be transferred to the High Court. That means that High Court Enforcement Officers will be instructed to apply for a writ of possession to enforce the order and carry out the eviction.

The High Court Enforcement Officers will write to you with at least 14 days' notice of the date when the eviction is set to take place. Unless you move out beforehand or apply to suspend the writ of possession, that is the date you will be evicted.

In some, but not all cases, you can apply for the eviction to be suspended although such an application is only likely to be successful if there has been some change in circumstances since the possession hearing, for example clearing or significantly reducing the arrears and having proposals to bring or keep the rent account in order. That application will need to be at the High Court or District Registry and details will be on the notice of the eviction date.]

Tenancy outcomes – Suspend warrant

The case had been in court before. The hearing on..............was the.............. hearing of your application to suspend a warrant for your eviction.

The outcome of the hearing

The judge agreed that the warrant should be suspended on terms that you pay your rent plus £....................per week/month off the arrears.

What happens next?

The court has ordered that the warrant should be suspended on terms that you must pay £....................against the arrears every week/month and that you must also pay your rent.

The first payment should be made by....................and payments thereafter must be made on the....................of each week/month.

If you do not keep to this order it is likely that your landlord will apply again to the court for you to be evicted.

If you were to miss even one week or be short by even £1, then the landlord would be entitled to ask the bailiffs to set a new date for your eviction with no further notice to yourself.

It is therefore very important that you make your payments strictly by the terms set by the court.

Important – Clearly it is in your best interests to keep to the terms of the order as your home will be at serious risk if you do not.

If for reasons outside of your control you are not able to make a payment, you should make contact with your landlord to explain why and keep a record of having contacted them.

If you receive help of any kind with your rent, you must ensure that remains in payment and if there is any shortfall between your help with the rent and the rent you have to pay, you must make up the difference.

You may wish to seek help with that from

It is sensible to remain in regular contact with your landlord to ensure that your rent account is in good order. If there is any problem, then it is still sensible to keep in touch with your landlord to explain what the problem is. Your landlord may be able to help and/or may hold off taking action if they know you are trying to sort things out.

If it becomes difficult to keep to the terms for the order and you want to propose different terms, you should talk to your landlord, and as long as you have sensible alternative proposals it would be preferable to make an application to the court to vary the terms rather than waiting for things to go wrong.

Mortgage outcomes – Suspended possession order

[You had managed to reach]/[I negotiated] an agreement with your mortgage lender as to payment of the arrears being that you would pay the current monthly instalment plus £..................... per month to the arrears.

The outcome of the hearing

An order for possession has been made but it has been suspended on terms that you pay your current monthly instalment plus .... per month off the arrears.

The court granted a money judgement against you for the outstanding balance of £................

What happens next?

The court has ordered that you must pay £............ against the arrears every month and that you must also pay your current monthly instalment. Your monthly instalment is due on the .... of each month and first payment is to be on ....

The court ordered that there be listed a review hearing on or after 6 months' time. You will need to have further proposals for the court as to payments against the arrears.

If you do not keep to this order, it is likely that your mortgage lender will apply to the court for you to be evicted.

If you were to miss payment by even one day or be short in your payment by even one pound then the mortgage lender would be entitled to ask the bailiffs to issue a warrant for eviction with no further notice to yourself. It is therefore very important that you make your payments *in full, on time* and *every month.*

Mortgage outcomes – Suspend warrant

The case had been in court before. The hearing on....................was the hearing of your further application to suspend a warrant for your eviction.

The outcome of the hearing

The judge agreed that the warrant should be suspended on terms that you pay your current monthly instalment plus £....................per month off the arrears.

What happens next?

The court has ordered that the warrant should be suspended on terms that you must pay £....................against the arrears every month and that you must also pay your current monthly instalment. The first payment should be made by....................and payments thereafter must be made on the....................of each month.

If you do not keep to this order, it is likely that your mortgage lender will apply again to the court for you to be evicted.

If you were to miss even one week or be short by even £1, then the mortgage lender would be entitled to ask the bailiffs to issue a warrant for eviction with no further notice to yourself. It is therefore very important that you make your payments strictly by the terms set by the court.

Mortgage outcomes – Outright possession order

I am sorry but we were not able to persuade the judge to refrain from making an outright possession order.

The outcome of the hearing

An order for possession has been made. The order takes effect on ....

What happens next?

Once the possession order takes effect on .... the lender can ask the court bailiffs to issue a warrant for eviction with no further notice to you. The court bailiffs will write to you with at least 14 days' notice of the date when the eviction is set to take place. Unless you move out beforehand or apply to suspend the warrant, that is the date you will be evicted.

In some cases you can apply for eviction to be suspended, although such an application is only likely to be successful if there has been some change in circumstances since the possession hearing, for example clearing or significantly reducing the mortgage arrears and having proposals to bring or keep the mortgage account in order.

It is still possible for you to try to sell the property yourself. If you make progress with that, you may be able to apply for more time for the sale to go through by applying to stay the warrant.

APPENDIX 5

Pre-action protocols[1]

Pre-Action Protocol for Possession Claims based on Mortgage or Home Purchase Plan Arrears in Respect of Residential Property

The Pre-Action Protocol describes the actions mortgage tenders and borrowers should take to resolve disputes with payment arrears before court proceedings are issued.
30 January 2017

Contents

I INTRODUCTION

Definitions

1.1 In this Protocol–

(a) 'possession claim' means a claim for the recovery of possession of property under Part 55 of the Civil Procedure Rules 1998;
(b) 'home purchase plan' means a method of purchasing a property by way of a sale and lease arrangement that does not require the payment of interest;
(c) 'bank holiday' means a bank holiday under the Banking and Financial Dealings Act 1971;
(d) 'business day' means any day except Saturday, Sunday, a bank holiday, Good Friday or Christmas day; and
(e) 'authorised tenant' means a tenant whose tenancy is authorised as between the borrower and the lender.

Preamble

2.1 This Protocol describes the behaviour the court will normally expect of the parties prior to the start of a possession claim within the scope of paragraph 3.1 below.

2.2 This Protocol does not alter the parties' rights and obligations.

2.3 It is in the interests of the parties that mortgage payments or payments under home purchase plans are made promptly and that difficulties are resolved wherever possible without court proceedings. However in some cases an order for possession may be in the interest of both the lender and the borrower.

Aims

3.1 The aims of this Protocol are to–

(a) ensure that a lender or home purchase plan provider (in this Protocol collectively referred to as 'the lender') and a borrower or home purchase plan customer (in this Protocol collectively referred to as 'the borrower') act fairly and reasonably with each other in resolving any matter concerning mortgage or home purchase plan arrears;

(b) encourage greater pre-action contact between the lender and the borrower in order to seek agreement between the parties, and where agreement cannot be reached, to enable efficient use of the court's time and resources; and

(c) encourage lenders to check who is in occupation of the property before issuing proceedings.

3.2 Where either party is required to communicate and provide information to the other, reasonable steps should be taken to do so in a way that is clear, fair and not misleading. If the lender is aware that the borrower may have difficulties in reading or understanding the information provided, the lender should take reasonable steps to ensure that information is communicated in a way that the borrower can understand.

Scope

4.1 This Protocol applies to arrears on–

(a) first charge residential mortgages and home purchase plans regulated by the Financial Conduct Authority under the Financial Services and Markets Act 2000 (as amended by the Financial Services Act, 2012);

(b) second charge mortgages over residential property and other secured loans regulated under the Consumer Credit Act 1974 on residential property; and

(c) unregulated residential mortgages.

4.2 Where a potential claim includes a money claim and a possession claim, this protocol applies to both.

4.3 The protocol does not apply to Buy To Let mortgages.

II ACTIONS PRIOR TO THE START OF A POSSESSION CLAIM

Initial contact and provision of information

5.1 Where a borrower falls into arrears, the lender must provide the borrower with–

(a) where appropriate, the required regulatory information sheet or the National Homelessness Advice Service/Shelter/Cymru booklet on mortgage arrears;
(b) information on the current monthly instalments and the amounts paid for the last 2 years; and
(c) information on the amount of arrears, which should include–
 (i) the total amount of the arrears;
 (ii) the total outstanding of the mortgage or the home purchase plan; and
 (iii) whether interest or charges have been or will be added, and, where appropriate, details or an estimate of the interest or charges that may be payable.

5.2 The lender should also seek information about whether the property is occupied by an authorised tenant.

5.3 The lender must advise the borrower to make early contact with the housing department of the borrower's Local Authority and, should, where relevant refer the borrower to appropriate sources of independent debt advice.

5.4 The parties, or their representatives, must take all reasonable steps to discuss with each other the reasons for the arrears, the borrower's financial circumstances and proposals for repayment of the arrears (see paragraph 7.1). For example, parties should consider whether the reasons for the arrears are temporary or long-term, and whether the borrower may be able to pay the arrears in a reasonable time.

5.5 The lender must consider a reasonable request from the borrower to change the date of regular payment (within the same payment period) or the method by which payment is made. The lender must either agree to such a request or, where it refuses such a request, it must, within a reasonable period of time, give the borrower a written explanation of its reasons for the refusal.

5.6 The lender must respond promptly to any proposal for payment made by the borrower. If the lender does not agree to such a proposal it should give reasons in writing to the borrower within 10 business days of the proposal.

5.7 If the lender submits a proposal for payment, the borrower must be given a reasonable period of time in which to consider such proposals. The lender must set out the proposal in sufficient detail to enable the borrower to understand the implications of the proposal.

5.8 If the borrower fails to comply with an agreement, the lender should warn the borrower, by giving the borrower 15 business days notice in writing, of its intention to start a possession claim unless the borrower remedies the breach in the agreement.

Postponing the start of a possession claim

6.1 A lender must not consider starting a possession claim for mortgage arrears where the borrower can demonstrate to the lender that the borrower has–

(a) submitted a claim to–
   (i) the Department for Works and Pensions ('DWP') for Support for Mortgage Interest (SMI) or if appropriate Universal Credit; or
   (ii) an insurer under a mortgage payment protection policy; or
   (iii) a participating local authority for support under a Mortgage Rescue Scheme, or other means of homelessness prevention support provided by the local authority,
   (iv) and has provided all the evidence required to process a claim;
(b) a reasonable expectation of eligibility for payment from the DWP or from an insurer or support from the local authority or welfare or charitable organisation such as the Veterans Welfare Scheme or Royal British Legion;
(c) an ability to pay a mortgage instalment not covered by a claim to the DWP or the insurer in relation to a claim under paragraph 6.1(1)(a) or (b);
(d) difficulty in respect of affordability or another specific personal or financial difficulty, and requires time to seek free independent debt advice, or has a confirmed appointment with a debt adviser and
(e) a reasonable expectation, providing evidence where possible, of an improvement in their financial circumstances in the foreseeable future (for example a new job or increased income from a lodger).

6.2 If a borrower can demonstrate that reasonable steps have been or will be taken to market the property at an appropriate price in accordance with reasonable professional advice, the lender must consider postponing starting a possession claim to allow the borrower a realistic period of time to sell the property. The borrower must continue to take all reasonable steps actively to market the property where the lender has agreed to postpone starting a possession claim.

6.3 Where, notwithstanding paragraphs 6.1 an 6.2, the lender has agreed to postpone starting a possession claim, the borrower should provide the lender with a copy of the particulars of sale, the Energy Performance Certificate ('EPC') or proof that an EPC has been commissioned and (where relevant) details of purchase offers received within a reasonable period of time specified by the lender. The borrower should give the lender details of the estate agent and the conveyancer instructed to deal with the sale. The borrower should also authorise the estate agent and the conveyancer to communicate with the lender about the progress of the sale and the borrower's conduct during the process.

6.4 Where the lender decides not to postpone the start of a possession claim, it must inform the borrower of the reasons for this decision at least 5 business days before starting proceedings.

Further matters to consider before starting a possession claim

7.1 Starting a possession claim should be a last resort and must not normally be started unless all other reasonable attempts to resolve the situation have failed. The parties should consider whether, given the individual circumstances of the borrower and the form of the agreement, it is reasonable and appropriate to do one or more of the following–

(a) extend the term of the mortgage;
(b) change the type of mortgage;
(c) defer payment of interest due under the mortgage;
(d) capitalise the arrears; or
(e) make use of any Government forbearance initiatives in which the lender chooses to participate.

7.2 Where there is an authorised tenant in occupation of the property, at the possession hearing the court will consider whether–

(a) further directions are required;
(b) to adjourn the possession claim until possession has been recovered against the tenant; or
(c) to make an order conditional upon the tenant's right of occupation.

Complaints to the Financial Services Ombudsman

8.1 The lender must consider whether to postpone the start of a possession claim where the borrower has made a genuine complaint to the Financial Ombudsman Service ('FOS') about the potential possession claim.

8.2 Where a lender does not intend to await the decision of the FOS, it must give notice to the borrower, with reasons, that it intends to start a possession claim.

Pre-Action Protocol for Possession Claims by Social Landlords

This Pre-Action Protocol describes the actions social landlords, such as local authorities and housing associations, should take before issuing a possession claim against a tenant.

13 January 2020

Table of contents

PART I AIMS AND SCOPE OF THE PROTOCOL

1.1 This Protocol applies to residential possession claims in England and Wales brought by social landlords (such as local authorities and housing associations). This Part sets out the aims and scope of the protocol. Part 2 relates to claims which are based solely on rent arrears. Part 3 applies to claims brought by social landlords where the court must, in principle, grant possession and where s89(1) Housing Act 1980 applies. The protocol does not apply to claims in respect of long leases .

1.2 Part 2 reflects the guidance on good practice given to social landlords in the collection of rent arrears. It recognises that it is in the interests of both social landlords and tenants to ensure that rent is paid promptly and that difficulties are resolved, wherever possible, without court proceedings.

1.3 Part 3 seeks to ensure that, in cases where human rights, public law or equality law matters are or may be raised, the necessary information is before the Court at the first hearing so that issues of proportionality may be dealt with summarily, if appropriate, or that appropriate directions for trial may be given.

1.4 The aims of the protocol are:

(a) to encourage more pre-action contact and exchange of information between landlords and tenants;

(b) to enable the parties to avoid litigation by settling the matter, if possible; and

(c) to enable court time to be used more effectively if proceedings are necessary.

1.5 Courts should take into account whether this protocol has been followed when considering what orders to make. Social landlords should also comply with guidance issued from time to time by the Regulator of Social Housing, the Ministry for Housing, Communities and Local Government and, in Wales, the Welsh Ministers.

(a) If the landlord is aware that the tenant has difficulty in reading or understanding information given, the landlord should take reasonable steps to ensure that the tenant understands any information given. The landlord should be able to demonstrate that reasonable steps have been taken to ensure that the information has been appropriately communicated in ways that the tenant can understand.

(b) If the landlord is aware that the tenant is particularly vulnerable, the landlord should consider at an early stage–

  (i) whether or not the tenant has the mental capacity to defend possession proceedings and the extent to which CPR 21 applies;

  (ii) whether or not any issues arise under the Equality Act 2010; and

  (iii) in the case of a local authority landlord, whether or not there is a need for a community care assessment in accordance with the Care Act 2014.

PART 2 POSSESSION CLAIMS BASED UPON RENT ARREARS

Initial contact

2.1 If the tenant falls into arrears, the landlord should contact the tenant, as soon as reasonably possible, to discuss: the cause of the arrears; the tenant's financial circumstances; the tenant's entitlement to benefits; and repayment of the arrears. Where contact is by letter, the landlord should write separately to each named tenant.

2.2 The landlord and tenant should try to agree affordable sums for the tenant to pay towards the arrears, based upon the tenant's income and expenditure (where such information has been supplied in response to the landlord's enquiries). The landlord should clearly set out, in pre-action correspondence, any time limits with which the tenant should comply.

2.3 The landlord should provide, on a quarterly basis, rent statements in a comprehensible format showing rent due and sums received for the past 13 weeks. The landlord should, upon request, provide the tenant with copies of rent statements in a comprehensible format, from the date when arrears first arose, showing all amounts of rent due, the dates and amounts of all payments made (whether through housing benefit, discretionary housing payments or directly by the tenant) and a running total of the arrears.

2.4 If the tenant meets the appropriate criteria, the landlord should apply for arrears to be paid by the Department for Work and Pensions ['DWP'] by deductions from the tenant's benefit.

2.5 The landlord should offer to assist the tenant in any claim that the tenant may have for housing benefit, discretionary housing payments or universal credit (housing element).

2.6 Possession proceedings for rent arrears should not be started against a tenant who can demonstrate that –

(a) the local authority or DWP have been provided with all the evidence required to process a housing benefit or universal credit (housing element) claim;

(b) there is a reasonable expectation of eligibility for housing benefit or universal credit (housing element); and

(c) they have paid other sums due that are not covered by housing benefit or universal credit (housing element).

The landlord should make every effort to establish effective ongoing liaison with housing benefit departments and the DWP and, with the tenant's consent, make direct contact with the relevant housing benefit department or DWP office before taking enforcement action.

The landlord and tenant should work together to resolve any housing benefit or universal credit (housing element) problems.

2.7 Bearing in mind that rent arrears may be part of a general debt problem, the landlord should advise the tenant to seek assistance from citizens advice bureaux, debt advice agencies or other appropriate agencies as soon as possible. Information on debt advice is available on the Money Advice Service website [www.moneyadviceservice.org.uk].

After service of statutory notices

2.8 After service of a statutory notice, but before the issue of proceedings, the landlord should make reasonable attempts to contact the tenant to discuss: the amount of the arrears; the cause of the arrears; repayment of the arrears; and the housing benefit or universal credit (housing element) position. The landlord should send the tenant a copy of this protocol.

2.9 If the tenant complies with an agreement to pay the current rent and a reasonable amount towards arrears, the landlord should agree to postpone issuing court proceedings for so long as the tenant keeps to such agreement. If the tenant ceases to comply with such an agreement, the landlord should warn the tenant of the intention to bring proceedings and give the tenant clear time limits within which to comply again and avoid proceedings.

Alternative dispute resolution

2.10 The parties should consider whether it is possible to resolve the issues between them by discussion and negotiation without recourse to litigation. The parties may be required by the court to provide evidence that alternative means of resolving the dispute were considered. Courts take the view that litigation should be a last resort, and that claims should not be issued prematurely when a settlement is still actively being explored.

2.11 The Civil Justice Council and the Judicial College have endorsed *The Jackson ADR Handbook* by Susan Blake, Julie Browne and Stuart Sime (2013, Oxford University Press). The Citizens Advice Bureaux website also provides information about ADR:

- the Civil Mediation Council [www.civilmediation.org/for-the-public/about-mediation/]
- the Citizens Advice website [www.citizensadvice.org.uk/law-and-courts/legal-system/]

Information is also available at: [www.civilmediation.justice.gov.uk] and [www.adviceguide.org.uk/england/law_e/law_legal_system_e/law_taking_legal action_e/alternatives_to_court.htm].

Court proceedings

2.12 Not later than ten days before the date set for the hearing of the possession claim, the landlord should–

(a) provide the tenant with up-to-date rent statements; and
(b) disclose what knowledge it possesses of the tenant's housing benefit or universal credit (housing element) position to the tenant.

2.13

(a) The landlord should inform the tenant of the date and time of any court hearing and provide an up-to-date rent statement and the terms of the order that will be applied for. The landlord should advise the tenant to attend the hearing as the tenant's home is at risk. Records of such advice should be kept.
(b) If the tenant complies with an agreement made, after the issue of proceedings, to pay the current rent and a reasonable amount towards arrears, the landlord should agree to adjourn the court proceedings for so long as the tenant keeps to such agreement.
(c) If the tenant ceases to comply with such agreement, the landlord should warn the tenant of the intention to restore the proceedings and give the tenant clear time limits within which to comply again and avoid restoration of the proceedings.

2.14 If the landlord unreasonably fails to comply with the terms of this protocol, the court may make one or more of the following orders–

(a) an order for costs;

(b) an order adjourning the claim; or

(c) an order striking out or dismissing the claim (other than a claim based on a mandatory ground).

2.15 If the tenant unreasonably fails to comply with the terms of this protocol, the court may take such failure into account when considering whether it is reasonable to make a possession order.

PART 3 MANDATORY GROUNDS FOR POSSESSION

3.1 This Part applies in cases where, if a social landlord proves its case, the court must, in principle, grant possession and where s.89(1) Housing Act 1980 applies

3.2 Before issuing any such possession claim a social landlord–

(a) should write to the occupants explaining why it currently intends to seek possession and requiring the occupants, within a specified time, to notify the landlord in writing of any personal circumstances or other matters which they wish to have taken into account. In appropriate cases, such a letter could accompany any notice to quit or notice seeking possession and so would not necessarily delay the issue of proceedings; and

(b) should consider any representations received and, if they decide to proceed with a claim for possession, give brief written reasons for doing so.

3.3 The social landlord should include with its claim form, or in any witness statement filed under CPR 55.8(3), a schedule stating–

(a) whether it has (by a statutory review procedure or otherwise) invited the defendant to make representations of any personal circumstances or other matters which they wished to be taken into account before the social landlord issued the proceedings;

(b) if representations were made, whether and how they were considered and with what outcome; and

(c) brief reasons for bringing proceedings.

Copies of any relevant documents which the social landlord wishes the court to consider in relation to the proportionality of the landlord's decision to bring the proceedings should be attached to the schedule.

APPENDIX 6

Civil Procedure Rules 1998 and practice directions[1]

1 The appendices contain material that is © Crown Copyright and is up to date to February 2021. These materials are available online at: www.justice.gov.uk/courts/procedure-rules/civil/rules.

Civil Procedure Rules 1998 Part 55 – Possession claims

Contents of this Part

Interpretation

55.1 In this Part–

(a) 'a possession claim' means a claim for the recovery of possession of land (including buildings or parts of buildings);

(b) 'a possession claim against trespassers' means a claim for the recovery of land which the claimant alleges is occupied only by a person or persons who entered or remained on the land without the consent of a person entitled to possession of that land but does not include a claim against a tenant or sub-tenant whether his tenancy has been terminated or not;

(c) 'mortgage' includes a legal or equitable mortgage and a legal or equitable charge and 'mortgagee' is to be interpreted accordingly;

(d) 'the 1985 Act' means the Housing Act 1985[1];(e) 'the 1988 Act' means the Housing Act 1988[2];

(f) 'a demotion claim' means a claim made by a landlord for an order under section 82A of the 1985 Act or section 6A of the 1988 Act ('a demotion order');

(g) 'a demoted tenancy' means a tenancy created by virtue of a demotion order; and

(h) 'a suspension claim' means a claim made by a landlord for an order under section 121A of the 1985 Act.

I GENERAL RULES

Scope

55.2

(1) The procedure set out in this Section of this Part must be used where the claim includes–

- (a) a possession claim brought by a–
  - (i) landlord (or former landlord);
  - (ii) mortgagee; or
  - (iii) licensor (or former licensor);
- (b) a possession claim against trespassers; or
- (c) a claim by a tenant seeking relief from forfeiture.

(Where a demotion claim or a suspension claim (or both) is made in the same claim form in which a possession claim is started, this Section of this Part applies as modified by rule 65.12. Where the claim is a demotion claim or a suspension claim only, or a suspension claim made in addition to a demotion claim, Section III of Part 65 applies).

(2) This Section of this Part

- (a) is subject to any enactment or practice direction which sets out special provisions with regard to any particular category of claim;

(b) does not apply where the claimant uses the procedure set out in Section II of this Part; and

(c) does not apply where the claimant seeks an interim possession order under Section III of this Part except where the court orders otherwise or that Section so provides.

Starting the claim

55.3

(1) In the County Court–

(a) the claimant may make the claim at any County Court hearing centre, unless paragraph (2) applies or an enactment provides otherwise;

(b) the claim will be issued by the hearing centre where the claim is made; and

(c) if the claim is not made at the County Court hearing centre which serves the address where the land is situated, the claim will be sent to the hearing centre serving that address when it is issued.

(Practice Direction 55A includes further direction in respect of claims which are not made at the County Court hearing centre which serves the address where the land is situated.)

(2) The claim may be started in the High Court if the claimant files with his claim form a certificate stating the reasons for bringing the claim in that court verified by a statement of truth in accordance with rule 22.1(1).

(3) Practice Direction 55A refers to circumstances which may justify starting the claim in the High Court.

(4) Where, in a possession claim against trespassers, the claimant does not know the name of a person in occupation or possession of the land, the claim must be brought against 'persons unknown' in addition to any named defendants.

(5) The claim form and form of defence sent with it must be in the forms set out in Practice Direction 55A.

Particulars of claim

55.4 The particulars of claim must be filed and served with the claim form.

(Part 16 and Practice Direction 55A provide details about the contents of the particulars of claim)

Hearing date

55.5

(1) Subject to paragraph (1A), the court will fix a date for the hearing when it issues the claim form.

(1A) If the claim is not made at the County Court hearing centre which serves the address where the land is situated, a date will be fixed for hearing when the claim is received by that hearing centre

(2) In a possession claim against trespassers the defendant must be served with the claim form, particulars of claim and any witness statements–
  (a) in the case of residential property, not less than 5 days; and
  (b) in the case of other land, not less than 2 days,
  before the hearing date.
(3) In all other possession claims–
  (a) the hearing date will be not less than 28 days from the date of issue of the claim form;
  (b) the standard period between the issue of the claim form and the hearing will be not more than 8 weeks; and
  (c) the defendant must be served with the claim form and particulars of claim not less than 21 days before the hearing date.
  (Rule 3.1(2)(a) provides that the court may extend or shorten the time for compliance with any rule)

Service of claims against trespassers

55.6 Where, in a possession claim against trespassers, the claim has been issued against 'persons unknown', the claim form, particulars of claim and any witness statements must be served on those persons by–
(a)
  (i) attaching copies of the claim form, particulars of claim and any witness statements to the main door or some other part of the land so that they are clearly visible; and
  (ii) if practicable, inserting copies of those documents in a sealed transparent envelope addressed to 'the occupiers' through the letter box; or
(b) placing stakes in the land in places where they are clearly visible and attaching to each stake copies of the claim form, particulars of claim and any witness statements in a sealed transparent envelope addressed to 'the occupiers'.

Defendant's response

55.7
(1) An acknowledgment of service is not required and Part 10 does not apply.
(2) In a possession claim against trespassers rule 15.2 does not apply and the defendant need not file a defence.
(3) Where, in any other possession claim, the defendant does not file a defence within the time specified in rule 15.4, he may take part in any hearing but the court may take his failure to do so into account when deciding what order to make about costs.
(4) Part 12 (default judgment) does not apply in a claim to which this Part applies.

The hearing

55.8

(1) At the hearing fixed in accordance with rule 55.5(1) or at any adjournment of that hearing, the court may–
  (a) decide the claim; or
  (b) give case management directions.

(2) Where the claim is genuinely disputed on grounds which appear to be substantial, case management directions given under paragraph (1)(b) will include the allocation of the claim to a track or directions to enable it to be allocated.

(3) Except where–
  (a) the claim is allocated to the fast track or the multi-track; or
  (b) the court orders otherwise,

  any fact that needs to be proved by the evidence of witnesses at a hearing referred to in paragraph (1) may be proved by evidence in writing.

  (Rule 32.2(1) sets out the general rule about evidence. Rule 32.2(2) provides that rule 32.2(1) is subject to any provision to the contrary)

(4) Subject to paragraph (5), all witness statements must be filed and served at least 2 days before the hearing.

(5) In a possession claim against trespassers all witness statements on which the claimant intends to rely must be filed and served with the claim form.

(6) Where the claimant serves the claim form and particulars of claim, the claimant must produce at the hearing a certificate of service of those documents and rule 6.17(2)(a) does not apply.

Allocation

55.9

(1) When the court decides the track for a possession claim, the matters to which it shall have regard include–
  (a) the matters set out in rule 26.8 as modified by the relevant practice direction;
  (b) the amount of any arrears of rent or mortgage instalments;
  (c) the importance to the defendant of retaining possession of the land;
  (d) the importance of vacant possession to the claimant; and
  (e) if applicable, the alleged conduct of the defendant

(2) The court will only allocate possession claims to the small claims track if all the parties agree.

(3) Where a possession claim has been allocated to the small claims track the claim shall be treated, for the purposes of costs, as if it were proceeding on the fast track except that trial costs shall be in the discretion of the court and shall not exceed the amount that would be recoverable under rule 45.38 (amount of fast track costs) if the value of the claim were up to £3,000.

(4) Where all the parties agree the court may, when it allocates the claim, order that rule 27.14 (costs on the small claims track) applies and, where it does so, paragraph (3) does not apply.

Possession claims relating to mortgaged residential property

55.10

(1) This rule applies where a mortgagee seeks possession of land which consists of or includes residential property.
(2) Within 5 days of receiving notification of the date of the hearing by the court, the claimant must send a notice to–
    (a) the property, addressed to 'the tenant or the occupier';
    (b) the housing department of the local authority within which the property is located; and
    (c) any registered proprietor (other than the claimant) of a registered charge over the property.
(3) The notice referred to in paragraph (2)(a) must–
    (a) state that a possession claim for the property has started;
    (b) show the name and address of the claimant, the defendant and the court which issued the claim form; and
    (c) give details of the hearing.
(3A) The notice referred to in paragraph 2(b) must contain the information in paragraph (3) and must state the full address of the property.
(4) The claimant must produce at the hearing–
    (a) a copy of the notices; and
    (b) evidence that they have been sent.
(4A) An unauthorised tenant of residential property may apply to the court for the order for possession to be suspended.

Electronic issue of certain possession claims

55.10A

(1) A practice direction may make provision for a claimant to start certain types of possession claim in certain courts by requesting the issue of a claim form electronically.
(2) The practice direction may, in particular–
    (a) provide that only particular provisions apply in specific courts;
    (b) specify–
        (i) the type of possession claim which may be issued electronically;
        (ii) the conditions that a claim must meet before it may be issued electronically;
    (c) specify the court where the claim may be issued;
    (d) enable the parties to make certain applications or take further steps in relation to the claim electronically;

- (e) specify the requirements that must be fulfilled in relation to such applications or steps;
- (f) enable the parties to correspond electronically with the court about the claim;
- (g) specify the requirements that must be fulfilled in relation to electronic correspondence;
- (h) provide how any fee payable on the filing of any document is to be paid where the document is filed electronically.

(3) The Practice Direction may disapply or modify these Rules as appropriate in relation to possession claims started electronically.

II ACCELERATED POSSESSION CLAIMS OF PROPERTY LET ON AN ASSURED SHORTHOLD TENANCY

When this section may be used

55.11

(1) The claimant may bring a possession claim under this Section of this Part where–

- (a) the claim is brought under section 21 of the 1988 Act[3] to recover possession of residential property let under an assured shorthold tenancy other than a demoted assured shorthold tenancy; and
- (b) all the conditions listed in rule 55.12(1) are satisfied.

(2) The claim–

- (a) may be brought in any County Court hearing centre; and
- (b) will be issued by the hearing centre where it is brought.

(3) In this Section of this Part, a 'demoted assured shorthold tenancy' means a demoted tenancy where the landlord is a registered social landlord or a private registered provider of social housing.

Conditions

55.12

The conditions referred to in rule 55.11(1)(b) are that–

- (a) the tenancy and any agreement for the tenancy were entered into on or after 28 February 1997;
- (b) the only purpose of the claim is to recover possession of the property and no other claim is made;
- (c) the tenancy did not immediately follow an assured tenancy which was not an assured shorthold tenancy;
- (d) the tenancy fulfilled the conditions provided by section 19A of the 1988 Act;
- (e) all the tenancies under which the defendant has occupied the property–
  - (i) were the subject of written agreements; or
  - (ii) arose by virtue of section 5 of the 1988 Act

Claim form

55.13

(1) The claim form must–

(a) be in the form set out in Practice Direction 55A; and

(b)

(i) contain such information; and

(ii) be accompanied by such documents,

as are required by that form.

(2) All relevant sections of the form must be completed.

(3) The court will serve the claim form by first class post (or an alternative service which provides for delivery on the next working day).

Defence

55.14

(1) A defendant who wishes to–

(a) oppose the claim; or

(b) seek a postponement of possession in accordance with rule 55.18,

must file his defence within 14 days after service of the claim form.

(2) The defence should be in the form set out in Practice Direction 55A.

Claim referred to judge

55.15

(1) On receipt of the defence the court will–

(a) send a copy to the claimant; and

(b) refer the claim and defence to a judge.

(2) Where the period set out in rule 55.14 has expired without the defendant filing a defence–

(a) the claimant may file a written request for an order for possession; and

(b) the court will refer that request to a judge.

(3) Where the defence is received after the period set out in rule 55.14 has expired but before a request is filed in accordance with paragraph (2), paragraph (1) will still apply.

(4) Where–

(a) the period set out in rule 55.14 has expired without the defendant filing a defence; and

(b) the claimant has not made a request for an order for possession under paragraph (2) within 3 months after the expiry of the period set out in rule 55.14,

the claim will be stayed.

Consideration of the claim

55.16

(1) After considering the claim and any defence, the judge will–
  (a) make an order for possession under rule 55.17;
  (b) where the judge is not satisfied as to any of the matters set out in paragraph (2)–
    (i) direct that a date be fixed for a hearing; and
    (ii) give any appropriate case management directions; or
  (c) strike out the claim if the claim form discloses no reasonable grounds for bringing the claim.

(1A) If–
  (a) the judge directs that a date be fixed for hearing in accordance either with paragraph (2) or rule 55.18(1); and
  (b) the claim has not been brought in the County Court hearing centre which serves the address where the land is situated,

  the judge will direct that the proceedings should be transferred to that hearing centre.

(2) The matters referred to in paragraph (1)(b) are that–
  (a) the claim form was served; and
  (b) the claimant has established that he is entitled to recover possession under section 21 of the 1988 Act against the defendant.

(3) The court will give all parties not less than 14 days' notice of a hearing fixed under paragraph (1)(b)(i).

(4) Where a claim is struck out under paragraph (1)(c)–
  (a) the court will serve its reasons for striking out the claim with the order; and
  (b) the claimant may apply to restore the claim within 28 days after the date the order was served on him

Possession order

55.17 Except where rules 55.16(1)(b) or (c) apply, the judge will make an order for possession without requiring the attendance of the parties.

Postponement of possession

55.18

(1) Where the defendant seeks postponement of possession on the ground of exceptional hardship under section 89 of the Housing Act 1980[6], the judge may direct a hearing of that issue.

(2) Where the judge directs a hearing under paragraph (1)–
  (a) the hearing must be held before the date on which possession is to be given up; and
  (b) the judge will direct how many days' notice the parties must be given of that hearing.

(3) Where the judge is satisfied, on a hearing directed under paragraph (1), that exceptional hardship would be caused by requiring possession to be given up by the date in the order of possession, he may vary the date on which possession must be given up.

Application to set aside or vary

55.19 The court may

(a) on application by a party within 14 days of service of the order; or

(b) of its own initiative,

set aside or vary any order made under rule 55.17.

III INTERIM POSSESSION ORDERS

When this section may be used

55.20

(1) This Section of this Part applies where the claimant seeks an Interim Possession Order.

(2) In this section–

  (a) 'IPO' means Interim Possession Order; and

  (b) 'premises' has the same meaning as in section 12 of the Criminal Law Act 1977[7].

(3) Where this Section requires an act to be done within a specified number of hours, rule 2.8(4) does not apply.

Conditions for IPO application

55.21

(1) An application for an IPO may be made where the following conditions are satisfied–

  (a) the only claim made is a possession claim against trespassers for the recovery of premises;

  (b) the claimant–

    (i) has an immediate right to possession of the premises; and

    (ii) has had such a right throughout the period of alleged unlawful occupation; and

  (c) the claim is made within 28 days of the date on which the claimant first knew, or ought reasonably to have known, that the defendant (or any of the defendants), was in occupation.

(2) An application for an IPO may not be made against a defendant who entered or remained on the premises with the consent of a person who, at the time consent was given, had an immediate right to possession of the premises.

The application

55.22

(1) Rules 55.3(1) and (4) apply to the claim.

(2) The claim form and the defendant's form of witness statement must be in the form set out in Practice Direction 55A.

(3) When he files his claim form, the claimant must also file–

(a) an application notice in the form set out in Practice Direction 55A; and

(b) written evidence.

(4) The written evidence must be given–

(a) by the claimant personally; or

(b) where the claimant is a body corporate, by a duly authorised officer.

(Rule 22.1(6)(b) provides that the statement of truth must be signed by the maker of the witness statement)

(5) The court will–

(a) issue–

(i) the claim form; and

(ii) the application for the IPO; and

(b) set a date for the hearing of the application.

(6) The hearing of the application will be as soon as practicable but not less than 3 days after the date of issue.

Service

55.23

(1) Within 24 hours of the issue of the application, the claimant must serve on the defendant–

(a) the claim form;

(b) the application notice together with the written evidence in support; and

(c) a blank form for the defendant's witness statement (as set out in Practice Direction 55A) which must be attached to the application notice.

(2) The claimant must serve the documents listed in paragraph (1) in accordance with rule 55.6(a).

(3) At or before the hearing the claimant must file a certificate of service in relation to the documents listed in paragraph (1) and rule 6.17(2)(a) does not apply.

Defendant's response

55.24

(1) At any time before the hearing the defendant may file a witness statement in response to the application.

(2) The witness statement should be in the form set out in Practice Direction 55A.

Hearing of the application

55.25

(1) In deciding whether to grant an IPO, the court will have regard to whether the claimant has given, or is prepared to give, the following undertakings in support of his application–
  (a) if, after an IPO is made, the court decides that the claimant was not entitled to the order to–
    (i) reinstate the defendant if so ordered by the court; and
    (ii) pay such damages as the court may order; and
  (b) before the claim for possession is finally decided, not to–
    (i) damage the premises;
    (ii) grant a right of occupation to any other person; and
    (iii) damage or dispose of any of the defendant's property.

(2) The court will make an IPO if–
  (a) the claimant has–
    (i) filed a certificate of service of the documents referred to in rule 55.23(1); or
    (ii) proved service of those documents to the satisfaction of the court; and
  (b) the court considers that–
    (i) the conditions set out in rule 55.21(1) are satisfied; and
    (ii) any undertakings given by the claimant as a condition of making the order are adequate.

(3) An IPO will be in the form set out in Practice Direction 55A and will require the defendant to vacate the premises specified in the claim form within 24 hours of the service of the order.

(4) On making an IPO the court will set a date for the hearing of the claim for possession which will be not less than 7 days after the date on which the IPO is made.

(5) Where the court does not make an IPO–
  (a) the court will set a date for the hearing of the claim;
  (b) the court may give directions for the future conduct of the claim; and
  (c) subject to such directions, the claim shall proceed in accordance with Section I of this Part.

Service and enforcement of the IPO

55.26

(1) An IPO must be served within 48 hours after it is sealed.

(2) The claimant must serve the IPO on the defendant together with copies of
  (a) the claim form; and
  (b) the written evidence in support, in accordance with rule 55.6(a).

(3) Rules 83.2, 83.3 and 83.26(1) to (9) do not apply to the enforcement of an IPO.
(4) If an IPO is not served within the time limit specified by this rule, the claimant may apply to the court for directions for the claim for possession to continue under Section I of this Part.

After IPO made

55.27

(1) Before the date for the hearing of the claim, the claimant must file a certificate of service in relation to the documents specified in rule 55.26(2).
(2) The IPO will expire on the date of the hearing of the claim.
(3) At the hearing the court may make any order it considers appropriate and may, in particular–
  (a) make a final order for possession;
  (b) dismiss the claim for possession;
  (c) give directions for the claim for possession to continue under Section I of this Part; or
  (d) enforce any of the claimant's undertakings.
(4) Unless the court directs otherwise, the claimant must serve any order or directions in accordance with rule 55.6(a).
(5) Rule 83.26(10) to (12) applies to the enforcement of a final order for possession.

Application to set aside IPO

55.28

(1) If the defendant has left the premises, he may apply on grounds of urgency for the IPO to be set aside before the date of the hearing of the claim.
(2) An application under paragraph (1) must be supported by a witness statement.
(3) On receipt of the application, the court will give directions as to–
  (a) the date for the hearing; and
  (b) the period of notice, if any, to be given to the claimant and the method of service of any such notice.
(4) No application to set aside an IPO may be made under rule 39.3.
(5) Where no notice is required under paragraph (3)(b), the only matters to be dealt with at the hearing of the application to set aside are whether–
  (a) the IPO should be set aside; and
  (b) any undertaking to re-instate the defendant should be enforced,

  and all other matters will be dealt with at the hearing of the claim.
(6) The court will serve on all the parties–
  (a) a copy of the order made under paragraph (5); and

(b) where no notice was required under paragraph (3)(b), a copy of the defendant's application to set aside and the witness statement in support.

(7) Where notice is required under paragraph (3)(b), the court may treat the hearing of the application to set aside as the hearing of the claim.

Stay of possession proceedings, coronavirus

55.29

(1) Subject to paragraph (2), all possession proceedings brought under this Part and all enforcement proceedings by way of writ or warrant of possession that are–

(a) stayed immediately prior to this rule coming into force; or

(b) brought after this rule comes into force and on or before 19 September 2020,

are stayed until 20 September 2020.

(2) Paragraph (1) does not apply to–

(a) a claim against trespassers to which rule 55.6 applies;

(b) proceedings under Section III of this Part;

(c) an application for case management directions that are agreed by all the parties; or

(d) a claim for injunctive relief.

(3) Paragraph (1) does not prevent the bringing of a claim notwithstanding that it may be stayed.

(4) For the purposes of the application of any rule to any proceedings that are stayed by paragraph (1)–

(a) time does not run; and

(b) no notice is required to be given by the court.

Practice Direction 55A – Possession claims

This Practice Direction supplements Part 55

Contents of this Practice Direction

SECTION I – GENERAL RULES

55.3 – STARTING THE CLAIM

1.1

(1) Except where the County Court does not have jurisdiction, possession claims should normally be brought in the County Court. Only exceptional circumstances justify starting a claim in the High Court.

(2) In the County Court, the claim will be issued by the County Court hearing centre where the claim is made, but will then be sent to the County Court hearing centre which serves the address where the land is situated. A claimant should consider the potential delay which may result if a claim is not made at the appropriate hearing centre in the first instance.

1.2 If a claimant starts a claim in the High Court and the court decides that it should have been started in the County Court, the court will normally either strike the claim out or transfer it to the County Court on its own initiative. This is likely to result in delay and the court will normally disallow the costs of starting the claim in the High Court and of any transfer.

1.3 Circumstances which may, in an appropriate case, justify starting a claim in the High Court are if–

(1) there are complicated disputes of fact;

(2) there are points of law of general importance; or

(3) the claim is against trespassers and there is a substantial risk of public disturbance or of serious harm to persons or property which properly require immediate determination.

1.4 The value of the property and the amount of any financial claim may be relevant circumstances, but these factors alone will not normally justify starting the claim in the High Court.

1.5 The claimant must use the appropriate claim form and particulars of claim form set out in Table 1 to Practice Direction 4. The defence must be in form N11, N11B, N11M or N11R, as appropriate.

1.6 High Court claims for the possession of land subject to a mortgage will be assigned to the Chancery Division.

1.7 A claim which is not a possession claim may be brought under the procedure set out in Section I of Part 55 if it is started in the same claim form as a possession claim which, by virtue of rule 55.2(1) must be brought in accordance with that Section.

(Rule 7.3 provides that a claimant may use a single claim form to start all claims which can be conveniently disposed of in the same proceedings)

1.8 For example a claim under paragraphs 4, 5 or 6 of Part I of Schedule 1 to the Mobile Homes Act 1983 may be brought using the procedure set out in Section I of Part 55 if the claim is started in the same claim form as a claim enforcing the rights referred to in section 3(1)(b) of the Caravan Sites Act 1968 (which, by virtue of rule 55.2(1) must be brought under Section I of Part 55).

1.9 Where the claim form includes a demotion claim, the claim must be started in the County Court for the district in which the land is situated.

55.4 – PARTICULARS OF CLAIM

2.1 In a possession claim the particulars of claim must:

(1) identify the land to which the claim relates;
(2) state whether the claim relates to residential property;
(3) state the ground on which possession is claimed;
(4) give full details about any mortgage or tenancy agreement; and
(5) give details of every person who, to the best of the claimant's knowledge, is in possession of the property.

Residential property let on a tenancy

2.2 Paragraphs 2.3 to 2.4B apply if the claim relates to residential property let on a tenancy.

2.3 If the claim includes a claim for non-payment of rent the particulars of claim must set out:

(1) the amount due at the start of the proceedings;

(2) in schedule form, the dates and amounts of all payments due and payments made under the tenancy agreement for a period of two years immediately preceding the date of issue, or if the first date of default occurred less than two years before the date of issue from the first date of default and a running total of the arrears;
(3) the daily rate of any rent and interest;
(4) any previous steps taken to recover the arrears of rent with full details of any court proceedings; and
(5) any relevant information about the defendant's circumstances, in particular:
   (a) whether the defendant is in receipt of social security benefits; and
   (b) whether any payments are made on his behalf directly to the claimant under the Social Security Contributions and Benefits Act 1992.

2.3A If the claimant wishes to rely on a history of arrears which is longer than two years, he should state this in his particulars and exhibit a full (or longer) schedule to a witness statement.

2.4 If the claimant knows of any person (including a mortgagee) entitled to claim relief against forfeiture as underlessee under section 146(4) of the Law of Property Act 1925 (or in accordance with section 38 of the Senior Courts Act 1981, or section 138(9C) of the County Courts Act 1984):
(1) the particulars of claim must state the name and address of that person; and
(2) the claimant must file a copy of the particulars of claim for service on him.

2.4A If the claim for possession relates to the conduct of the tenant, the particulars of claim must state details of the conduct alleged.

2.4B If the possession claim relies on a statutory ground or grounds for possession, the particulars of claim must specify the ground or grounds relied on.

Land subject to a mortgage

2.5 If the claim is a possession claim by a mortgagee, the particulars of claim must also set out:
(1) if the claim relates to residential property whether:
   (a) a land charge of Class F has been registered under section 2(7) of the Matrimonial Homes Act 1967;
   (b) a notice registered under section 2(8) or 8(3) of the Matrimonial Homes Act 1983 has been entered and on whose behalf; or
   (c) a notice under section 31(10) of the Family Law Act 1996 has been registered and on whose behalf; and

   if so, that the claimant will serve notice of the claim on the persons on whose behalf the land charge is registered or the notice or caution entered.

(2) the state of the mortgage account by including:
  (a) the amount of:
    (i) the advance;
    (ii) any periodic repayment; and
    (iii) any payment of interest required to be made;
  (b) the amount which would have to be paid (after taking into account any adjustment for early settlement) in order to redeem the mortgage at a stated date not more than 14 days after the claim started specifying the amount of solicitor's costs and administration charges which would be payable;
  (c) if the loan which is secured by the mortgage is a regulated consumer credit agreement, the total amount outstanding under the terms of the mortgage; and
  (d) the rate of interest payable:
    (i) at the commencement of the mortgage;
    (ii) immediately before any arrears referred to in paragraph (3) accrued;
    (iii) at the commencement of the proceedings.

(3) if the claim is brought because of failure to pay the periodic payments when due:
  (a) in schedule form, the dates and amounts of all payments due and payments made under the mortgage agreement or mortgage deed for a period of two years immediately preceding the date of issue, or if the first date of default occurred less than two years before the date of issue from the first date of default and a running total of the arrears;
  (b) give details of:
    (i) any other payments required to be made as a term of the mortgage (such as for insurance premiums, legal costs, default interest, penalties, administrative or other charges);
    (ii) any other sums claimed and stating the nature and amount of each such charge; and
    (iii) whether any of these payments is in arrears and whether or not it is included in the amount of any periodic payment.

(4) whether or not the loan which is secured by the mortgage is a regulated consumer credit agreement and, if so, specify the date on which any notice required by sections 76 or 87 of the Consumer Credit Act 1974 was given;

(5) if appropriate details that show the property is not one to which section 141 of the Consumer Credit Act 1974 applies;

(6) any relevant information about the defendant's circumstances, in particular:
  (a) whether the defendant is in receipt of social security benefits; and

(b) whether any payments are made on his behalf directly to the claimant under the Social Security Contributions and Benefits Act 1992;

(7) give details of any tenancy entered into between the mortgagor and mortgagee (including any notices served); and

(8) state any previous steps which the claimant has taken to recover the money secured by the mortgage or the mortgaged property and, in the case of court proceedings, state:

(a) the dates when the claim started and concluded; and

(b) the dates and terms of any orders made.

2.5A If the claimant wishes to rely on a history of arrears which is longer than two years, he should state this in his particulars and exhibit a full (or longer) schedule to a witness statement.

Possession claim against trespassers

2.6 If the claim is a possession claim against trespassers, the particulars of claim must state the claimant's interest in the land or the basis of his right to claim possession and the circumstances in which it has been occupied without licence or consent.

Possession claim in relation to a demoted tenancy by a housing action trust or a local housing authority

2.7 If the claim is a possession claim under section 143D of the Housing Act 1996 (possession claim in relation to a demoted tenancy where the landlord is a housing action trust or a local housing authority), the particulars of claim must have attached to them a copy of the notice to the tenant served under section 143E of the 1996 Act.

55.5 – HEARING DATE

3.1 The court may exercise its powers under rules 3.1(2)(a) and (b) to shorten the time periods set out in rules 55.5(2) and (3).

3.2 Particular consideration should be given to the exercise of this power if:

(1) the defendant, or a person for whom the defendant is responsible, has assaulted or threatened to assault:

(a) the claimant;

(b) a member of the claimant's staff; or

(c) another resident in the locality;

(2) there are reasonable grounds for fearing such an assault; or

(3) the defendant, or a person for whom the defendant is responsible, has caused serious damage or threatened to cause serious damage to the property or to the home or property of another resident in the locality.

3.3 Where paragraph 3.2 applies but the case cannot be determined at the first hearing fixed under rule 55.5, the court will consider what steps are needed to finally determine the case as quickly as reasonably practicable.

55.6 – SERVICE IN CLAIMS AGAINST TRESPASSERS

4.1 If the claim form is to be served by the court and in accordance with rule 55.6(b) the claimant must provide sufficient stakes and transparent envelopes.

55.8 – THE HEARING

5.1 Attention is drawn to rule 55.8(3). Each party should wherever possible include all the evidence he wishes to present in his statement of case, verified by a statement of truth.

5.2 If relevant the claimant's evidence should include the amount of any rent or mortgage arrears and interest on those arrears. These amounts should, if possible, be up to date to the date of the hearing (if necessary by specifying a daily rate of arrears and interest). However, rule 55.8(4) does not prevent such evidence being brought up to date orally or in writing on the day of the hearing if necessary.

5.3 If relevant the defendant should give evidence of:

(1) the amount of any outstanding social security or housing benefit payments relevant to rent or mortgage arrears; and

(2) the status of:

- (a) any claims for social security or housing benefit about which a decision has not yet been made; and
- (b) any applications to appeal or review a social security or housing benefit decision where that appeal or review has not yet concluded.

5.4 If:

(1) the maker of a witness statement does not attend a hearing; and

(2) the other party disputes material evidence contained in his statement,

the court will normally adjourn the hearing so that oral evidence can be given.

5.5 The claimant must bring 2 completed copies of Form N123 to the hearing.

CONSUMER CREDIT ACT CLAIMS RELATING TO THE RECOVERY OF LAND

7.1 Any application by the defendant for a time order under section 129 of the Consumer Credit Act 1974 may be made:

(1) in his defence; or

(2) by application notice in the proceedings.

ENFORCEMENT OF CHARGING ORDER BY SALE

7.2 A party seeking to enforce a charging order by sale should follow the procedure set out in rule 73.10 and the Part 55 procedure should not be used.

SECTION II– ACCELERATED POSSESSION CLAIMS OF PROPERTY LET ON AN ASSURED SHORTHOLD TENANCY

55.18 – POSTPONEMENT OF POSSESSION

A8.1 In the County Court, the claim will be issued by the County Court hearing centre where the claim is made, but will then be sent to the County Court hearing centre which serves the address where the land is situated. A claimant should consider the potential delay which may result if a claim is not made at the appropriate hearing centre in the first instance.

8.1 If the judge is satisfied as to the matters set out in rule 55.16(2), he will make an order for possession in accordance with rule 55.17, whether or not the defendant seeks a postponement of possession on the ground of exceptional hardship under section 89 of the Housing Act 1980.

8.2 In a claim in which the judge is satisfied that the defendant has shown exceptional hardship, he will only postpone possession without directing a hearing under rule 55.18(1) if–

(1) he considers that possession should be given up 6 weeks after the date of the order or, if the defendant has requested postponement to an earlier date, on that date; and

(2) the claimant indicated on his claim form that he would be content for the court to make such an order without a hearing.

8.3 In all other cases if the defendant seeks a postponement of possession under section 89 of the Housing Act 1980, the judge will direct a hearing under rule 55.18(1).

8.4 If, at that hearing, the judge is satisfied that exceptional hardship would be caused by requiring possession to be given up by the date in the order of possession, he may vary that order under rule 55.18(3) so that possession is to be given up at a later date. That later date may be no later than 6 weeks after the making of the order for possession on the papers (see section 89 of the Housing Act 1980).

SECTION III– INTERIM POSSESSION ORDERS

9.1 The claim form must be in form N5, the application notice seeking the interim possession order must be in form N130 and the defendant's witness statement must be in form N133.

9.2 The IPO will be in form N134 (annexed to this practice direction).

SECTION IV– ORDERS FIXING A DATE FOR POSSESSION

10.1 This paragraph applies where the court has made an order postponing the date for possession under section 85(2)(b) of the Housing Act 1985 (secure tenancies) or under section 9(2)(b) of the Housing Act 1988 (assured tenancies).

10.2 If the defendant fails to comply with any of the terms of the order which relate to payment, the claimant, after following the procedure set out in paragraph 10.3, may apply for an order fixing the date upon which the defendant has to give up possession of the property. Unless the court further postpones the date for possession, the defendant will be required to give up possession on that date.

10.3 At least 14 days and not more than 3 months before applying for an order under paragraph 10.2, the claimant must give written notice to the defendant in accordance with paragraph 10.4.

10.4 The notice referred to in paragraph 10.3 must–

(1) state that the claimant intends to apply for an order fixing the date upon which the defendant is to give up possession of the property;

(2) record the current arrears and state how the defendant has failed to comply with the order referred to in paragraph 10.1 (by reference to a statement of the rent account enclosed with the notice);

(3) request that the defendant reply to the claimant within 7 days, agreeing or disputing the stated arrears; and

(4) inform the defendant of his right to apply to the court–

   (a) for a further postponement of the date for possession; or

   (b) to stay or suspend enforcement.

10.5 In his reply to the notice, the defendant must–

(1) where he disputes the stated arrears, provide details of payments or credits made;

(2) where he agrees the stated arrears, explain why payments have not been made.

10.6 An application for an order under paragraph 10.2 must be made by filing an application notice in accordance with Part 23. The application notice must state whether or not there is any outstanding claim by the defendant for housing benefit.

10.7 The claimant must file the following documents with the application notice–

(1) a copy of the notice referred to in paragraph 10.3;

(2) a copy of the defendant's reply, if any, to the notice and any relevant subsequent correspondence between the claimant and the defendant;

(3) a statement of the rent account showing–
   (a) the arrears that have accrued since the first failure to pay in accordance with the order referred to in paragraph 10.2; or
   (b) the arrears that have accrued during the period of two years immediately preceding the date of the application notice, where the first such failure to pay occurs more than two years before that date.

10.8 Rules 23.7(service of a copy of an application notice) and 23.10 (right to set aside or vary an order made without service of the application notice) and paragraphs 2.3, 2.4 and 2.5 of Practice Direction 23A (dealing with applications without a hearing) do not apply to an application under this Section.

10.9 On being filed, the application will be referred to the District Judge who–

(1) will normally determine the application without a hearing by fixing the date for possession as the next working day; but
(2) if he considers that a hearing is necessary–
   (a) will fix a date for the application to be heard; and
   (b) direct service of the application notice and supporting evidence on the defendant.

10.10 The court does not have jurisdiction to review a decision that it was reasonable to make an order for possession.

Updated: Monday, 30 January 2017

Practice Direction 55B – Possession Claims Online

This Practice Direction supplements CPR rule 55.10A.

Contents of this Practice Direction

Scope of this practice direction

1.1 This practice direction provides for a scheme ('Possession Claims Online') to operate in the County Court–

(1) enabling claimants and their representatives to start certain possession claims under CPR Part 55 by requesting the issue of a claim form electronically via the PCOL website; and

(2) where a claim has been started electronically, enabling the claimant or defendant and their representatives to take further steps in the claim electronically as specified below.

1.2 In this practice direction–

(1) 'PCOL website' means the website which may be accessed via the Business Link website, and through which Possession Claims Online will operate.

~~Information on the PCOL website~~

~~**2.1** The PCOL website contains further details and guidance about the operation of Possession Claims Online.~~

~~**2.2** In particular the PCOL website sets out–~~

~~(1) the specified courts; and~~

~~(2) the dates from which Possession Claims Online will be available in each specified court.~~

~~2.3 The operation of Possession Claims Online in any specified court may be restricted to taking certain of the steps specified in this practice direction, and in such cases the PCOL website will set out the steps which may be taken using Possession Claims Online in that specified court.~~

Security

3.1 Her Majesty's Courts and Tribunals Service will take such measures as it thinks fit to ensure the security of steps taken or information stored electronically. These may include requiring users of Possession Claims Online–

(1) to enter a customer identification number or password;

(2) to provide personal information for identification purposes; and

(3) to comply with any other security measures,

before taking any step online.

Fees

4.1 A step may only be taken using Possession Claims Online on payment of the prescribed fee where a fee is payable. Where this practice direction provides for a fee to be paid electronically, it may be paid by–

(1) credit card;

(2) debit card; or

(3) any other method which Her Majesty's Courts and Tribunals Service may permit.

4.2 A defendant who wishes to claim exemption from payment of fees must do so through an organisation approved by Her Majesty's Courts and Tribunals Service before taking any step using PCOL which attracts a fee. If satisfied that the defendant is entitled to fee exemption, the organisation will submit the fee exemption form through the PCOL website to Her Majesty's Courts and Tribunals Service. The defendant may then use PCOL to take such a step.

(Her Majesty's Courts and Tribunals Service website contains guidance as to when the entitlement to claim an exemption from payment of fees arises. The PCOL website will contain a list of organisations through which the defendant may claim an exemption from fees).

Claims which may be started using Possession Claims Online

5.1 A claim may be started online if–

(1) it is brought under Section I of Part 55;

(2) it includes a possession claim for residential property by–

  (a) a landlord against a tenant, solely on the ground of arrears of rent (but not a claim for forfeiture of a lease); or

  (b) a mortgagee against a mortgagor, solely on the ground of default in the payment of sums due under a mortgage, relating to land the address for which is served by a County Court hearing centre;

(3) it does not include a claim for any other remedy except for payment of arrears of rent or money due under a mortgage, interest and costs;

(3A) the claimant has an address for service in the United Kingdom;

(4) the defendant has an address for service in England and Wales; and

(5) the claimant is able to provide a postcode for the property.

5.2 A claim must not be started online if a defendant is known to be a child or protected party.

Starting a claim

6.1 A claimant may request the issue of a claim form by–

(1) completing an online claim form at the PCOL website;

(2) paying the appropriate issue fee electronically at the PCOL website or by some other means approved by Her Majesty's Courts and Tribunals Service.

6.2 The particulars of claim must be included in the online claim form and may not be filed separately. It is not necessary to file a copy of the tenancy agreement, mortgage deed or mortgage agreement with the particulars of claim.

6.2A In the case of a possession claim for residential property that relies on a statutory ground or grounds for possession, the claimant must specify, in section 4(a) of the online claim form, the ground or grounds relied on.

6.3 Subject to paragraphs 6.3A and 6.3B, the particulars of claim must include a history of the rent or mortgage account, in schedule form setting out–

(1) the dates and amounts of all payments due and payments made under the tenancy agreement, mortgage deed or mortgage agreement either from the first date of default if that date occurred less than two years before the date of issue or for a period of two years immediately preceding the date of issue; and

(2) a running total of the arrears.

6.3A Paragraph 6.3B applies where the claimant has, before commencing proceedings, provided the defendant in schedule form with–

(1) details of the dates and amounts of all payments due and payments made under the tenancy agreement, mortgage deed or mortgage account–

   (a) for a period of two years immediately preceding the date of commencing proceedings; or

   (b) if the first date of default occurred less than two years before that date, from the first date of default; and

(2) a running total of the arrears.

6.3B Where this paragraph applies the claimant may, in place of the information required by paragraph 6.3, include in his particulars of claim a summary only of the arrears containing at least the following information–

(1) The amount of arrears as stated in the notice of seeking possession served under either section 83 of the Housing Act 1985 or section 8 of the Housing Act 1988, or at the date of the claimant's letter before action, as appropriate;
(2) the dates and amounts of the last three payments in cleared funds made by the defendant or, if less than three payments have been made, the dates and amounts of all payments made;
(3) the arrears at the date of issue, assuming that no further payments are made by the defendant.

6.3C Where the particulars of claim include a summary only of the arrears the claimant must–

(1) serve on the defendant not more than 7 days after the date of issue, a full, up-to-date arrears history containing at least the information required by paragraph 6.3; and
(2) either–
    (a) make a witness statement confirming that he has complied with sub-paragraph (1) or (2) of paragraph 6.3A as appropriate, and including or exhibiting the full arrears history; or
    (b) verify by way of oral evidence at the hearing that he has complied with sub-paragraph (1) or (2) of paragraph 6.3A as appropriate and also produce and verify the full arrears history.

(Rule 55.8(4) requires all witness statements to be filed and served at least 2 days before the hearing.)

6.4 If the claimant wishes to rely on a history of arrears which is longer than two years, he should state this in his particulars and exhibit a full (or longer) schedule to a witness statement.

6.5 When an online claim form is received, an acknowledgment of receipt will automatically be sent to the claimant. The acknowledgment does not constitute notice that the claim form has been issued or served.

6.6 When the court issues a claim form following the submission of an online claim form, the claim is 'brought' for the purposes of the Limitation Act 1980 and any other enactment on the date on which the online claim form is received by the court's computer system. The court will keep a record, by electronic or other means, of when online claim forms are received.

6.7 When the court issues a claim form it will–

(1) serve a printed version of the claim form and a defence form on the defendant; and

(2) send the claimant notice of issue by post or, where the claimant has supplied an e-mail address, by electronic means.

6.8 The claim shall be deemed to be served on the fifth day after the claim was issued irrespective of whether that day is a business day or not.

6.9 Where the period of time within which a defence must be filed ends on a day when the court is closed, the defendant may file his defence on the next day that the court is open.

6.10 The claim form shall have printed on it a unique customer identification number or a password by which the defendant may access the claim on the PCOL website.

6.11 PCOL will issue the proceedings in the appropriate County Court hearing centre by reference to the post code provided by the claimant and that court shall have jurisdiction to hear and determine the claim and to carry out enforcement of any judgment irrespective of whether the property is within or outside the jurisdiction of that court.

(CPR 30.2(1) authorises proceedings to be transferred from one county court to another.)

Defence

7.1 A defendant wishing to file–

(1) a defence; or

(2) a counterclaim (to be filed together with a defence) to a claim which has been issued through the PCOL system,

may, instead of filing a written form, do so by–

(a) completing the relevant online form at the PCOL website; and

(b) if the defendant is making a counterclaim, paying the appropriate fee electronically at the PCOL website or by some other means approved by Her Majesty's Courts and Tribunals Service.

7.2 Where a defendant files a defence by completing the relevant online form, he must not send the court a hard copy.

7.3 When an online defence form is received, an acknowledgment of receipt will automatically be sent to the defendant. The acknowledgment does not constitute notice that the defence has been served.

7.4 The online defence form will be treated as being filed–

(1) on the day the court receives it, if it receives it before 4 p.m. on a working day; and

(2) otherwise, on the next working day after the court receives the online defence form.

7.5 A defence is filed when the online defence form is received by the court's computer system. The court will keep a record, by electronic or other means, of when online defence forms are received.

Statement of truth

8.1 CPR Part 22 requires any statement of case to be verified by a statement of truth. This applies to any online claims and defences and application notices.

8.2 CPR Part 22 also requires that if an applicant wishes to rely on matters set out in his application notice as evidence, the application notice must be verified by a statement of truth. This applies to any application notice completed online that contains matters on which the applicant wishes to rely as evidence.

8.3 Attention is drawn to–

(1) paragraph 2 of Practice Direction 22, which stipulates the form of the statement of truth; and

(2) paragraph 3 of Practice Direction 22, which provides who may sign a statement of truth; and

(3) CPR 32.14, which sets out the consequences of making, or causing to be made, a false statement in a document verified by a statement of truth, without an honest belief in its truth.

Signature

9.1 Any provision of the CPR which requires a document to be signed by any person is satisfied by that person entering his name on an online form.

Communication with the court electronically by the messaging service

10.1 If the PCOL website specifies that a court accepts electronic communications relating to claims brought using Possession Claims Online the parties may communicate with the court using the messaging service facility, available on the PCOL website ('the messaging service').

10.2 The messaging service is for brief and straightforward communications only. The PCOL website contains a list of examples of when it will not be appropriate to use the messaging service.

10.3 Parties must not send to the court forms or attachments via the messaging service.

10.4 The court shall treat any forms or attachments sent via the messaging service as not having been filed or received.

10.5 The court will normally reply via the messaging service where–

(1) the response is to a message transmitted via the messaging service; and

(2) the sender has provided an e-mail address.

Electronic applications

11.1 Certain applications in relation to a possession claim started online may be made electronically ('online applications'). An online application may be made if a form for that application is published on the PCOL website ('online application form') and the application is made at least five clear days before the hearing.

11.2 If a claim for possession has been started online and a party wishes to make an online application, he may do so by–

(1) completing the appropriate online application form at the PCOL website; and

(2) paying the appropriate fee electronically at the PCOL website or by some other means approved by Her Majesty's Courts and Tribunals Service.

11.3 When an online application form is received, an acknowledgment of receipt will automatically be sent to the applicant. The acknowledgment does not constitute a notice that the online application form has been issued or served.

11.4 Where an application must be made within a specified time, it is so made if the online application form is received by the court's computer system within that time. The court will keep a record, by electronic or other means, of when online application forms are received.

11.5 When the court receives an online application form it shall–

(1) serve a copy of the online application endorsed with the date of the hearing by post on the claimant at least two clear days before the hearing; and

(2) send the defendant notice of service and confirmation of the date of the hearing by post; provided that

(3) where either party has provided the court with an e-mail address for service, service of the application and/or the notice of service and confirmation of the hearing date may be effected by electronic means.

Request for issue of warrant

12.1 Where–

(1) the court has made an order for possession in a claim started online; and

(2) the claimant is entitled to the issue of a warrant of possession without requiring the permission of the court

the claimant may request the issue of a warrant by completing an online request form at the PCOL website and paying the appropriate fee electronically at the PCOL website or by some other means approved by Her Majesty's Courts and Tribunals Service.

12.2 A request under paragraph 12.1 will be treated as being filed–

(1) on the day the court receives the request, if it receives it before 4 p.m. on a working day; and

(2) otherwise, on the next working day after the court receives the request.

(Rule 83.2 sets out certain circumstances in which a warrant of possession may not be issued without the permission of the court.)

Application to suspend warrant of possession

13.1 Where the court has issued a warrant of possession, the defendant may apply electronically for the suspension of the warrant, provided that:

(1) the application is made at least five clear days before the appointment for possession; and

(2) the defendant is not prevented from making such an application without the permission of the court.

13.2 The defendant may apply electronically for the suspension of the warrant, by–

(1) completing an online application for suspension at the PCOL website; and

(2) paying the appropriate fee electronically at the PCOL website or by some other means approved by Her Majesty's Courts and Tribunals Service.

13.3 When an online application for suspension is received, an acknowledgment of receipt will automatically be sent to the defendant. The acknowledgment does not constitute a notice that the online application for suspension has been served.

13.4 Where an application must be made within a specified time, it is so made if the online application for suspension is received by the court's computer system within that time. The court will keep a record, by electronic or other means, of when online applications for suspension are received.

13.5 When the court receives an online application for suspension it shall–

(1) serve a copy of the online application for suspension endorsed with the date of the hearing by post on the claimant at least two clear days before the hearing; and

(2) send the defendant notice of service and confirmation of the date of the hearing by post; provided that

(3) where either party has provided the court with an e-mail address for service, service of the application and/or the notice of service and confirmation of the hearing date may be effected by electronic means.

Viewing the case record

14.1 A facility will be provided on the PCOL website for parties or their representatives to view–

(1) an electronic record of the status of claims started online, which will be reviewed and, if necessary, updated at least once each day; and

(2) all information relating to the case that has been filed by the parties electronically.

14.2 In addition, where the PCOL website specifies that the court has the facility to provide viewing of such information by electronic means, the parties or their representatives may view the following information electronically–

(1) court orders made in relation to the case; and
(2) details of progress on enforcement and subsequent orders made.

Updated: Monday, 30 January 2017

Practice Direction 55C – Coronavirus: temporary provision in relation to possession proceedings

This practice direction supplements CPR Part 55

Contents of this practice direction

General – introductory and interpretation

1.1 This practice direction is made under rule 55.A1 and provides for temporary modification of Part 55 during the period beginning with 20 September 2020 (the end of the stay imposed by rule 55.29) and ending on 30 July 2021 ('the interim period').

1.2 During the interim period, Part 55 has effect subject to this practice direction.

1.3 In this practice direction–

'stayed claim' means a claim which was brought on or before 19 September 2020 (including an appeal from a decision in such a claim) and which is accordingly subject to the stay imposed by rule 55.29;

'new claim' means a claim brought after 19 September 2020.

1.4 Paragraphs 2.1 to 3.1 and 5.1 to 5.4 of this practice direction apply only to stayed claims (and attention is drawn to paragraph 2.2, which provides that paragraph 2.1– and therefore the requirement for a reactivation notice– does not apply to stayed claims brought on or after 3 August 2020 or stayed claims in which a final possession order has been made).

1.5 Paragraph 4.1 of this practice direction applies to all claims whenever brought.

1.6 Paragraph 6.1 of this practice direction applies to all claims, including stayed claims, brought on or after 3 August 2020.

1.7 Paragraph 6.2 of this practice direction applies only to new claims to which Section II of Part 55 applies.

No listing, relisting, hearing or referral in stayed claims without reactivation notice

2.1 Subject to paragraph 2.2, and unless the court directs otherwise, no stayed claim is to be–

(a) listed;

(b) relisted;

(c) heard; or

(d) referred to a judge under rule 55.15,

until one of the parties files and serves a written notice (a 'reactivation notice') confirming that they wish the case to be listed, relisted, heard or referred.

2.2 Paragraph 2.1 does not apply to a stayed claim–

(a) which was brought on or after 3 August 2020; or

(b) in which a final order for possession has been made.

2.3 A reactivation notice must–

(a) confirm that the party filing and serving it wishes the case to be listed, relisted, heard or referred; and

(b) except in proceedings relating to an appeal, set out what knowledge that party has as to the effect of the Coronavirus pandemic on the Defendant and their dependants.

2.4 Except in proceedings relating to an appeal, where a reactivation notice is filed and served by the Claimant and the claim is based on arrears of rent, the Claimant must provide with the notice an updated rent account for the previous two years.

2.5 Unless the court orders otherwise, any trial date set prior to 27 March 2020 (the date on which Practice Direction 51Z came into force) shall be vacated and the case stayed unless a party complies with the provisions of paragraphs 2.1, 2.3, 2.4 and 5.1 not less than 42 days prior to the hearing date.

2.6 If by 4.00 p.m. on 30 April 2021 no reactivation notice has been filed and served in relation to a stayed claim to which paragraph 2.1 applies, that claim will be automatically stayed.

2.7 A stay under paragraph 2.5 or 2.6 is not a sanction for breach; and an application to lift the stay is accordingly not an application for relief from sanctions under rule 3.9.

Notice of listed or relisted hearings in stayed claims

3.1 The court must, unless it directs otherwise, give at least 21 days' notice to the parties of any hearing listed or relisted in response to a reactivation notice.

All claims where no hearing listed

4.1 During the interim period, rule 55.5 applies with the following modifications–

(a) paragraph (1) is modified to read–

> '(1) Subject to paragraph (1A), the court will fix a date for the hearing when or after it issues the claim form.'; and

(b) paragraph (3)(b) (standard period between issue and hearing of eight weeks) does not apply.

Stayed claims where case management directions made

5.1 In relation to a stayed claim to which paragraph 2.1 applies and in which case management directions were made before 20 September 2020, a party filing and serving a reactivation notice must file and serve with it–

(a) a copy of the last directions order together with new dates for compliance with the directions taking account of the stay before 20 September 2020; and

(b) either–

  (i) a draft order setting out additional or alternative directions (including proposing a new hearing date) which are required; or

  (ii) a statement in writing that no new directions are required and that an existing hearing date can be met; and

(c) a statement in writing whether the case is suitable for hearing by video or audio link.

5.2 If the other parties do not agree with any of the matters advanced under paragraph 5.1(a), (b) and (c), they must file and serve a response within 14 days of service of the reactivation notice.

5.3 If no party has complied with paragraph 5.1 by 4.00 p.m. on 30 April 2021, the claim will be automatically stayed.

5.4 A stay under paragraph 5.3 is not a sanction for breach; and an application to lift the stay is accordingly not an application for relief from sanctions under rule 3.9.

New claims and stayed claims brought on or after 3 August 2020 – demonstrating compliance with relevant Pre-Action Protocol and providing information as to effect of pandemic

6.1 In any claim (whether a new claim or a stayed claim) brought on or after 3 August 2020, the Claimant must–

(a) bring to the hearing two copies of a notice–

  (i) in a claim to which the Pre-Action Protocol for Possession Claims by Social Landlords is applicable, confirming that the Claimant has complied with that Pre-Action Protocol and detailing how the Claimant has done so; and

(ii) in all claims, setting out what knowledge that party has as to the effect of the Coronavirus pandemic on the Defendant and their dependants; and

(b) serve on the Defendant not less than 14 days prior to the hearing the notices referred to in sub-paragraph (a) setting out what knowledge that party has as to the effect of the Coronavirus pandemic on the Defendant and their dependants.

6.2 In any claim (whether a new claim or a stayed claim) brought on or after 3 August 2020 to which Section II of Part 55 applies the Claimant must file with the claim form for service with it a notice setting out what knowledge that party has as to the effect of the Coronavirus pandemic on the Defendant and their dependants.

(For a claim to which the Pre-Action Protocol for Possession Claims based on Mortgage or Home Purchase Plan Arrears in Respect of Residential Property is applicable, paragraph 5.5 of Practice Direction 55A requires the Claimant to bring to the hearing two completed copies of Form N123 (the mortgage pre-action protocol checklist).)

Updated: 10 February 2021

APPENDIX 7

Notice periods[1]

1 These materials are available from the Ministry of Housing, Communities and Local Government online at: www.gov.uk/government/publications/understanding-the-possession-action-process-guidance-for-landlords-and-tenants.

Section 21 Housing Act 1988 notices – England and Wales

In England, your Section 21 notice will only be valid if you have:

Given your tenant a minimum of 6 months' notice to leave if you served your notice on or after 29 August 2020 until at least 31 March 2021. This is because of coronavirus (COVID-19).

If you served your notice on or after the 26 March 2020 until 28 August 2020, you should have provided your tenant with a minimum of 3 month's notice. This is because of coronavirus (COVID-19).

If you served your notice before 26 March 2020, you should have provided your tenant with a minimum of 2 months' notice.

Allowed at least 4 months to elapse, since the start of the original tenancy, before serving the section 21 notice.

Protected the tenant's deposit in a government-approved deposit protection scheme[2] and given the tenant information about how the deposit is held. You must provide the tenant with certain details about the deposit known as 'prescribed information'. This includes details of the deposit protection scheme, confirmation of the amount held, your contact details and information on how the tenant can get their deposit back when they leave.

Obtained a licence for the property from the local authority, if the property needed one.

Started court proceedings in time. The court process must generally be started within ten months of serving the notice, if the notice is served on or after 29 August 2020.

If you served notice on or before 28 August 2020, you must generally make a claim for possession in the court within 6 months of giving the notice.

However, in the case of a periodic tenancy where more than 6 months' notice is required, the proceedings may be started up to 4 months after the date specified in the notice as the date after which the tenant must leave the property.

Provided the tenant with the right documents giving information about the property and their rights and responsibilities as a renter. This includes a valid gas safety certificate if there is a gas installation in the property, an energy performance certificate, and the version of the 'How to Rent' guide which was most up to date when your contract started or was renewed.

Completed the required repairs and allowed at least 6 months to elapse, if you received an improvement notice or notice of emergency remedial action from the local authority following a complaint made by the tenant.

2 https://www.gov. uk/tenancy-deposit-protection

Repaid to the tenant (or otherwise properly accounted for) any prohibited payments that you may have charged them. The law says that you are only allowed to take certain permitted payments. These are set out in the Tenant Fees Act 2019 guidance for landlords.[3]

In Wales, your Section 21 notice will only be valid if you have:

Given the tenant at least 3 months' notice to leave, if you gave notice from the 26 March to 23 July. If you served notice on or after 24 July 2020 until at least 31 March 2021, you must have given your tenant at least 6 months' notice months' notice to leave. The notice must be given in writing.

If you served your notice before 26 March 2020, you should have provided your tenant with a minimum of 2 months' notice.

In a fixed term tenancy, you can serve a Section 21 notice at any time, but it cannot end until the end of the fixed term. In a periodic tenancy notice can be given at any time, but the appropriate notice period must be given and the date specified in the notice as the date after which the tenant must leave the property, must by the last day of a period of the tenancy.

Protected the tenant's deposit in a government-approved deposit protection scheme[4] and given the tenant information about how the deposit is held. You must provide the tenant with certain details about the deposit known as 'prescribed information'. This includes details of the deposit protection scheme, confirmation of the amount held, your contact details and information on how the tenant can get their deposit back when they leave.

Registered or obtained a license under the Rent Smart Wales scheme, where the Section 21 notice is given after 23 November 2016.

Obtained other licences from the local authority, if the property needed one, such as in HMO accommodation.

Repaid to the tenant (or otherwise properly accounted for) any prohibited payments that you may have charged them. The law says that you are only allowed to take certain permitted payments. The list of prohibited or allowable payments is set out in the Renting Homes (Fees Etc.) (Wales) Act 2019 guidance for landlords and agents.[5]

3 https://assets.publishing.service.gov.uk/government/ uploads/system/uploads/attachment_data/file/819634/TFA_Landlord_and_ Agent_Guidance_190722.pdf

4 https://www.gov. uk/tenancy-deposit-protection

5 https://gov.wales/sites/default/files/ publications/2019-08/letting-fees-guidance-for-landlords-and-letting-agents. pdf

Minimum notice period lengths for tenancies in England [social landlord]

Notice period lengths under Section 83 and 83ZA of the Housing Act 1985 (Secure and Flexible Tenancies)

Legislation: Section 83, Housing Act 1985 / For grounds see Schedule 2 to the Act / Applicable to secure tenancies

Users: Local authorities and where tenancy granted pre-1988 Act, private registered providers of social housing

Ground	Pre-coronavirus act 2020 notice period: Until 26 march 2020	Modified notice period: 26 March 2020 – 28 August 2020	Modified notice period: 29 August 2020 – 31 March 2021
Where court considers reasonable			
1: Rent arrears or breach of tenancy	4 weeks	3 months	(a) 4 weeks where arrears are at least 6 months and no other ground is specified (apart from ground 2) (b) 6 months where arrears are less than 6 months
2: Nuisance/annoyance, illegal/immoral use of property	None – proceedings may be commenced immediately after service of notice	3 months	None – proceedings may be commenced immediately after service of notice
2ZA: Rioting	4 weeks	3 months	At least 4 weeks where no other ground is specified (apart from ground 2)
2A: Domestic abuse (social tenancies only – where victim has permanently left the property)	4 weeks	3 months	At least 4 weeks where no other ground is specified (apart from ground 2)

Ground	Pre-coronavirus act 2020 notice period: Until 26 march 2020	Modified notice period: 26 March 2020 – 28 August 2020	Modified notice period: 29 August 2020 – 31 March 2021
3: Deterioration of property (tenant at fault)	4 weeks	3 months	6 months
4: Deterioration of furniture (tenant at fault)	4 weeks	3 months	6 months
5: False statement	4 weeks	3 months	At least 4 weeks where no other ground is specified (apart from ground 2)
6: Assignment by mutual exchange for a premium	4 weeks	3 months	6 months
7: Tied accommodation and misconduct	4 weeks	3 months	6 months
8: Temporary home while works being carried out	4 weeks	3 months	6 months
Where suitable alternative accommodation is available			
9: Overcrowding	4 weeks	3 months	6 months
10: Demolition/redevelopment	4 weeks	3 months	6 months
10A: Regeneration	4 weeks	3 months	6 months
11: Charity and has not met objectives	4 weeks	3 months	6 months
Where suitable alternative accommodation is available and court considers reasonable			
12: Tied accommodation/employment	4 weeks	3 months	6 months
13: Accessible accommodation and tenant doesn't require it	4 weeks	3 months	6 months

Ground	Pre-coronavirus act 2020 notice period: Until 26 march 2020	Modified notice period: 26 March 2020 – 28 August 2020	Modified notice period: 29 August 2020 – 31 March 2021
14: Housing association, accommodation for people who have difficulty in meeting specific housing needs and tenant no longer requires it	4 weeks	3 months	6 months
15: Housing for people with special needs, and tenant no longer requires it	4 weeks	3 months	6 months
15A: Succession, property too big (Only applies in England)	4 weeks	3 months	6 months
16: Succession, property too big (Only applies in Wales)	4 weeks	3 months	6 months

Legislation: Section 83ZA, Housing Act 1985 / Applicable to secure tenancies

Users: Local authorities and where tenancy granted pre-1988 Act, private registered providers of social housing

Ground	Pre-coronavirus act 2020 notice period: Until 26 march 2020	Modified notice period: 26 March 2020 – 28 August 2020	Modified notice period: 29 August 2020 – 31 March 2021
Mandatory ground for serious ASB	At least 4 weeks	3 months	At least 4 weeks if the tenancy is periodic At least 1 month if the tenancy is for a fixed term

Notice period lengths under section 128 of the Housing Act 1996 (Introductory Tenancies)

Legislation: Section 128 Housing Act 1996 / Applicable to introductory tenancies

Users: Local authorities

Ground	Pre-coronavirus act 2020 notice period: Until 26 march 2020	Modified notice period: 26 March 2020 – 28 August 2020	Modified notice period: 29 August 2020 – 31 March 2021
Possession of introductory tenancy	At least 4 weeks	3 months	Where the landlord has provided an ASB reason, 4 weeks Otherwise, 6 months

Notice period lengths under section 143E of the Housing Act 1996 (Demoted Tenancies)

Legislation: Section 143E, Housing Act 1996 / Applicable to demoted local authority tenancies

Users: Local authorities

Ground	Pre-coronavirus act 2020 notice period: Until 26 march 2020	Modified notice period: 26 March 2020 – 28 August 2020	Modified notice period: 29 August 2020 – 31 March 2021
Possession of demoted tenancy	At least 4 weeks	3 months	Where the landlord has provided an ASB reason, 4 weeks Otherwise, 6 months

Notice period lengths under section 107C of the Housing Act 1985 (Flexible Tenancies)

Legislation: Section 107D, Housing Act 1985 / Applicable to flexible tenancies – a type of secure fixed term tenancy

Users: Local authorities

Ground	Pre-coronavirus act 2020 notice period: Until 26 march 2020	Modified notice period: 26 March 2020 – 28 August 2020	Modified notice period: 29 August 2020 – 31 March 2021
Recovery of possession on expiry of flexible tenancy. A flexible tenancy is a type of secure fixed term tenancy.	2 months	3 months	6 months

Notice period lengths under Section 8 of the Housing Act 1988 (Assured and Assured Shorthold Tenancies)

Legislation: Section 8, Housing Act 1988 / For grounds see Schedule 2 to the Act / Applicable to assured and assured shorthold tenancies

Users: Private sector and private registered providers of social housing (housing associations)

Ground	Pre-coronavirus Act 2020 notice period: until 26 March 2020	Modified notice period: 26 March 2020 – 28 August 2020	Modified notice period: 29 August 2020 – 31 March 2021
Mandatory (judge must award possession if ground met)			
1: Landlord wants to move in	2 months	3 months	6 months
2: Mortgage repossession	2 months	3 months	6 months
3: Out of season holiday let	2 weeks	3 months	6 months
4: Let to student by an educational institution	2 weeks	3 months	6 months
5: Property required for use by minister of religion	2 months	3 months	6 months
6: Demolition / redevelopment	2 weeks	3 months	6 months
7: Death of tenant	2 months	3 months	3 months
7a: Serious anti-social behaviour	4 weeks (periodic tenancy) 1 month (fixed term tenancy)	3 months	4 weeks (periodic tenancy) 1 month (fixed term tenancy)
7b: No right to rent in the UK	2 weeks	3 months	3 months
8: Serious rent arrears at time of service of notice and possession proceedings	2 weeks	3 months	(a) 4 weeks where arrears are at least 6 months (b) 6 months where arrears are less than 6 months

Ground	Pre-coronavirus Act 2020 notice period: until 26 March 2020	Modified notice period: 26 March 2020 – 28 August 2020	Modified notice period: 29 August 2020 – 31 March 2021
Discretionary (judge can decide whether to award possession, if ground met)			
9: Alternative accommodation available	2 months	3 months	6 months
10: Some rent arrears at the time of service of notice and possession proceedings	2 weeks	3 months	(a) 4 weeks where arrears are at least 6 months (b) 6 months where arrears are less than 6 months
11: Persistent late payment of rent	2 weeks	3 months	(a) 4 weeks where arrears are at least 6 months (b) 6 months where arrears are less than 6 months
12: Breach of tenancy agreement	2 weeks	3 months	6 months
13: Tenant deteriorated property	2 weeks	3 months	6 months
14: Nuisance/annoyance, illegal/immoral use of property	None – proceedings may be commenced immediately after service of notice	3 months	None – proceedings may be commenced immediately after service of notice
14A: Domestic abuse (social tenancies only – where victim has permanently left the property)	2 weeks	3 months	2 weeks
14ZA: Rioting	2 weeks	3 months	2 weeks
15: Tenant has deteriorated furniture	2 weeks	3 months	6 months
16: Employment	2 months	3 months	6 months
17: False statement	2 weeks	3 months	2 weeks

Minimum notice period lengths under Section 8 of the Housing Act 1988 in England [private landlord]

Legislation: Section 8, Housing Act 1988 / For grounds see Schedule 2 to the Act / Applicable to assured and assured shorthold tenancies

Users: Private sector and private registered providers of social housing

Ground	Pre-coronavirus Act 2020 notice period: until 26 March 2020	Modified notice period: 26 March 2020 – 28 August 2020	Modified notice period: 29 August 2020 – 31 March 2021
Mandatory (judge must award possession if ground met)			
1: Landlord wants to move in	2 months	3 months	6 months
2: Mortgage repossession	2 months	3 months	6 months
3: Out of season holiday let	2 weeks	3 months	6 months
4: Let to student by an educational institution	2 weeks	3 months	6 months
5: Property required for use by minister of religion	2 months	3 months	6 months
6: Demolition / redevelopment	2 weeks	3 months	6 months
7: Death of tenant	2 months	3 months	3 months
7a: Serious anti-social behaviour	4 weeks (periodic tenancy) 1 month (fixed term tenancy)	3 months	4 weeks (periodic tenancy) 1 month (fixed term tenancy)
7b: No right to rent in the UK	2 weeks	3 months	3 months
8: Serious rent arrears at time of service of notice and possession proceedings	2 weeks	3 months	(a) 4 weeks where arrears are at least 6 months (b) 6 months where arrears are less than 6 months

Ground	Pre-coronavirus Act 2020 notice period: until 26 March 2020	Modified notice period: 26 March 2020 – 28 August 2020	Modified notice period: 29 August 2020 – 31 March 2021
Discretionary (judge can decide whether to award possession, if ground met)			
9: Alternative accommodation available	2 months	3 months	6 months
10: Some rent arrears at the time of service of notice and possession proceedings	2 weeks	3 months	(a) 4 weeks where arrears are at least 6 months (b) 6 months where arrears are less than 6 months
11: Persistent late payment of rent	2 weeks	3 months	(a) 4 weeks where arrears are at least 6 months (b) 6 months where arrears are less than 6 months
12: Breach of tenancy agreement	2 weeks	3 months	6 months
13: Tenant deteriorated property	2 weeks	3 months	6 months
14: Nuisance/annoyance, illegal/immoral use of property	None – proceedings may be commenced immediately after service of notice	3 months	None – proceedings may be commenced immediately after service of notice
14A: Domestic abuse (social tenancies only – where victim has permanently left the property)	2 weeks	3 months	2 weeks
14ZA: Rioting	2 weeks	3 months	2 weeks
15: Tenant has deteriorated furniture	2 weeks	3 months	6 months
16: Employment	2 months	3 months	6 months
17: False statement	2 weeks	3 months	2 weeks

Minimum notice period lengths for tenancies in Wales [social landlord]

Notice period lengths under Section 83 and 83ZA of the Housing Act 1985 (Secure Tenancies)

Legislation: Section 83, Housing Act 1985 / For grounds see Schedule 2 to the Act / Applicable to secure tenancies

Users: Local authorities and where tenancy granted pre-1988 Act, private registered providers of social housing

Ground	Pre-coronavirus act 2020 notice period: Until 26 march 2020	Modified notice period: 26 March 2020 – 28 September 2020	Modified notice period: 29 September 2020 – 31 March 2021
Where court considers reasonable			
1: Rent arrears or breach of tenancy	4 weeks	3 months	6 months
2: Nuisance/annoyance, illegal/immoral use of property	None – proceedings may be commenced immediately after service of notice	3 months	None – proceedings may be commenced immediately after service of notice
2A: Domestic abuse (social tenancies only – where victim has permanently left the property)	4 weeks	3 months	At least 4 weeks where no other ground is specified (apart from ground 2)
3: Deterioration of property (tenant at fault)	4 weeks	3 months	6 months
4: Deterioration of furniture (tenant at fault)	4 weeks	3 months	6 months
5: False statement	4 weeks	3 months	6 months
6: Assignment by mutual exchange for a premium	4 weeks	3 months	6 months
7: Tied accommodation and misconduct	4 weeks	3 months	6 months
8: Temporary home while works being carried out	4 weeks	3 months	6 months

Ground	Pre-coronavirus act 2020 notice period: Until 26 march 2020	Modified notice period: 26 March 2020 – 28 September 2020	Modified notice period: 29 September 2020 – 31 March 2021
Where suitable alternative accommodation is available			
9: Overcrowding	4 weeks	3 months	6 months
10: Demolition/ redevelopment	4 weeks	3 months	6 months
10A: Regeneration	4 weeks	3 months	6 months
11: Charity and has not met objectives	4 weeks	3 months	6 months
Where suitable alternative accommodation is available and court considers reasonable			
12: Tied accommodation/employment	4 weeks	3 months	6 months
13: Accessible accommodation and tenant doesn't require it	4 weeks	3 months	6 months
14: Housing association, accommodation for people who have difficulty in meeting specific housing needs and tenant no longer requires it	4 weeks	3 months	6 months
15: Housing for people with special needs, and tenant no longer requires it	4 weeks	3 months	6 months
15A: Succession, property too big (Only applies in England)	4 weeks	3 months	6 months
16: Succession, property too big (Only applies in Wales)	4 weeks	3 months	6 months

Legislation: Section 83ZA, Housing Act 1985 / Applicable to secure tenancies

Users: Local authorities and where tenancy granted pre-1988 Act, private registered providers of social housing

Ground	Pre-coronavirus act 2020 notice period: Until 26 march 2020	Modified notice period: 26 March 2020 – 28 September 2020	Modified notice period: 29 September 2020 – 31 March 2021
Mandatory ground for serious ASB	At least 4 weeks	3 months	At least 4 weeks if the tenancy is periodic At least 1 month if the tenancy is for a fixed term

Notice period lengths under section 128 of the Housing Act 1996 (Introductory Tenancies)

Legislation: Section 128 Housing Act 1996 / Applicable to introductory tenancies

Users: Local authorities

Ground	Pre-coronavirus act 2020 notice period: Until 26 march 2020	Modified notice period: 26 March 2020 – 28 September 2020	Modified notice period: 29 September 2020 – 31 March 2021
Possession of introductory tenancy	At least 4 weeks	3 months	Where the landlord has provided an ASB reason, 4 weeks Otherwise, 6 months

Notice period lengths under section 143E of the Housing Act 1996 (Demoted Tenancies)

Legislation: Section 143E, Housing Act 1996 / Applicable to demoted local authority tenancies

Users: Local authorities

Ground	Pre-coronavirus act 2020 notice period: Until 26 march 2020	Modified notice period: 26 March 2020 – 28 September 2020	Modified notice period: 29 September 2020 – 31 March 2021
Possession of demoted tenancy	At least 4 weeks	3 months	Where the landlord has provided an ASB reason, 4 weeks Otherwise, 6 months

Notice period lengths under Section 8 of the Housing Act 1988 (Assured and Assured Shorthold Tenancies) [in Wales]

Legislation: Section 8, Housing Act 1988 / For grounds see Schedule 2 to the Act / Applicable to assured and assured shorthold tenancies

Users: Private sector and private registered providers of social housing (housing associations)

Ground	Pre-coronavirus Act 2020 notice period: until 26 March 2020	Modified notice period: 26 March 2020 – 23 July 2020	Modified notice period: 24 July – 28 September 2020	Modified notice period: 29 September 2020 – 31 March 2021
Mandatory (judge must award possession if ground met)				
1: Landlord wants to move in	2 months	3 months	6 months	6 months
2: Mortgage repossession	2 months	3 months	6 months	6 months
3: Out of season holiday let	2 weeks	3 months	6 months	6 months
4: Let to student by an educational institution	2 weeks	3 months	6 months	6 months
5: Property required for use by minister of religion	2 months	3 months	6 months	6 months
6: Demolition / redevelopment	2 weeks	3 months	6 months	6 months
7: Death of tenant	2 months	3 months	6 months	6 months
7a: Serious anti-social behaviour	4 weeks (periodic tenancy) 1 month (fixed term tenancy)	3 months	3 months	4 weeks (periodic tenancy) 1 month (fixed term tenancy)
8: Serious rent arrears at time of service of notice and possession proceedings	2 weeks	3 months	6 months	6 months

Ground	Pre-coronavirus Act 2020 notice period: until 26 March 2020	Modified notice period: 26 March 2020 – 23 July 2020	Modified notice period: 24 July – 28 September 2020	Modified notice period: 29 September 2020 – 31 March 2021
Discretionary (judge can decide whether to award possession, if ground met)				
9: Alternative accommodation available	2 months	3 months	6 months	6 months
10: Some rent arrears at the time of service of notice and possession proceedings	2 weeks	3 months	6 months	6 months
11: Persistent late payment of rent	2 weeks	3 months	6 months	6 months
12: Breach of tenancy agreement	2 weeks	3 months	6 months	6 months
13: Tenant deteriorated property	2 weeks	3 months	6 months	6 months
14: Nuisance/annoyance, illegal/immoral use of property	None – proceedings may be commenced immediately after service of notice	3 months	3 months	None – proceedings may be commenced immediately after service of notice
14A: Domestic abuse (social tenancies only – where victim has permanently left the property)	2 weeks	3 months	6 months	2 weeks
14ZA: Rioting	2 weeks	3 months	2 weeks	
15: Tenant has deteriorated furniture	2 weeks	3 months	6 months	6 months
16: Employment	2 months	3 months	6 months	6 months
17: False statement	2 weeks	3 months	6 months	6 months

Minimum notice period lengths under Section 8 of the Housing Act 1988 in Wales [private landlord]

Legislation: Section 8, Housing Act 1988 / For grounds see Schedule 2 to the Act / Applicable to assured and assured shorthold tenancies

Users: Private sector and private registered providers of social housing

Ground	Pre-coronavirus Act 2020 notice period: until 26 March 2020	Modified notice period: 26 March 2020 – 23 July 2020	Modified notice period: 24 July 2020 – 28 September 2020	Modified notice period: 29 September 2020 – 31 March 2021
Mandatory (judge must award possession if ground met)				
1: Landlord wants to move in	2 months	3 months	6 months	6 months
2: Mortgage repossession	2 months	3 months	6 months	6 months
3: Out of season holiday let	2 weeks	3 months	6 months	6 months
4: Let to student by an educational institution	2 weeks	3 months	6 months	6 months
5: Property required for use by minister of religion	2 months	3 months	6 months	6 months
6: Demolition / redevelopment	2 weeks	3 months	6 months	6 months
7: Death of tenant	2 months	3 months	6 months	6 months
7a: Serious anti-social behaviour	4 weeks (periodic tenancy) 1 month (fixed term tenancy)	3 months	3 months	4 weeks (periodic tenancy 1 month (fixed term tenancy)
8: Serious rent arrears at time of service of notice and possession proceedings	2 weeks	3 months	6 months	6 months

Ground	Pre-coronavirus Act 2020 notice period: until 26 March 2020	Modified notice period: 26 March 2020 – 23 July 2020	Modified notice period: 24 July 2020 – 28 September 2020	Modified notice period: 29 September 2020 – 31 March 2021
Discretionary (judge can decide whether to award possession, if ground met)				
9: Alternative accommodation available	2 months	3 months	6 months	6 months
10: Some rent arrears at the time of service of notice and possession proceedings	2 weeks	3 months	6 months	6 months
11: Persistent late payment of rent	2 weeks	3 months	6 months	6 months
12: Breach of tenancy agreement	2 weeks	3 months	6 months	6 months
13: Tenant deteriorated property	2 weeks	3 months	6 months	6 months
14: Nuisance/annoyance, illegal/immoral use of property	None – proceedings may be commenced immediately after service of notice	3 months	3 months	None – proceedings may be commenced immediately after service of notice
14A: Domestic abuse (social tenancies only – where victim has permanently left the property)	2 weeks	3 months	6 months	2 weeks
15: Tenant has deteriorated furniture	2 weeks	3 months	6 months	6 months
16: Employment	2 months	3 months	6 months	6 months
17: False statement	2 weeks	3 months	6 months	6 months

APPENDIX 8

Background – the general stay on possession proceedings and the Master of the Rolls Working Group

Introduction

On 27 March 2020, a general stay was announced by the Master of Rolls on possession proceedings in response to the COVID-19 public health crisis. It had been recognised earlier that block possession lists of the kind covered by the Housing Possession Court Duty Scheme (HPCDS) were not safe. There was a further recognition that it was not in the public interest for possession proceedings and evictions to go ahead in the midst of a public health crisis and where people were locked down and unable to go to work.

New and continuing mortgage cases were barred by the Financial Conduct Authority (FCA) until31 October 2020 and evictions in mortgage cases banned until 31 March 2021. Borrowers have until 31 March 2021 to apply for a payment break.

These measures were necessary but also created a backlog of housing possession cases. At the same time economic conditions meant that in August 2020 over 320,000 households, who were not in arrears of rent in March, were now falling behind with their rent and therefore were at risk of possession proceedings and eviction.

The first stay was brought about by the introduction of Civil Procedure Rules 1998 (CPR) Practice Direction (PD) 51Z 'Stay of possession proceedings, coronavirus', on 27 March 2020. PD 51Z was amended on 20 April 2020 and then replaced on 25 June 2020 by a fresh stay brought about by CPR 55.29 'Stay of possession proceedings, coronavirus'. That stay was then extended to 20 September 2020 simply by amending the dates in CPR 55.29.

The stay on possession proceedings had its sceptics, and there were attempts to strike it down. On 30 April 2020, the Court of Appeal heard the case of *Arkin v Marshall and Marshall* [2020] EWCA Civ 620, in which the appellant argued that that particular case was not of the usual run of possession cases and so should not be subject to the stay or, in the alternative, the general stay was ultra vires. Judgment was handed down on 11 May 2020 and the appeal dismissed. Subsequent appeals brought by litigants seeking to dismantle the stay were also dismissed.

Shortly after the first stay was announced, the Master of the Rolls convened a Working Group on Possession Proceedings under the stewardship of Knowles J (Sir Robin Knowles). The mission of the Working Group was to produce arrangements to allow, as far as possible, the safe and orderly lifting of the general stay on proceedings from 21 September 2020. The Working Group produced 'Overall Arrangements for Possession Proceedings in England And Wales: "The Overall Arrangements"' on 17 September 2020. The Overall Arrangements state:

> 4. The strategy reflected in the Overall Arrangements is directed to (a) reducing volume in the system by enabling earlier advice and increas-

ing settlement, (b) taking account, within limits that the law has imposed, of the effect of the pandemic on all parties, and (c) maintaining confidence in the fairness of outcomes. These objectives are also relevant beyond the legal system, including to the economy and to homelessness.

This was to be achieved in consultation with relevant government departments, the judiciary, landlord representatives and tenant representatives.

The innovations of the Overall Arrangements can be listed as follows:

- housing possession lists limited to 10 'substantive (S) hearings', 10 'review (R) dates' and any emergency warrant suspension or other hearings;
- the advent of the R date opportunity for advice and assistance;
- facilitated negotiation/mediation;
- alignment of the rules for county court and High Court enforcement of possession orders (although substantial work on this had been underway prior to 2020 by way of a detailed consultation exercise).

The arrangements drawn up by Knowles J are designed to meet the objectives of the project while drawing a balance between the interest of tenants and landlords. Knowles J is known for his commitment to access to justice and his involvement with organisations promoting pro bono and other advice. The arrangements very much reflect that commitment.

To understand the R date, it is necessary to know how and why it came about. The Master of the Rolls Working Group was keen to build in early advice and assistance into the arrangements they were developing, to open up possession proceedings after the various general stays were lifted. It was crucial that this advice could be delivered through the existing HPCDS contracts with the Legal Aid Agency (LAA) and with as little adjustment to the existing rules and contract as possible. This allowed for the advice to be delivered by experienced duty advisers, and meant it would be free of charge to defendants and would not be means tested. That could only be achieved if the opportunity for this advice and assistance was delivered at something akin to a 'hearing'. At the same time, it was important that the advice could be provided prior to there being any risk of the tenant of eviction or, as was argued by members of the Working Group, any undue expectation being placed on defendant and the position of their case when the matter came to a substantive hearing.

Guidance was also issued by the Master of the Rolls to civil judges as to the listing priorities for when the courts opened up possession proceedings again from 21 September 2020: 'Possession Proceeding Listing Priorities in the County Court', issued 17 September 2020. These are as follows:

(a) Cases with allegations of anti-social behaviour, including Ground 7A of Schedule 2 to the Housing Act 1988 and Section 84A of the Housing Act 1985.
(b) Cases with extreme alleged rent arrears accrued, that is, arrears equal to at least
  (i) 12 months' rent, or
  (ii) 9 months' rent where that amounts to more than 25% of a private landlord's total annual income from any source.
(c) Cases involving alleged squatters, illegal occupiers or persons unknown.
(d) Cases involving an allegation of domestic violence where possession of the property is alleged to be important for particular reasons which are set out in the claim form (and with domestic violence agencies alerted).
(e) Cases with allegations of fraud or deception.
(f) Cases with allegations of unlawful subletting.
(g) Cases with allegations of abandonment of the property, non-occupation or death of defendant.
(h) Cases concerning what was allocated by an authority as 'temporary accommodation' and is specifically needed by the authority for reallocation as 'temporary accommodation'.

Documentation

Master of the Rolls

As mentioned, the work of the Master of the Rolls Working Group on Possession Proceedings led to a document called the 'Overall Arrangements' and that may be found on the Master of the Rolls' website: www.judiciary.uk/announcements/resumption-of-possession-cases/.

Also on the same page is the guidance to civil judges as to listing priorities set out above.

HM Courts & Tribunals Service

In chapter 3 above we discuss changes to the CPR which include the need for a 'reactivation notice' for cases issued prior to 3 August 2020 and held by the general stay. The form for reactivation notices is here: www.gov.uk/government/publications/reactivation-notice-for-property-possession.

That page also includes other notices sent by the court relating to proceedings started before 3 August 2020.

Ministry of Housing, Communities and Local Government

As we set out above, the work done by the Working Group was in consultation with relevant government departments, and the Ministry of Housing, Communities and Local Government (MHCLG) has issued guidance to both landlords and tenants in relation to possession proceedings, which can be found here: www.gov.uk/government/publications/understanding-the-possession-action-process-guidance-for-landlords-and-tenants.

There are four documents aimed at social landlords, private landlords, social tenants and private tenants respectively. They deal with the procedures involved in seeking possession of residential property, including notices and court processes, but they also seek to persuade landlords and tenants to try to find other ways to resolve disputes that would otherwise lead to possession actions. Those attempts at persuasion reflect much work done in the background with social landlords, in particular to try to reduce the number of claims issued.

The documents include very helpful tables regarding notice periods (also reproduced at appendix 7 above).

The documents are guidance, and their utility for duty advisers (apart from the tables with notice periods) will be mostly if not exclusively limited to discretionary cases where they could be used to indicate to judges that a landlord might not have abided by the guidance and so should not be awarded the order sought. It cannot have any effect in mandatory cases or to override existing civil procedure rules and practice directions.

Financial Conduct Authority

The FCA has also issued guidance in relation to mortgage cases: 'Mortgages and Coronavirus: Additional Guidance for Firms', September 2020, which can be found here: www.fca.org.uk/publications/finalised-guidance/mortgages-coronavirus-additional-guidance-firms-finalised-guidance. This guidance will be very helpful to duty advisers who are regularly seeing mortgage cases in their lists, and this document may well be capable of being persuasive in arguments brought in mortgage cases – see chapter 11 above.

National Residential Landlords Association

The National Residential Landlords Association (NRLA) has issued guidance to its members: 'Regaining Possession – ending tenancies responsibly', 22 September 2020, which can be found here: www.nrla.org.uk/resources/ending-your-tenancy/regaining-possession-responsibly. Some of the links are for NRLA members only, but from a duty adviser's point of view, the document 'Pre-Action Plan: Managing arrears and avoiding possession claims' which is open to all and which includes the 'nine golden rules' for dealing with rent disputes, will be of interest. Again, the utility of this document for duty advisers will be limited to discretionary cases (which form a minority of private landlord possession claims brought on rent arrears grounds) because the guidance cannot have any influence on mandatory cases for possession.

Legal Aid Agency

The LAA HPCDS contract itself has not changed, but the contract guidance has been updated to make sure the contract works with the Overall Arrangements: 'Housing Possession Court Duty Scheme Guidance for Service Providers', and can be found here: https://assets.publishing.service.gov.uk/government/uploads/system/uploads/attachment_data/file/923187/Housing_Possession_Court_Duty_Scheme_Provider_Guidance_-_for_use_from_20th_September_2020_v5.pdf.

Both advisers and administrators of HPCDS schemes need to make themselves familiar with this document in order to understand the contractual requirements and procedures.

The Overall Arrangements and the CPR

We deal with the CPR, including relatively new CPR PD 55C 'Coronavirus: Temporary Provision in Relation to Possession Proceedings', in chapter 3. However, it is worth discussing briefly how the Overall Arrangements document relates to the rules. The Overall Arrangements are guidance issued by the Master of the Rolls' office to help the court and the judiciary manage the opening up of proceedings. They are not rules or directions. It is unclear to the authors as to the consequences of a court not following these arrangements either in spirit or letter.

What is clear is that in relation to post-stay claims, the court's general case management powers at CPR Part 3 are doing a lot of the work in making the Overall Arrangements effective. CPR 3.1, 3.2, 3.3 and 3.4 are the mechanics by which R dates and S hearings occur, along with everything in between.

It may well be that we will need to see the Overall Arrangements in action and in the breach to understand how the courts of first instance and any appeal courts would deal with deviation from the arrangements.

Mediation

At the time of writing, the Mediation scheme had just gone live and this account deals with what was known about the scheme as at February 2021.

This scheme is another innovation brought about as a result of the Coronavirus public health crisis and, along with the R date, represents another attempt to see if claims for possession can be resolved between the parties without the need for a substantive hearing. The arrangements are controversial. Most advisers representing tenants are sceptical of mediation in possession proceedings for many reasons including the power imbalance between the parties and the fact that it is hard to see how a landlord's wish to evict a tenant can be resolved by mediation. There is a great concern that moves towards mediation are designed to further erode legal aid for tenants and therefore erode tenants' legal rights.

The opportunity for some properly helpful assistance for tenants between the R date and S hearing, such as could be provided by for example a funded 'crisis navigator' scheme, was unfortunately not considered.

Instead the government approached the Working Group with £3m to put towards "mediation" and it was made clear that if the duty advice sector did not take up the offer to participate in the scheme then other organisations including large corporate interests, experienced in securing government contracts, would fulfil the scheme. It was initially proposed that duty advisers would act as mediators on cases referred by other duty advisers. Payments for both the referrer and the adviser undertaking the mediation were proposed.

Under time pressure and with reluctance those on the WG aligned with tenant advice groups agreed that they would encourage members to undertake the work if they wished to and that careful monitoring of its efficacy would be done.

The MoJ and MHCLG then withdrew their initial proposal conducted an open tender for a different mediation scheme. The successful bidders were the Society of Mediators - https://www.societyofmediators.com/

A separate process is ongoing to tender for work to monitor the scheme and that process had not concluded at the time of writing.

How it works

Although the scheme had gone live at the time of writing, virtually no details of how the mediation scheme would work had been released and details of how it works are sketchy. This is what was known in February 2021:

- A duty adviser may identify cases from those where they have advised on an R date list, which in their view would benefit from mediation.
- If the landlord or their representative agrees to mediation and the defendant also agrees, then the case may be referred for mediation.
- The mediation will take place between the R date and the S hearing and mediation should not alter the timescale of the proceedings at all.
- At the time of writing there is no payment proposed for the work of the duty adviser to make a referral. However the duty adviser will need to explain the process and principles behind mediation to both the claimant and the defendant.

The procedure to make a referral is simply to email the claim number to a dedicated email address – possession.support@justice.gov.uk – on the R date. HMCTS will make all other arrangements.

If the mediation results in an agreement then currently it is proposed that the S hearing will not be required because a consent order will be filed. If not the S hearing will proceed as usual. The judge is not informed of the mediation unless there is an agreement reached.

Our specific concerns about this scheme aside from the scepticism we set out above are:

- We do not know enough about the mediation process and what 'success' in mediation would look like to have confidence to refer cases.
- We are concerned about possession orders being agreed through mediation leading to problems with homelessness application and intentional homelessness decisions.
- We do not know what level of knowledge and experience mediators will have of for example benefits and debt law which we think are essential to understanding the position of a defendant.
- We do not know whether cases with more than one defendant could or should be referred given that the interest of more than one defendant are not necessarily in alignment.
- We have deep concerns about the result of mediation being approved without a hearing, particularly if possession orders are not ruled out as being a 'successful' result of mediation.
- Duty advisers will not be remunerated for the work done to refer. The major part of the that work would be advising the claimant of what mediation is and how it works and advising the defendant of what mediation is and how it works and cautioning about what they may be asked to agree to, and what they might be unwise to agree to. Fees for duty work are already low and more work for the same fixed fee is extremely unwelcome.

APPENDIX 9

Master of the Rolls Working Group's Overall Arrangements[1]

1 This document is available online at: www.judiciary.uk/wp-content/uploads/2020/09/Possession-Proceedings-Overall-Arrangements-Version-1.0-17.09.20.pdf. An overview of the arrangements from the Master of the Rolls is available here: www.judiciary.uk/announcements/resumption-of-possession-cases/.

Overall Arrangements for Possession Proceedings in England and Wales: 'The Overall Arrangements'

The Master of the Rolls (as Head of Civil Justice) Working Group on Possession Proceedings

17 September 2020: Version 1.0

Introduction

1. The stay of possession proceedings comes to an end on 20 September 2020. The legal system faces a combination of (a) accrued demand from the stay, (b) the possible increase in demand caused by economic consequences of the pandemic and (c) reduced physical court capacity because of social distancing. The challenge, and its scale, does not have a precedent.

2. This document summarises the arrangements ('Overall Arrangements') identified and developed to address the challenge, within the time available.

3. A Working Group appointed by the Master of the Rolls as Head of Civil Justice and with cross sector membership has sought to bring together contributions from government and government agencies, judiciary and court service, profession and advice sector, user groups and experts. The Working Group has also engaged with a wide range of associations and representative bodies, and at national (England and Wales), regional and local level. Regional and local user group meetings, led by the regional and local Judiciary and Court Service, play a crucial part.

4. The strategy reflected in the Overall Arrangements is directed to (a) reducing volume in the system by enabling earlier advice and increasing settlement, (b) taking account, within limits that the law has imposed, of the effect of the pandemic on all parties, and (c) maintaining confidence in the fairness of outcomes. These objectives are also relevant beyond the legal system, including to the economy and to homelessness.

5. The Overall Arrangements involve and are supported by the following, in combination:

1) Amendments by the Civil Procedure Rule Committee (CPRC) to rules and practice directions.
2) The introduction by the Judiciary of new case management and listing arrangements, including a scheme of prioritisation.
3) The inclusion of specific procedures to enable the Court to receive enhanced information of any effect of the pandemic on the parties.
4) Increased user communication through the Court Service (HMCTS), including guidance.
5) The publication of guidance by the Ministry of Housing, Communities & Local Government (MHCLG), and the Financial Conduct Authority

(FCA, with UK Finance), and the development and publication of voluntary best practice by a number of national associations.

6) Adjustments in relation to legal aid duty scheme legal advice (a) to enable earlier provision, (b) to enable remote provision where needed, (c) to remove gaps in geographical coverage, and (d) to extend to some Accelerated Possession Claims.
7) Specific designation, deployment, preparation and training of staff through the Court Service.
8) Judicial preparation and training through the Judicial College.
9) Arrangements for monitoring, including to identify when and where adjustments are needed and if contingency arrangements need to be brought in.
10) Contingency arrangements, including the assembly of an additional cadre of judges.

6. In practice and throughout the operation of the Overall Arrangements everyone, collectively, has a critically important role in tackling the challenge. This includes by (a) helping the parties, (b) identifying additional solutions and (c) enabling court process and hearings to operate efficiently (both for possession proceedings and for other parts of the legal system).

Re-starting existing cases

7. No claim for possession should be re-started without careful efforts to reach compromise.

8. Claims brought before 3 August 2020 will not be listed, relisted or referred to a Judge until a party files and serves a 'Reactivation Notice' confirming that they wish the case to proceed. There is no rush – this may be done at any time from 21 September 2020 until at least 29 January 2021. A template Reactivation Notice will be available from the Court Service. If a Reactivation Notice has been provided to the Court by a party before 21 September 2020 the Courts can be expected to put it to one side and not deal with it before 21 September 2020; then, on or after 21 September 2020 (as resources allow) the Court will process the filing of it unless requested not to do so by the party who provided it.

9. In existing claims where case management directions were made before 21 September 2020, a party filing and serving a Reactivation Notice must propose new dates for directions and proposed hearing date, or state that no new directions are required and that an existing hearing date can be met.

Starting new cases

10. No new claim for possession should be started without careful efforts to reach compromise. Regulations both in England and in Wales provide (extended) notice periods before most new claims may be commenced.

11. Where a Pre-Action Protocol applies it should be complied with, and compliance will be expected to be shown.

All cases

12. For all cases there are guidelines to pre- and post-issue best practice. These include guidance to be published by MHCLG and by a number of associations.

13. Some claims have now been postponed by up to 6 months by reason of the stay, expiring 20 September 2020. In addition:

(a) Claims by mortgage lenders are subject to regulatory or voluntary schemes under which, as a matter of good practice and with appropriate exceptions for priority cases, claims are postponed to 30 October 2020. After 30 October 2020 claims will still need to proceed in an orderly sequence with proper conduct and best practice observed. The FCA has published further guidance on 14 September 2020.

(b) The National Residential Landlords Association will publish a 'Pre-Action Plan: Managing arrears and avoiding possession claims' by 18 September 2020. This sets out 9 'golden rules' and emphasises that 'in unprecedented times . . . it is incumbent on tenants and landlords to engage with each other, trying all available avenues to reach an agreement before seeking repossession through the courts.' It will also set out 5 steps to take before notice is issued (including under s21 and s8, ground 8).

(c) Other national landlord and lender associations remain committed to encouraging their members only to bring forward cases where absolutely necessary.

(d) MHCLG will publish by 18 September 2020 four sets of Guidance for private landlords, social housing landlords, tenants of private landlords and tenants of social housing landlords. The Guidance encourages advice, discussion and compromise, with court proceedings as a last resort.

14. HMCTS will publish guidance, with a particular emphasis on the specific availability of advice and the importance of exploring settlement, as follows:

(a) within notices of Review Date and Substantive Hearing Date (see below);

(b) within 'key points' leaflets for claimants and defendants respectively.

HMCTS will arrange for materials to be available in the Welsh language as well as in the English language.

The Courts

15. The parties will be offered a physical hearing for substantive hearings. This is subject to 3 exceptions:

(a) If contingency arrangements need to be introduced (see below).

(b) The existing provisions for Accelerated Possession Claims (see below) to be dealt with without a hearing in certain circumstances.

(c) Where the parties agree (subject to the Court) that a hearing should be by telephone or video.

16. Court centres will as far as possible allocate to possession proceedings the same number of courtroom/days per week as before March 2020. Where strictly necessary, the Court Service will arrange suitable additional premises.

17. Every courtroom and Judge handling a possession list will have a member of staff/usher attached to that courtroom and Judge throughout the day.

18. Only court centres able to conduct hearings with social distancing will be used. Each court centre will have, guided by the relevant health authority and adjusting as needed, a safety and active cleaning procedure running through the day. Parties must not attend a court building where that would conflict with pandemic health guidelines applying to the party.

19. The Court Service has designated 160 staff to serve as liaison staff members for these Overall Arrangements at each court centre. It is intended that there should be a dedicated possessions email address at each court centre to facilitate information and document flow.

20. Where a party is at the court centre, a legal representative may appear for that party either at Court or (where the facilities allow) by video link.

21. Where a party's legal representative is at the court centre, the party may appear either at Court or (where the facilities allow) by video link or by telephone.

22. The preferred starting point at least for the opening months is to use full-time District Judges and Deputy District Judges who sit extensively at the particular court centre. This is for a number of reasons including (a) because new arrangements are involved, (b) because of the potential for difficult 'pandemic-related' issues, and (c) because it will promote consistency and shared judicial knowledge. Designated Civil Judges (DCJs) have sought to prepare the ground regionally and locally for this approach.

23. In addition, a cadre of 200 additional Deputy District Judges (and Property Tribunal Judges) has been assembled to assist as required.

24. Special preparation/training through the Judicial College is being provided to assist all Judges involved.

Enhanced information

25. The claimant is now required to set out what knowledge the claimant has as to the effect of the pandemic on the defendant and dependants. This includes in all existing cases where a Reactivation Notice is served, and in all new claims, including all Accelerated Possession Claims.

26. Under a new facility for Covid-19 Case Marking (see below) the Court file will be marked to highlight any case that is or is claimed to be a direct consequence of Covid19.

27. The rules now also contain new requirements in appropriate cases for an updated rent account for the previous two years.

28. Court communications will emphasise to a defendant that if he/she has difficulty in completing the forms for a defence, a short statement explaining his/her circumstances and why an order should not be made will suffice.

Covid-19 Case Marking

29. Covid-19 Case Marking serves these ends:

(a) The Marking may highlight settlement suitability.

(b) Marking by the defendant will be available to claimants who have agreed as a matter of policy to give special consideration to such cases.

(c) Marking by the claimant will draw attention to cases where it is the claimant that may be in particular difficulty as a result of the pandemic.

(d) The Marking will be available to the Court to assist with listing (whether to take earlier or later), with case management and with exercising any discretion available in decision making.

(e) The Marking will assist in monitoring.

30. Any defendant or private claimant will be entitled to request that the case is Covid-19 Case Marked. The request can be made at any stage and by any means, but the defendant[1] or private claimant[2] will be required to provide specified information. The party making the request must inform all other parties. The request will result in the Marking unless there is an objection. If there is an objection the Court will decide, on the documents, whether the case should be Covid-19 Case Marked when the file is next before a Judge.

31. A Judge may also, with a request from any party, at any stage direct that the case is to be Covid-19 Case Marked. The Court Service will advise the parties when this occurs.

Listing cases

32. Generally speaking, the Court will not fix a date when it issues the claim form.

33. The former standard period between issue and hearing of eight weeks does not apply.

34. There will be no 'block lists'.

35. Listing dates will not start to be provided by court centres until the end of the stay, i.e. from 21 September 2020.

36. At least 21 days' notice is required of a hearing in a stayed claim listed or relisted in response to a Reactivation Notice.

37. Cases (stayed and new) will ordinarily proceed with a Review (please see below) and then (where necessary) a Substantive Hearing (please see below). (For Accelerated Possession Claims please see separately below.)

38. Unless there are existing case management directions that provide otherwise, for both stayed claims and new claims the first date to be listed is the Review (R) Date. (For Accelerated Possession Claims please see separately below.)

39. Generally, the Substantive (S) Hearing Date will be fixed on the Review (R) Date, although at some court centres the Substantive (S) Hearing Date may be advised in the same communication as the Review Date is advised. On either approach the Substantive (S) Hearing Date should be 28 days after the Review (R) Date.

40. Courts will list up to around 3 months ahead. The balance of reactivated or newly issued claims will be held in reserve to be listed for a Review on a rolling basis as each week passes.

41. Where possible, cases listed on a particular day or part of a day will be of the same type of claimant: e.g. Social Landlords, Private Landlords, Mortgage Lenders.

42. Notice of listing will include:

(a) Details for the defendant of duty scheme advice arrangements.
(b) The point that if the defendant takes up the offer of early advice on the Review Date (please see below) and the case can be resolved, no Substantive Hearing will be needed.
(c) Emphasis that the defendant's home is at risk and that help is available that is free.
(d) Case management and listing requirements for the claimant (please see below).

Prioritisation

43. As a guideline the following cases will be listed with priority:

(a) Cases with allegations of anti-social behaviour, including Ground 7A of Schedule 2 to the Housing Act 1988 and Section 84A of the Housing Act 1985.
(b) Cases with extreme alleged rent arrears accrued, that is, arrears equal to at least (i) 12 months' rent or (ii) 9 months' rent where that amounts to more than 25% of a private landlord's total annual income from any source.
(c) Cases involving alleged squatters, illegal occupiers or persons unknown.
(d) Cases involving an allegation of domestic violence where possession of the property is alleged to be important for particular reasons which are set out in the claim form (and with domestic violence agencies alerted).
(e) Cases with allegations of fraud or deception.
(f) Cases with allegations of unlawful subletting.
(g) Cases with allegations of abandonment of the property, non-occupation or death of defendant.

(h) Cases concerning what was allocated by an authority as 'temporary accommodation' and is specifically needed by the authority for reallocation as 'temporary accommodation'.

Other circumstances may warrant priority, and further amplification of this guideline may be published.

44. Subject to the above, priority will be given to claims issued before the stay commenced in March 2020.

45. When the Court reaches a decision over the priority or urgency of a case, it will have regard to the impact not only on the claimant and defendant in that case but to the effect on other claimants and defendants in other cases.

Legal advice and assistance for defendants

46. Non means tested free of charge legally aided advice and assistance will be available to the defendant through revised duty scheme arrangements, at two points:

(a) (as a new arrangement) early advice one month (28 days) before the first substantive hearing (i.e. on what will be known as the R or Review Date), and also;

(b) (as now) advice at the first substantive hearing if there needs to be one (i.e. at what will be known as the S or Substantive Hearing Date).

47. By 18 September 2020 the Legal Aid Agency will have removed gaps in existing coverage of duty scheme legal advice for defendants by issuing contracts in the areas concerned.

48. All legal aid duty scheme contracts have been adjusted to allow the advice and assistance to be provided flexibly, including face to face (at Court building or suitable off-site location), video or phone (adviser calling back where necessary to address call costs problems and manage demand across the day).

The Review (R) Date

49. 14 days before the date listed as the Review (R) Date the claimant will be required:

(a) to provide to the Court an electronic bundle (with a paper bundle allowed as an alternative);

(b) to confirm to the Court that a paper bundle had been provided to the defendant (with an electronic copy in addition where the defendant is able to receive that);

(c) to confirm to the Court that the bundle includes all required material, specifically including enhanced information about the defendant now required;

(d) to confirm to the Court that the claimant will be available during the Review Date to discuss the case (by telephone would be sufficient) with the defendant or a duty scheme (or other) adviser.

50. The Review Date is an important new opportunity for the defendant to obtain free of charge duty scheme advice, and for the claimant and the defendant to reach agreement (with the assistance of the duty adviser). (If the bundle provided by the claimant to the court and the defendant has not reached a duty scheme adviser who is advising a defendant, the Court will make a copy available to the duty adviser (note the Privacy Notice at https://www.judiciary.uk/about-the-judiciary/judiciary-anddata-protection-privacy-notice/).

51. On the Review Date a very short Review appointment will be listed by the Court. This will be conducted by a Judge on the documents and without attendance by the parties. The Review is for 5 minutes. No court fee will be payable in relation to a Review or any order made on the Review Date.

52. The Review will be at the end of the sitting day so that if on that day the claimant and the defendant resolve the case, or agree directions, then the Court will be available to make the orders required. This will still be without attendance of the parties; the agreed order should be provided (usually by the duty scheme adviser who has assisted the defendant to resolve the case or agree directions) to the member of staff/ usher attached to the Judge and courtroom throughout the day.

53. To ensure that compromise is not deterred, local authorities will be expected to take the approach, guided by MHCLG that signing a consent order or agreeing an order for possession where the property is unaffordable is not, in itself, a reason to find an applicant intentionally homeless.

54. If the case is not resolved by agreement, the Judge will consider the bundle provided by the claimant and the Court file. If the claimant's documents are in order the case will proceed to a Substantive Hearing 28 days later. If the claimant's documents are not in order the Court can be expected to dismiss the claim (with liberty to apply for reconsideration at an oral hearing) or may give directions.

The Substantive (S) Hearing Date

55. Where a Substantive (S) Hearing is listed, all parties must attend.

56. The hearing is for 15 minutes, with additional time between hearings for Covid-19 safety procedures.

57. Unless the claimant and the defendant resolve the case, the Court will decide the claim or give further case management directions. Where the issues are complex or the evidence or argument requires, these directions may be towards a fuller substantive hearing with an individual time estimate and listing.

58. It can be expected that the question of adjournment will be considered, without the need for an application to adjourn, in any case where (a) there is no sign that advice has yet been made available to the defendant and (b) the consequences of the order may be serious in the context of the pandemic.

59. All concerned need to keep in mind that the court's discretion at the point of decision or order is currently limited by statute. In the result, as the law stands there are material cases where the judiciary may not have discretion, or may have only very limited discretion, to take into account the effect of the pandemic on a defendant.

Accelerated Possession Claims

60. In accordance with existing rules, in some cases (Accelerated Possession Claims) an order for possession may be made without a hearing by a Judge to whom the papers have been referred for this course to be considered.

61. Within the Overall Arrangements, Accelerated Possession Claims are however subject to the following:

(a) Accelerated Possession Claims issued before 3 August 2020 will require a Reactivation Notice as with all other stayed claims.
(b) As a guideline, Accelerated Possession Claims will be dealt with having regard to the priorities listed in the section on Prioritisation above.
(c) Each court centre will refer Accelerated Possession Claims to a Judge at manageable frequency.
(d) Judges will use the time freed up where Substantive (S) Hearing slots are vacated, to deal with Accelerated Possession Claims referred to them for consideration.
(e) Where the parties agree or there is no objection, the Judge to whom an Accelerated Possession Claim has been referred for consideration may direct that a Review (R) Date be listed to enable the Defendant to receive duty scheme advice and assistance.

62. If on consideration of an Accelerated Possession Claim referred to the Judge for consideration the Judge directs a Substantive Hearing (giving any appropriate case management directions, and with the parties to attend) that will be listed as a Substantive (S) Hearing unless otherwise directed.

Eviction where an order for possession is made

63. Notice of eviction, of at least 14 days, is now required both in the County Court and in the High Court. In both cases, a new form now provides in both Courts for clear information to the defendant of the date of the proposed eviction and the right to apply to the court for suspension or postponement, and of available routes to advice.

64. Whilst any application will be considered on its merits, generally speaking, in current circumstances and in light of current challenges, parties will be encouraged to recognise that applications to transfer proceedings from the County Court to the High Court may not be able to be treated as of high priority.

65. Safety of defendants, occupants and High Court Enforcement Officers (HCEOs)/bailiffs in the specific case will be carefully considered by HCEOs/bailiffs. The Ministry of Justice has issued guidance to ensure that no enforcement of possession orders will proceed (a) where local lockdown measures are in place to protect public health (in areas where the public health risks could be greater), and (b) other than in the most serious cases, over the Christmas period.

Monitoring and adjustments

66. Participation in regional and local court user groups is encouraged throughout the duration of the Overall Arrangements.

67. HMCTS, led nationally, will collect data and monitor agreed points across the Overall Arrangements to ensure reporting to local, regional and national Judiciary, and to allow evaluation.

68. With the benefit of data collection and monitoring, adjustments to the Overall Arrangements will be made in light of experience. Nationally, judicial members of the MR's Working Group will continue to meet weekly with HMCTS national senior management. The full cross-sector MR's Working Group will convene from time to time as circumstances require.

69. If the pandemic occasions future adjustments in HMG advice to the public, or to legal requirements, e.g. regional or temporary return of 'lockdown', then required adjustments to the Overall Arrangements will be made, with advice from the MR's Working Group.

Full contingency arrangements

70. Full contingency arrangements include:

(a) the use of additional buildings at scale (some initial advance scoping has been undertaken by HMCTS);
(b) the use of remote hearings at scale; and
(c) deploying the additional cadre of Judges at scale (rather than simply to assist).

71. Full contingency arrangements will be used only where an assessment is made at national Judicial level that they are required. This recognises that access to advice will in practice diminish if they are used. The MR's Working Group will provide advice.

SCHEDULE

Milestones

Please note that the dates given are subject to exceptions for certain types of case and in certain circumstances

14-18 September	Guidance published by MHCLG, the FCA, and by associations. Overall Arrangements published in final form by the Master of the Rolls' cross-sector Working Group. Template Reactivation Notices published by the Court Service.
18 September	Remaining Template Documents, guidance and leaflets published by the Court Service.
20 September	The final day of the stay of possession proceedings.
21 September	Courts will start to deal with possession proceedings, including initially: i. Issuing reactivated claims lodged but not issued because of the stay, and new claims (NB the claimant must ensure that required notice periods have expired before a claim is issued; required notice periods can now be up to 6 months). ii. Serving claims. iii. Hearing stayed cases that had case management directions (in accordance with those directions or any amendment to those directions). iv. Hearing applications to suspend or stay a warrant, and appeals. v. Listing for Review both reactivated claims and new claims.
6 October	Earliest date for evictions (claimants who have already obtained a warrant following an existing possession order, and allowing 14 days' notice, and assuming no outstanding application to suspend or stay the warrant).
19 October	First Review (R) Dates (allowing 21 days' notice) (generally speaking, these will be priority cases first). Duty scheme free early advice available to all defendants on the Review Date for their case.
16 November	First Substantive (S) Hearing Dates following first Review Dates.

Illustrative timeline for a claim

When	What
From 21 September 2020	New proceedings issued and served (or Reactivation Notice served by Claimant (or Defendant) in stayed claims issued before 3 August 2020).
At any point	Covid-19 Marking on the initiative of the Claimant, Defendant or at the direction of a Judge.
By (claim served plus 14 days)	Defence filed.
After issue	**R** (Review) Date fixed (priority cases first).
By (**R** minus 21 days)	Notice of **R** (Review) Date to Claimant and Defendant.
By (**R** minus 14 days)	Claimant lodges bundle with Court and provides a copy to Defendant.
R	Review (**R**) listed – no attendance before Judge; free early advice available to Defendants under duty scheme; negotiation; agreed order made where achieved and appropriate; Substantive (**S**) Hearing fixed unless claim resolved or other directions.
R plus 28 days	Substantive (**S**) Hearing – attendance required before Judge; further free advice and assistance available to Defendants under duty scheme.
After **S**	As directed by the Court (if case continues).

Typical listing for a Court Possession Proceedings Day

1000	Urgent hearings to suspend/stay/set aside/vary/postpone
1045	Hearing **S**1
1105	Hearing **S**2
1125	Hearing **S**3
1145	Hearing **S**4
1205	Hearing **S**5
1225	Hearing **S**6
1245	Hearing **S**7
1300-1400	Lunch adjournment
1400	Hearing **S**8
1420	Hearing **S**9
1450	Hearing **S**10
1510	Reviews **R**1-10 [All on the documents; no attendance before the Judge]
1600	Hearings end

Urgent hearings to suspend/stay may also be taken where any S hearings have been vacated or are ineffective, although these will also be used for considering Accelerated Possession Claims (see below). Appeals, applications to suspend/stay/vary/postpone will also be dealt with on other days where required.

Footnotes

1 Covid-19 Case Marking by a Defendant will require the following information from the Defendant:

- brief details of the particular hardship faced by the Defendant;
- whether there were material arrears outstanding before March 2020;
- whether the Defendant has been placed on furlough, and whether the Defendant offered or paid a related proportion of rent or borrowing arrears;
- whether the Defendant has obtained universal credit since March 2020, and whether the Defendant offered or paid a related proportion of rent or borrowing arrears;
- whether the Defendant has been unable to earn by reason of Covid-19;
- whether the Defendant has been shielding;
- what proposals the Defendant has to pay the rent or borrowing arrears.

2 Covid-19 Case Marking by a Claimant will require the following information from the Claimant:

- brief details of the particular hardship faced by the Claimant;
- whether the Claimant has received assistance under a Covid-19 scheme, including (where a Landlord) with any borrowing by the Landlord in respect of the property.

APPENDIX 10

Insolvency and duty advice

Debt Relief Orders

Although these are rare, we wanted to cover everything that might possibly come up in the duty possession list. We hope this detail is useful.

Since 2009 individual debtors on a low income and with qualifying debts of £20,000 or less have been able to apply for Debt Relief Orders (DRO) through an authorised DRO intermediary. Information about DROs which is useful for duty advisers to know can be found here – https://www.citizensadvice.org.uk/debt-and-money/debt-solutions/debt-relief-orders

Homeowners are not eligible for a DRO and so this section relates to tenant defendants facing possession on the grounds of rent arrears.

The making of a DRO sets a moratorium period of 12 months after which the qualifying debts are discharged. Rent arrears are a qualifying debt and so can fall under a DRO but the ongoing rent still remains payable.

Duty advisers whose client is subject to a DRO need to be aware of the following:

- A DRO does not prevent the court making a possession order based on rent arrears which are subject to the moratorium under a DRO or discharged following the moratorium. The courts cannot make a money judgment for those arrears (because they are subject to the moratorium or they are discharged) but the court can make a possession order *based on* those arrears.
- The court can take the view that, but for the DRO the defendant would owe £xx.xx in rent arrears and consider that based on those arrears it is reasonable for a possession order to be made. It follows that the court could make a mandatory order for possession based on an appropriate level of arrears notwithstanding the DRO and proceed with enforcement. can proceed.
- If readers want to look into this further, then see *Sharples v Places for People Homes Ltd: Godfrey v A2 Dominion Homes Ltd* [2011] EWCA Civ 813.
- A court cannot make an order for possession suspended or postponed on condition of payment towards arrears which are covered by a DRO. However, the court can make an order conditional upon payment of ongoing rent liability and costs.
- A defendant who has obtained a DRO after a suspended or postponed possession order may apply to vary the postponed or suspended order to take account of the fact that the condition of payments to the arrears which have become subject to the DRO should no longer be imposed.

- Important – a claimant faced with the position that arrears of rent cannot be recovered because of a DRO may wish to use that fact to argue that an outright order for possession is appropriate rather than a conditional order, or that a warrant should proceed to be executed. Citizens Advice's website advises that a defendant may wish to continue paying towards arrears of rent in order to keep their home, notwithstanding that there is a mortarium on the debt or it is discharged.
- With that advice from Citizens Advice in mind, a duty adviser will want to think carefully about making submissions to the court about using a defendant's intention to apply for a DRO in order to seek relief from other debts and concentrate on paying the rent. This positive step to sort out finances may persuade a judge that it is not reasonable for a possession order to be made or that a possession order should be postponed or suspended.

Bankrupt tenants and duty advice

The situation for bankrupt tenants facing possession proceedings on the grounds of rent arears is similar to the position set out above. The bankruptcy does not prevent the claimant from seeking possession based on the arrears which are provable in the bankruptcy but does restrict what the court can do in respect of any money claim. The court could only make a condition possession order based on payments to arrears accrued after the bankruptcy order, not those which are provable in the bankruptcy.

For the purposes of this book, it suffices to say that most tenancies do not automatically vest in the trustee in bankruptcy (which means that the tenant retains statutory security of tenure) but at the same time the defendant should be advised that they must inform the trustee of the outcome of any hearing because the trustee's consent is required in the payment of rent, court costs and any payments to post bankruptcy rent arrears. In some cases, it may be appropriate to request an adjournment to seek that consent from the trustee if it has not already been given.

It should go without saying that the defendant should be referred for specialist advice if they have not already had it.

Bankrupt borrowers, tenants of bankrupt borrowers and duty advice

While relatively rare, cases involving bankrupt borrowers may come to the attention of the duty adviser in a number of different ways, including the tenant of a bankrupt borrower seeking advice. It is even conceivable that a tenant of a bankrupt borrower may be bankrupt themselves.

There may be proceedings brought by a lender, a trustee in bankruptcy (TiB) or by a bankrupt borrower against their tenant. There may be applications in existing proceedings made by any of these or by an authorised tenant (whose tenancy predates the relevant mortgage) or by an unauthorised tenant. Hearings may be attended and participated in by all or any of these parties as well as other joint owners, and/or other members of the borrower's and/or tenant's household.

A bankrupt borrower is entitled to attend any hearing and address any court on what order shall be made and the terms of the order. The full range of protections under the Administration of Justice Acts 1970 and 1973 are available - see *Nationwide BS v Purvis* [1998] BPIR 625, CA.

Occupiers or tenants of relevant premises must be notified of proceedings and so may attend to seek to defend the claim or seek time before a possession order is made and may apply to the court to try to stop or delay enforcement.

Issues for a duty adviser may also be:

- Are there joint owners whose position needs to be considered?
- Are there other household members who may have a beneficial or other interest that means possession should not be given up?
- For example, has another household member made a substantial contribution to the initial purchase or to the upkeep of the property?
- Are there exceptional circumstances (perhaps engaging Human Rights) of other household members that can support an application to provide for more time before sale; including ill health or an important event like pending exams for children?
- Has every relevant party been notified of the proceedings, for example has a lender notified the TiB of proceedings against a bankrupt borrower?
- Is the tenant an authorised tenant and, if so, is that relevant to the proceedings before the court?
- Does the tenant or their household have exceptional circumstances (perhaps engaging Human Rights) which the court should take account of when disposing of the proceedings?

There are more than likely to be scenarios that the authors have not conceived of, let alone encountered. The issues that can arise and are relevant to such proceedings are complicated and involve competing interests. They are not matters that can be safely disposed of by a judge in the limited time at a first instance possession hearing. Consequently, the duty adviser's task is to set out an outline of the issues on behalf of the client that has consulted them and ask the court to adjourn for the parties to get legal advice, such that on the next occasion the court can try to disentangle the competing interests of the parties.

The Debt Respite Scheme (Breathing Space Moratorium and Mental Health Crisis Moratorium) (England and Wales) Regulations 2020

Caution – in this section we seek to draw out relevant points for duty advisers arising from these forthcoming regulations. We have not seen them in action yet of course and the detail of how they work is beyond the scope of this book. Duty advisers will need to keep in touch with their local friendly authorised debt advisers to work out strategies for using the regulations for their clients' benefit. In addition, those working in Wales will have to keep an eye on the progress with the coming into force of the Renting Homes (Wales) Act 2016 for the impact of the regulations on rent arrears based possession notices.

On 4 May 2021 The Debt Respite Scheme (Breathing Space Moratorium and Mental Health Crisis Moratorium) (England and Wales) Regulations 2020 will come into force. The stated purpose of the regulations is to give debtors a breathing space to try to find advice and a solution to their financial problems. The regulations may be of assistance to defendants to possession proceedings and those advising them.

The regulations set out two types of breathing space which are described in the regulations as a 'breathing space moratorium' and 'mental health crisis moratorium'. In the guidance they are respectively described as a 'standard breathing space' and a 'mental health crisis breathing space'. Government guidance – https://www.gov.uk/government/publications/debt-respite-scheme-breathing-space-guidance/debt-respite-scheme-breathing-space-guidance-for-money-adviser – says this about the two types moratoria/breathing spaces:

> *A standard breathing space is available to any client with problem debt. It gives them legal protections from creditor action for up to 60 days. The protections include pausing most enforcement action and contact from creditors and freezing most interest and charges on their debts.*
>
> *A mental health crisis breathing space is only available to a client who is receiving mental health crisis treatment. If an Approved Mental Health Professional (AMHP) certifies a client is in mental health crisis treatment, the client or someone else might ask you for a mental health crisis breathing space on the client's behalf. The mental health crisis breathing space has some stronger protections than the standard breathing space. It lasts as long as the client's mental health crisis treatment, plus 30 days (no matter how long the crisis treatment lasts).*

In either case a moratorium/breathing space can only be arranged by a debt adviser who is authorised by the Financial Conduct Authority. For a mental health crisis breathing space to be applied for then the client will need to have been certified as receiving mental health crisis treatment by an Approved Mental Health Professional (AMHP).

The eligibility criteria for a moratorium/breathing space are:

- be an individual
- owe a qualifying debt to a creditor
- live or usually reside in England or Wales
- not have a debt relief order (DRO), an individual voluntary arrangement (IVA), an interim order, or be an undischarged bankrupt at the time they apply
- not already have a breathing space, and not have had a standard breathing space in the last 12 months at the time they apply

and the mental health crisis moratorium/breathing space application requires the additional certification from the AMHP.

During the period of the moratorium/breathing space the debtor has ongoing liabilities which must still be paid:

- a mortgage secured against your client's primary residence (this does not include arrears accrued up to the start of the breathing space)
- a lease or rental agreement for your client's primary residence (this does not include arrears of rent for the property accrued up to the start of the breathing space)
- an insurance agreement
- any taxes, duties and national insurance contributions
- any local taxes rates for local authority
- water, sewerage, electricity, gas, heating oil or solid fuel bills

Any other debts or bills that fall due to be paid during the period of the breathing space are not ongoing liabilities.

The list of debts qualifying for a moratorium/breathing space includes rent and mortgage arrears and incudes those arrears even if under a joint liability so one client can apply for a breathing space on the whole of a joint rent or mortgage liability.

While ongoing rent or mortgage payments must be made during the period of a moratorium/breathing space, any steps amounting to enforcement of a rent or mortgage debt must stop including for our purposes:

- steps to collect a breathing space debt
- steps to enforce a court order or tribunal judgment about a breathing space debt
- steps to obtain a warrant or writ
- steps to start any action or legal proceedings for a breathing space debt
- steps to serve a notice to take possession of your client's property for rent

arrears or take possession of their property for rent arrears if a notice has already been served

- Steps to contacts your client about the enforcement of a breathing space debt

The relevant regulation is rather long but worth setting out in full for reference:

Effect of a moratorium

(1) A moratorium has the effect specified in this regulation in relation to moratorium debt during a moratorium period.

(2) Subject to paragraph (3), during a moratorium period a creditor may not, in relation to any moratorium debt, take any of the steps specified in paragraph (6) in respect of the debt unless–
  (a) these Regulations specify otherwise, or
  (b) the county court or any other court or tribunal where legal proceedings concerning the debt have been or could be issued or started has given permission for the creditor to take the step.

(3) A court or tribunal may not give permission for a creditor or agent to take any of the steps specified in paragraph (6)(a) or (b).

(4) Subject to paragraph (5), for the purposes of paragraph (2)(b), a court or tribunal may–
  (a) determine an application for permission to take a step specified in paragraph (6)(c) or (d) in any way that it thinks fit,
  (b) give permission subject to such conditions as it thinks fit, and
  (c) make such orders as may be necessary to give effect to the determination of the application.

(5) A court or tribunal may only grant permission under paragraph 2(b) for a creditor or agent to take a step specified in paragraph (6)(c) or for a creditor to instruct an agent to take a step specified in paragraph (6)(c) where the court considers that–
  (a) it is reasonable to allow the creditor or their agent to take the step, and
  (b) the step will not–
    (i) be detrimental to the debtor to whom the moratorium relates, or
    (ii) significantly undermine the protections of the moratorium.

(6) The steps mentioned in paragraph (2) that a creditor is prevented from taking are any steps to–
  (a) require a debtor to pay interest that accrues on a moratorium debt during a moratorium period,
  (b) require a debtor to pay fees, penalties or charges in relation to a moratorium debt that accrue during a moratorium period,

(c) take any enforcement action in respect of a moratorium debt (whether the right to take such action arises under a contract, by virtue of an enactment or otherwise), or
(d) instruct an agent to take any of the actions mentioned in sub-paragraphs (a) to (c).

(7) A creditor or agent takes enforcement action if they take any of the following steps in relation to a moratorium debt–
(a) take a step to collect a moratorium debt from a debtor,
(b take a step to enforce a judgment or order issued by a court or tribunal before or during a moratorium period regarding a moratorium debt,
(c) enforce security held in respect of a moratorium debt,
(d) obtain a warrant,
(e) subject to regulation 12(4)(d), sell or take control of a debtor's property or goods,
(f) start any action or legal proceedings against a debtor relating to or as a consequence of non-payment of a moratorium debt,
(g) make an application for a default judgment in respect of a claim for money against the debtor,
(h) take steps to install a pre-payment meter under paragraph 7(3)(a) of Schedule 2B to the Gas Act 1986 or paragraph 2(1)(a) of Schedule 6 to the Electricity Act 1989 to take payments in respect of a moratorium debt, or use a pre-payment meter already installed to take such payments, unless a debtor had provided their consent for the installation of the pre-payment meter before the moratorium started,
(i) take steps to disconnect a debtor's premises from a supply of gas under paragraph 7(3)(b) of Schedule 2B to the Gas Act 1986 or electricity under paragraph 2(1)(b) of Schedule 6 to the Electricity Act 1989 unless the debtor had taken the supply of gas or electricity illegally,
(j) serve a notice to take possession of a dwelling-house let to a debtor on grounds 8, 10 or 11 in Schedule 2 to the Housing Act 1988 or take possession of a dwelling-house let to a debtor having served such a notice,
(k) serve a notice to take possession of a dwelling let to a debtor or take possession of a dwelling let to a debtor having served such a notice—
   (i) on the ground of breach of contract specified in section 157 of the Renting Homes (Wales) Act 2016 where that breach relates to rent arrears, or
   (ii) on the grounds specified in section 181(2) of the Renting Homes (Wales) Act 2016, or

(iii) on the grounds specified in section 187(2) of the Renting Homes (Wales) Act 2016,

(l) contact a debtor for the purpose of enforcement of a moratorium debt,

(m) make an application in respect of a debtor for commitment to prison under regulation 16 of the Non-Domestic Rating (Collection and Enforcement) (Local Lists) Regulations 1989 or regulation 47 of the Council Tax (Administration and Enforcement) Regulations 1992, or

(n) take any of the steps in this paragraph in relation to a joint debtor.

(8) For the purposes of paragraph (7)(f), legal proceedings against a debtor includes a bankruptcy petition.

(9) Where a moratorium debt is a secured debt, paragraph (6)(a) applies only to interest that accrues on any arrears on the debt during a moratorium period.

(10) After the end of a moratorium period, neither a creditor nor their agent is entitled to–

(a) require a debtor to pay interest, fees, penalties or charges referred to in paragraph (6)(a) and (b) that accrued during the moratorium period, or

(b) treat the non-payment during the moratorium period by the debtor of interest, fees, penalties or charges as a default by the debtor under, or a breach of, the agreement between the debtor and the creditor.

(11) Subject to paragraph (13)(c), to the extent it applies to a moratorium debt, during a moratorium period, the Secretary of State and the Commissioners for Revenue and Customs must not direct that a new arrangement should be put in place for a debtor's benefit to be paid, wholly or in part, to a third party under regulation 35 of the Social Security (Claims and Payments) Regulations 1987.

(12) Any action taken contrary to this regulation shall be null and void.

(13) Nothing in this regulation affects the following to the extent that they relate to a debtor–

(a) a charging order made before the start of the moratorium under the Charging Orders Act 1979or regulations 50 and 51 of the Council Tax (Administration and Enforcement) Regulations 1992,

(b) an attachment of earnings order made before the start of the moratorium under the Attachment of Earnings Act 1971or regulation 37 of the Council Tax (Administration and Enforcement) Regulations 1992,

(c) a deduction from earnings made under–

(i) Parts 8 or 8A of the Social Security (Payments on account, Overpayments and Recovery) Regulations 1988,

(ii) Part 3 of the Social Security Administration Act 1992, or
(iii) Part 6 of the Social Security (Overpayments and Recovery) Regulations 2013,

where a deduction notice has been served before the start of the moratorium under that Act or those Regulations, or

(d) the debtor's universal credit paid, wholly or in part, to a third party under regulation 60 of and Schedules 6 and 7 to the Universal Credit, Personal Independence Payment, Jobseeker's Allowance and Employment and Support Allowance (Claims and Payments) Regulations 2013.

(14) In this regulation, "benefit" means any payment made to a debtor under the Social Security Contributions and Benefits Act 1992, the Jobseekers Act 1995, the Welfare Reform Act 2007 or the Welfare Reform Act 2012.

(15) This regulation is subject to regulation 11.

In a case where legal proceedings are ongoing the creditor must tell the court that a breathing space has started. Court proceedings can continue to an extent, but the court must make sure that the case does not get to the enforcement stage unless the court has allowed an application under regulation 7 (4) by the creditor for enforcement to continue.

Where the defendant has not yet applied for a breathing space but may be eligible and can make ongoing payments to rent or mortgage liabilities, the regulation may be usefully referred to as support for asking for an adjournment for time for a defendant to get advice about their financial position. The court can be told that a defendant will seek advice from an authorised debt adviser to apply and that in the meantime it would not be reasonable for a possession order to be made. The court can be told that the regulations are drafted such that the defendant is obliged to continue to pay the rent or mortgage during the breathing space. As we said about DROs above, the prospect of a positive step to sort out finances such as this may persuade a judge that it is not reasonable for a possession order to be made or that a possession order should be postponed or suspended.

Where the defendant is or was in a moratorium/breathing space period, the duty adviser may be able to bring to the court's attention any conduct of or steps taken by a claimant that are not in accordance with regulation 7 set out above. For example, if a notice of seeking possession on rent arrears grounds was served during a moratorium/breathing space period that it will be null and void by virtue of regulation 7 (12).

Where the defendant is in a moratorium/breathing space period the regulations may prevent enforcement of a possession order and any step taken to apply for a warrant or writ of eviction should usually be null and void unless the clamant has had permission from the court to take those steps.

The duty adviser may find themselves at court in a position of seeking to oppose an application made by the claimant to take steps in the proceedings pursuant to regulation 4. We may anticipate that claimants may make such applications in advance, in a similar way to the applications we see now for permission for High Court enforcement.

Index

Note: references to the main text are to paragraph number. References to the Appendices are to page number.